Susie,

Growing Your Business

Gurd luck! Go on, create the future you want for the business and for you

Gerard

Growing Your Business is designed to help owner-managers develop growth strategies for their businesses by providing frameworks, ideas, inspiration and hands-on assignments. Its contents are a distillation of the authors' knowledge and experience in successfully helping hundreds of owner-managers to grow and develop their businesses and themselves over the last 20 years.

Filled with case studies and examples of businesses involved with the world-renowned Business Growth and Development Programme (BGP) at Cranfield School of Management, the book covers all industry sectors and includes high-profile names such as Karan Bilimoria of Cobra Beer, Angus Thirlwell of Hotel Chocolat and Lara Morgan of Pacific Direct.

As well as an ideal text for courses and modules in small business development and business growth at the undergraduate and MBA levels, this book also stands on its own as an invaluable 'workbook' that can enable owner-managers to develop their own growth strategy and take their business to the next level.

Gerard Burke is the Programme Director of BGP and the Director of CREDO, the part of Cranfield School of Management which works exclusively with owner-managers and their businesses.

Liz Clarke, David Molian and **Paul Barrow** are core members of the BGP delivery team and are all visiting fellows at Cranfield School of Management.

Growing Your Business

A Handbook for Ambitious Owner-Managers

GERARD BURKE, LIZ CLARKE,
DAVID MOLIAN and PAUL BARROW

Routledge
Taylor & Francis Group

NEW YORK AND LONDON

First published 2008
by Routledge
270 Madison Ave, New York, NY 10016

Simultaneously published in the UK
by Routledge
2 Park Square, Milton Park, Abingdon, Oxon OX14 4RN

Routledge is an imprint of the Taylor & Francis Group, an informa business

Typeset in Minion Pro and Helvetica Neue Pro by Prepress Projects Ltd

Printed and bound by The Cromwell Press, Trowbridge, Wiltshire

Library of Congress Cataloging in Publication Data
Burke, Gerard.
    Growing your business : a handbook for ambitious owner-managers / by Gerard Burke, Paul Barrow, Liz Clarke David Molian.
      p. cm.
    1. Small business–Management. 2. Business planning. 3. Management. I. Barrow, Paul, 1948– II. Clarke, Liz, MBA. III. Title.
    HD62.7.B834 2008
    658.4'012–dc22
    2007026731

ISBN 10: 0-415-40517-3 (hbk)
ISBN 10: 0-415-40518-1 (pbk)
ISBN 10: 0-203-93868-2 (ebk)

ISBN 13: 978-0-415-40517-1 (hbk)
ISBN 13: 978-0-415-40518-8 (pbk)
ISBN 13: 978-0-203-93868-3 (ebk)

Contents

Figures

Tables

Introduction

In 1979, Professor David Birch of the Massachusetts Institute of Technology (MIT) published *The Job Generation Process*. His findings were to have a massive impact on government thinking in most developed economies.

Contrary to the accepted wisdom that big businesses create jobs, Birch found that two-thirds of the increase in employment in the United States between 1969 and 1976 had been in firms with fewer than 20 workers. In other words, smaller, independently owned businesses are the real engine of job creation and, hence, economic growth and wealth creation.

This startling discovery, backed up by many subsequent studies, has resulted in the government of almost every country in the developed world espousing the virtues of enterprise and encouraging their citizens to be more entrepreneurial. These governments have established a whole range of initiatives to stimulate new enterprises and to provide support to small businesses (e.g. the work of the Small Business Administration in the USA or the Small Business Service in the UK).

As a result, enterprise and entrepreneurship, in its various different forms, is becoming more and more prolific and universal. For instance, there are now over 22 million independently owned businesses in Europe, and more than 1 in 15 of all Europeans, Japanese and Americans in work own and run a business of their own.

We wholeheartedly congratulate all of this entrepreneurial activity and, most importantly, the entrepreneurs themselves who take the brave steps to start their own businesses. They are extraordinary people who achieve remarkable things.

Nevertheless, encouraging more and more entrepreneurial individuals to start new ventures will not, by itself, achieve the economic aspirations of governments or of individual entrepreneurs – as demonstrated by the large numbers of businesses that fail in the first few years! In order to create sustainable jobs and wealth, for the national economy, for the local community and for the entrepreneurs themselves, these businesses not only need to be started, they also need to survive and to grow.

Interestingly, business survival and business growth are linked. Professor David Storey, in his comprehensive 1994 study *Understanding the Small Business Sector*, noted that 'the fundamental characteristic, other than size per se, which distinguishes small firms from large is their higher probability of ceasing to trade'. In other words, bigger businesses are more likely to survive. One could reasonably surmise that bigger businesses are in a better position to survive the loss of a key customer or a key member of staff, and have a wider range of products/services and more financial strength which allows them to ride out drops in demand and the ups and downs of the economic cycle. Furthermore, Professor Storey also found that failure rates were lowest among firms expressing a desire to grow.

Being more likely to survive is clearly a good thing from the entrepreneur's perspective! Having a bigger business also has a number of other advantages for the entrepreneur. A bigger business is likely to be more valuable, to have the potential to make more money and to be more capable of having a significant impact on the world around it.

So, business growth seems to be a 'good thing' for everyone!

Unfortunately, growing a business is not that easy! In reality, the challenges of growing a business are often even more difficult to overcome than the challenges of starting a business in the first place. Entrepreneurs with aspirations to grow have to learn how to manage and lead the business, they face greater complexity and probably more competition, they need to find, retain and motivate other people to share the increased workload, and they need to continue to invest in the growth of the business.

Is it any wonder, then, that so many entrepreneurs are happy to have got through the start-up stages and are content to stay pretty much as they are. They are working for themselves, running their own business, generating sufficient income to support their own family and lifestyle, and perhaps employing a few other people and supporting their families. These entrepreneurs may feel that they have achieved everything that they set out to when they started their business. They may have no further ambitions for the business and may be perfectly happy to run it in this way until they retire. These entrepreneurs are usually called 'lifestyle' entrepreneurs, and many can be found among tradespeople (for example, plumbers, carpenters, hairdressers), people with specific skills (for example, artists, music teachers) and, indeed, the traditional 'professions' (for example, solicitors, accountants, architects). Even so, there are very few lifestyle entrepreneurs who would not like to get a little bit more out of their business!

There are other entrepreneurs who are hugely ambitious and, right from the start, have a goal to build a very large business. For example, from the very beginning, Karan Bilimoria had an ambition for Cobra Beer to be available in every Indian restaurant and to become the first global Indian beer brand.

There are also a large number of entrepreneurs and owner-managers whose scale of ambition lies somewhere in between these two. They may be running profitable businesses with significant turnovers, while at the same time being ambitious for the business to be bigger and/or more profitable so that they would feel more secure and more fulfilled. The participants on the Business Growth and Development Programme (BGP), which we have run for many years at Cranfield School of Management, are often in this category.

This book is for all of these entrepreneurs and owner-managers, from those who are looking to get a little bit more out of their business to those with truly global ambitions. It is intended as a guidebook for those about to set out on the journey of business growth and for those who are part-way through that journey.

The Challenges of Growth

Over the past 20 years of running BGP, we have worked with hundreds of owner-managers and studied thousands more. Over that time, we have distilled what we believe to be the key challenges of sustained, profitable growth and identified the ways in which successful businesses overcome them.

Growth Challenge 1: The Planning Vacuum

Research studies consistently demonstrate that owner-managed businesses with strategies and plans grow sales and profits faster than those without. However, over two-thirds of owner-managed businesses with a turnover of less than £10 million that we have studied do not have a plan at all!

Growth Challenge 2: Muddled Marketing

Many small firms lack true market focus. Nine out of ten of the fastest growing and most profitable smaller businesses achieve these results by focusing on their core products/services and their core markets. They serve a well-defined niche with a product/service which delivers distinctive benefits to customers in that niche. They develop better and better understanding of the needs of those customers and build up superior reputations. They grow by selling more of the same product/service to their existing customers and people just like them. In other words, they 'stick to the knitting'. Entering new markets and developing innovative new products/services may well play an important role at certain specific stages of growth but only at the right time and only as part of an overall strategy.

Growth Challenge 3: Mismanaged Change

All business growth and development calls for change. Just like human beings, businesses pass through different phases as they grow and develop. Each phase requires a different management approach. Sometimes, strong leadership is required; at other times a more consultative style is necessary. Some phases demand more formalized systems and processes, while others require looser control and informal cooperation.

Unfortunately, our experience shows that most owner-managers try to run their growing business in much the same way as they did when they started. As a rule, the result of the owner-manager not being able to adapt and develop their own management style as the business grows is that sustained growth will not happen, and the business, its management and its employees will not achieve their full potential.

Growth Challenge 4: The Wrong Objectives

Many businesses do not even have clear objectives. Even those that do often have the wrong ones! All too often sales growth is the primary, or even sole, target without regard to other critical measures such as gross margin, profit and cash generation. With more sales turnover comes increased costs in terms of labour, materials, working capital and overheads. In fact, many businesses grow turnover at the expense of profitability! We call this the 'busy fool' syndrome. For most of us, greater profit, less work and fewer problems are much more desirable outcomes than rapid sales growth and lower margins.

Growth Challenge 5: Meddling and Misspent Time

Most owner-managers work long hours. But does successful growth mean working harder or working smarter? Our studies strongly suggest that too many owner-managers spend too much of their time undertaking day-to-day operational tasks and interfering with work which they are paying others to do. The typical owner-manager spends 90 per cent of the time on day-to-day operations, 10 per cent of the time on improving those operations and precious little on future strategy. However much effort is put into routine tasks, the effect on the business's performance will only ever be marginal. By far the most important and valuable task for the owner-manager is to work on the future strategy for the business.

Growth Challenge 6: No Financial Strategy – and Poor Controls

More than half of owner-managed businesses in the UK rely exclusively on a bank overdraft as their means of long-term finance. No wonder UK banks are among the most profitable in Europe! The reliance on short-term financing for long-term support appears to be for three main reasons.

First, since most owner-managed businesses have no strategy or plan, they have little idea when they will need extra cash. And the easiest money the business can get in a hurry is an overdraft.

Second, there is widespread lack of understanding about the range of financing instruments available to smaller businesses, above and beyond short-term bank borrowing.

Third, there is also a strong belief that taking outside investment capital is not only expensive but can also lead to losing control of the business. And for many business founders having control was one of the main reasons they set up on their own!

The problem of no financing strategy is often compounded by inadequate or inappropriate financial and business controls. Often there are no controls because that is the way it was when the business started. Clearly, as the business grows and becomes more complex and sophisticated, these controls also need to change.

Overcoming the Challenges

Few businesses enjoy a meteoric and untroubled rise from one person with a dream to professionally managed multimillion-pound enterprise. The pitfalls along the way are many – and some are fatal! However, most of the challenges that lie ahead for the growth-hungry business are predictable. So, even if they cannot be prevented, they can generally be managed to an acceptable level.

The remedies to managing these challenges require a degree of strategic thinking on the part of the owner-manager and a proactive approach to managing people, markets and money. As we have seen, for the owner-manager who takes time to anticipate and plan for the challenges ahead, the rewards can be great. The business can become easier to manage as it grows, as well as being more profitable and more fun to run!

Our overall approach to addressing the challenges of growth is predicated on the belief that good preparation and planning will be a significant aid in dealing with each of these challenges. In other words, you are more likely to grow successfully if you have researched carefully, analysed rigorously and planned thoroughly. On the other hand, we are not saying that having a great plan is all you need to grow a business! On the contrary, as you will see as you progress through the book, you also need a good business proposition, an appropriate personality, an effective team around you, and, perhaps, a little bit of luck. But, then as the great golfer Gary Player said, 'The more I practise, the luckier I get!'

Structure of the Book

As on all journeys, it is important to know where you are starting from, to know where you are heading and to have a map of how to get there. The journey of business growth is no different. Therefore, at the highest level, the planning process presented in this book consists of three key stages:

- Where are we now?
- Where are we going?
- How do we get there?

These three stages form an appropriate structure for this book. As a result, the book is split in to three parts corresponding to these three stages of planning.

Within each of the stages, there are four key themes to which we return. We call these the four Ms. They are:

- *Markets.* In this theme, we look at the external environment in which the business operates, we consider the market niche that the business is addressing, we look at the product/service that the business offers, and we consider customers, suppliers and competitors.
- *Money and measures.* Under this topic, we look at the basic financial information of the business and how to use that information to manage the business dynamically and to benchmark against competitors. We also broaden this out to include other non-financial performance measures.
- *Management.* No business can grow without great people. The management theme is about finding and recruiting those people, organizing, motivating and rewarding them once you have got them, and about building them into a high-performing team.
- *Me.* The fourth, and arguably the most important theme, is Me. In an owner-managed business it is simply not possible to disentangle the business objectives and strategy from the personal goals and drivers of the owner-manager. This theme deals with the owner-manager's own management and leadership style and with the articulation of his or her personal goals and drivers.

How to Use this Book

This is not an academic book. It is a practical book which is aimed at people who are seriously interested in actually growing their business. We hope to inspire owner-managers to grow their businesses more successfully and quickly, by sharing insights from other high-growth businesses and by providing a guide to the process of developing a growth strategy and a plan to implement that strategy.

Assignments

Perhaps the most practical part of the book is the assignments which can be found at the end of each chapter. These assignments suggest work to be done in applying the ideas introduced in that chapter. In all cases, we have written these assignments on the assumption that the reader is an owner-manager with a business that he or she is trying to grow.

By completing the assignments at the end of all the chapters, you will have most of what you need in order to put together a growth strategy and plan for your business.

Examples

In addition to the ideas, tools and techniques which are presented in the main body of the text, you will find that there is a liberal sprinkling of examples taken from real life. Furthermore, we find that, in the case of owner-managers, the owner-manager's own story is often as valuable and full of insights as the theory.

Acknowledgements

Throughout the book, the thinking we set out, and the suggestions we make, have been heavily influenced by our work on BGP at Cranfield School of Management and with individual owner-managers.

BGP is aimed specifically at ambitious owner-managers of businesses with a turnover between £0.5 million and £20 million. It has been run every year since 1988 and in that time has helped nearly 1,000 owner-managers to achieve their business and personal aspirations. Many of these owner-managers have gone on to great things and some of their stories are used as examples in the book. Overall, businesses which participate in BGP grow their sales and profits more quickly than their peers and they grow sales and profits more quickly after the programme than they did before. As a result of their success, BGP is now firmly established as the biggest and most successful programme for ambitious owner-managers in the UK. We thank the individual BGP past participants who are mentioned in the book for allowing us to tell their stories.

We have also drawn examples from many other published sources. One particular source of examples has been the highly informative website of Real Business, one of the leading UK magazines for entrepreneurs and owner-managers. We are grateful for the opportunity to use these examples to illustrate our thinking.

Through BGP, we are privileged and humbled to spend most of our working lives with truly remarkable individuals and their businesses. It is true to say that we have learned from them at least as much as they have learned from us! We are truly grateful. They are our inspiration. We hope that, through this book, we can share some of that inspiration with you!

part one
Where Are We Now?

Entrepreneurs and owner-managers have an almost irrepressible desire to move directly from spotting an opportunity to attempting to exploit it. This is rather like seeing an interesting place marked on a map and immediately setting off towards it (hopefully!) without knowing where you are starting from, how far you are away from the place of interest or whether there might be even more exciting destinations somewhere else on the map!

You can have all the grand intentions in the world but, like the Irishman being asked the way to Cork, who said, 'I wouldn't start from here!', you still have to start from where you are now. It is even worse than this, because where you have been – your history – is still hanging around and potentially getting in the way of your plans for the future.

You can think of this part of the planning process as taking stock. It is also sometimes called a position audit.

The chapters and assignments in Part One are intended to help you establish the current position of your business. They pose the sort of questions which need answering in order to establish your strengths and weaknesses, the opportunities and threats in your markets, your financial position, your organizational capability and your management and leadership style.

Of course, in considering these ideas and questions, you may well identify some areas of immediate potential improvement. Our advice is to go right ahead and make those improvements straight away rather than wait until you have completed the whole growth strategy and plan. You might as well start getting the benefits immediately!

one
Your Business and its Markets

This chapter is primarily concerned with the relationship between your business and the environment in which it operates: it is about placing your business within the bigger picture. Every business that stays in business meets the needs of a group, or groups, of customers. Those needs can vary hugely not just across industries but within an industrial sector. Smaller businesses typically succeed through serving the needs of an identified group of customers, and grow by finding more customers like their existing ones. However, the ability to grow and build a business is, inevitably, influenced by outside forces. The environment in which a business operates may be benign, as a result of factors such as favourable government legislation, a strong economy or new, enabling technologies. Equally, the environment may be a challenging one, perhaps as a result of tighter regulation, a slowdown in the economy and new technologies which disrupt the existing structure of the market. By their very nature smaller businesses – and, come to that, many larger ones – cannot alter or even modify such outside forces. But, they can anticipate, assess and often exploit environmental changes through systematic evaluation, planning and adaptation.

We begin by examining your business purpose. What are you in business to achieve, and do your aspirations need revisiting? We then consider how your business operates: does it sell direct or through others, and does it serve other businesses or consumers, or both? We review the industry in which you operate and how you are positioned to extract value. The final section reviews the broader external environment as it currently affects your business. At various points in the chapter there are assignments for you to complete, to apply the frameworks presented to analyse your business. In the chapter that follows, we will look at the market segments your business serves, how you fare against your competitors and your marketing strategy.

What Does Your Business Do ... and How Does It Do It?

Your Business Purpose

Ask an employee of Cobra Beer (learn more about Cobra Beer by visiting www.cobrabeer. com) what their business stands for and, without blinking, they will reply: 'To aspire and achieve against all odds, with integrity'.

It is one of the first things which every new employee learns when they join this remarkable company. In nine words, this short sentence condenses the story of a business that was begun in 1988 by an Indian resident in the UK, Karan Bilimoria, who had a dream and a £20,000 student overdraft! He aspired to create a new kind of beer, a lager that would both be the perfect accompaniment to the cuisine of the Indian sub-continent and appeal to ale drinkers. He has achieved a business that in 2006 sold more than £100m of beer at retail value in over 60 countries around the world. He has done so by building a company in the teeth of the most competitive beer market in the world. And he has succeeded in doing so in accordance with his own personal code of ethics. Despite its dominant position in the tandoori restaurant sector, Cobra never demands exclusivity. 'The customer must have a choice', says Karan, when he returns to talk every year on BGP. 'We have always said, "try us, give us a chance."'

Cobra has more than earned the right to customers' trust, having won numerous awards for its products, its advertising and as one of Britain's best companies in which to work. At every major crossroads or decision point in the company's history, Karan and the senior team have always revisited their corporate statement. Is this course of action in line with what we stand for? If we are forced to choose between alternatives, which fits better with our beliefs and values? In 2004 the business even made the company credo tangible, when the story of aspiration and achievement was retold through images on the Cobra beer bottle (and won yet more awards in the process!).

For the Cobra team their vision of the business is not a marketing gesture but an affirmation of what their business is. And the Cobra credo is like the tip of the iceberg. Underneath the surface is a set of clear objectives, which cascade into numerous tasks, all of which move the business towards achieving the vision. Without detailed objectives the credo would be empty rhetoric; thanks to the credo, a thousand actions every day are marshalled in a coherent direction.

You are probably familiar with the terms vision and mission statement, company credo, statement of purpose and the like. You may already have such a statement in your business. You may regard them with a certain cynicism. In this book – and on BGP itself – we are less concerned with what such statements are called, and much more with the purposes they serve. First, they define – or redefine – the goals of the business. In our experience, owner-managers often find themselves so swallowed up in the minutiae of running their businesses that they lose sight of what they are trying to achieve. Sometimes it is good just to remind yourself of what you are in business for. Is the goal the same as when you started or acquired the business? If it is different, how and why is it different?

The second purpose they serve is to clarify the opportunity you are trying to capture and, perhaps, what makes you distinct from your competitors. Again, is there a danger that, in the daily swim through treacle that so much of business life consists of, you no longer see this as clearly? Sometimes it can take a setback or reversal in a company's fortunes for that clarity to be recaptured. The co-founders of Hotel Chocolat (www.hotelchocolat.com), the delivered chocolate gifts business, relearned their business purpose as a result of an unsuccessful diversification into supplying other businesses. 'It made us re-examine our values', says joint managing director Angus Thirlwell, who participated in BGP in 2000. 'In fact it was a very positive experience for us, as it reaffirmed our values and culture and sharpened our appetite to do more of the sort of business that we found to be fun'. Their conclusions are encapsulated in a company culture table, displayed prominently in the offices for employees and visitors alike to see (Table 1.1).

Defining Your Business Purpose

Large companies spend long weekends at expensive retreats wrestling with the fine print of their vision statements. You can do so more quickly and certainly more cheaply! Statements of business purpose and objectives are statements of direction, intended to focus your attention on essentials, and to define your specific competence(s) in relation to the markets/customers you plan to serve. They signal to your employees, as much as the outside world, where their priorities lie. They are essentially 'what' statements. The details of 'how' we achieve what we say we will achieve follow from these statements of intent. Figure 1.1, the pyramid of goals, illustrates this.

TABLE 1.1 Hotel Chocolat Statement of Values

We are	We are not
Leaders	Followers
Adders of value through our ideas	Wage slaves to other companies
Always seeking to improve	Red tape merchants
Exciting, excited and excitable	Dull and predictable
Building something worthwhile	Short-termist
Driven by our vision and teamwork	Driven by fear and politics

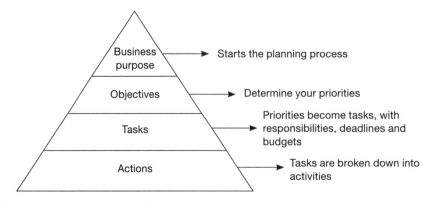

FIGURE 1.1 The Pyramid of Goals.

So let us review the current state of your thinking about what you are in business to achieve.

Assignment 1.1 Your Business Purpose

How clearly can you answer the following?

1. Write your current statement of business purpose, if you have one. Does it refer to your products/services and to the customers whose needs you serve? If you have no such statement of purpose, try to draft one, incorporating your products/services and the customers they serve.
2. Consider your principal objectives when you started or acquired the business. How well have you succeeded in achieving them? Should they be redefined?
3. What do you think is the business purpose of the most successful business in your market (apart from yours!)?

An effective statement of purpose should be realistic, achievable, but demanding and communicate also at the emotional level. Consider this. Apart from the owners, who is inspired to work for a business which has only dry financial goals as its stated purpose? Brevity, if at all possible, is also a virtue! When it is complete to your satisfaction, do not lock it away in a drawer as the company's secret formula for success. In our experience, great businesses like Cobra and Hotel Chocolat actively share their aspirations with their employees, promote them at internal meetings and publicize them through their branding and marketing literature.

Your Business Model

Let us move on now to how your business operates. We will begin by identifying some different, basic kinds of business through a typology often described as the business model, represented in the simple diagram shown in Figure 1.2.

Customer type

	Business	Consumer
Direct	For example, commercial property developer	For example, clothing catalogue retailer
Indirect	For example, company car windscreen replacement, sold through insurance companies	For example, food or beverages manufacturer selling through shops

Route to market

FIGURE 1.2 Business Model Matrix.

Along the horizontal axis is the type of customer you do business with. Business customers (and we also include public sector and other types of organizations in this category) buy on behalf of their organization and they spend the organization's money. Consumers, on the other hand, spend their own money, purchasing goods and services for their own consumption. Along the vertical axis is the way that you reach your final purchaser, either directly or through an intermediary. If it is through an intermediary, you will have two kinds of customer to satisfy: the intermediary you sell to and the customer who consumes your product or service. Although the number of people employed in selling direct to end consumers is huge, the majority of businesses sell business-to-business.

At start-up, the choice of business model is usually straightforward. Subject to the market sector and the nature of the opportunity, a business normally opts for one of the four boxes in this matrix. But this can change over time. Consider the case of Hotel Chocolat. In the early days, the firm focused on supplying promotional confectionery and chocolates direct to other companies, i.e the business began life in the top-left box. In the 1990s the founders of Hotel Chocolat diversified in two ways. First, they started to supply supermarkets, so moving into the bottom right-hand box. The second diversification took the form of selling direct to consumers through mail order, taking them into the top right-hand box. By the mid-1990s the business model and branding strategy had evolved to look like Figure 1.3.

The choice of business model is driven both by the perceived opportunity and by the skills and competences inherent in the business. Let us review briefly each box in turn, in terms of the factors needed to succeed.

- Business/direct (top left): the firm has strong selling skills and in-depth understanding of a particular industry or set of industries. Target customers can be identified and sold to at a cost that allows the firm to make a sustainable margin.
- Business/indirect (bottom left): the firm is focused on development and production and can build strong alliances or partnerships with others that provide

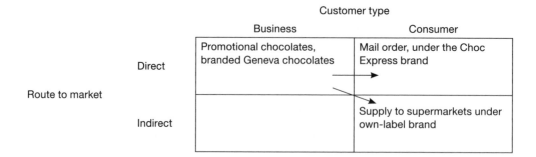

FIGURE 1.3 Business Model Matrix for Hotel Chocolat, mid-1990s.

the necessary route(s) to market. Margins have to be sufficient to incentivize business partners or agents, and the firm must evolve the systems and structure to support its channels to market.

■ Consumer/direct (top right): the firm needs not only direct selling skills but also a deep understanding of consumer behaviour, typically developed through consumer market research.

■ Consumer/indirect (bottom right): direct selling is less important than the ability to manage key accounts. Frequently the immediate customer will also expect its supplier to have a detailed consumer understanding, and to support sales through consumer marketing activities.

A Business Model that Works for You

After an unhappy couple of years, Hotel Chocolat decided to withdraw from supplying supermarkets. The two partners felt the margins were insufficient to compensate for the work that was involved and that their core skill was in building a brand through direct contact with the end customer. Selling through supermarkets meant supplying customers with products under their brand, not that of Hotel Chocolat, and remaining at arm's length from the consumer. Instead the company refocused on selling direct and as a result has grown rapidly and profitably.

The case of Hotel Chocolat is not atypical. Many enterprises alter their business model over time, and there is a good chance that you have done so as well. Compare your selling structure and channels to market with what you started with, or inherited if you acquired the business. Have these elements changed partly or even significantly? If the business model is fundamentally the same, has that helped or impeded your capacity to grow? If the business model has altered, has the change increased your ability to service the market or have changes actually diluted your firepower?

Assignment 1.2: Your Business Model

1. Describe your current business model, using the framework presented in Figure 1.2. Is this the business model which has always existed, or has it altered significantly?

2. Make a note of the competences for success identified for each box of the matrix. Have these altered in line with changes in the model? Where do you think you are strong and weak?

If you have not thought of your business in this way before, this may be a challenging exercise. You may feel you cannot yet give definitive answers. If so, do not worry. The questions are designed to start you on the path of taking stock, and by the end of this first part, where you are now, you should be in good shape to complete your analysis. Thinking about your business model can certainly sharpen your view on the basic nature of your business activities. Following BGP, Hotel Chocolat partners, Angus Thirlwell and Peter Harris decided that they had spread themselves too thinly by diversifying too early in the company's life cycle. The future, they decided, lay not in broadening their business activity, but in deepening it, selling more of the same kinds of product to similar types of customer, using channels they already understood.

BGP business-to-business company Pacific Direct has taken a similar road. A worldwide supplier of hotel and air travel toiletries, post BGP company founder Lara Morgan refined her business model. She decided that the business should deal only with prestige brands and sell only to the premium sector. The strategy has paid off handsomely. In January 2005, to celebrate achieving over £1 million in profit, she took the entire workforce to Barbados for two weeks!

Which Industry Are You In?

To some owner-managers the answer is so obvious that they wonder why the question is asked at all. 'I sell shoes/make ball-bearings/install IT systems...' could all be replies from people who can say precisely which industry they are in. But for others it is not always so clear-cut. This could be because their business is so specialized that it could only loosely be described as belonging to an industry. One example is Cambridge Regulatory Services, which specializes in advising multinational pharmaceutical companies in how to apply for and obtain regulatory clearance for their products within the UK. This company does not do research and development, nor does it sell pharmaceutical products. Yet its fate and fortunes are tightly linked to the industry which it serves.

In other cases a firm provides services or products to a number of different industries, which makes it hard to characterize. Endoline Machinery, for instance, supplies end-of-line packaging equipment to food companies and pharmaceutical firms as its two major groups of customers. The balance of Endoline's business between these two industries varies depending on the cycle of each. 'We're classified as a smallish mechanical engineering business', says Endoline Managing Director and BGP past participant Tony Hacker. 'Is that a helpful way of thinking about which industry I'm in? Sometimes yes, but sometimes it makes better sense to consider what we do as part of the supply chain serving a particular market or industry sector.'

The Industry Value Chain

Within any given industrial sector there are a number of players who buy and sell to each other. The automotive sector, for instance, is structured in a clear hierarchy. At the top are the tier 1 companies, the Fords and DaimlerChryslers, who assemble and brand the vehicles we drive. They are supplied in turn by tier 2 businesses, which provide sub-assemblies such as gearboxes or windscreens. The chain of supply then cascades all the way to the thousands of suppliers who produce individual components such as screws and springs. Within that industry everyone understands where they sit within the extended chain of supply, who they buy from and who they sell to.

The physical chain of supply also translates into a chain of commercial value, or the value chain. To stick with cars, supplier A buys raw materials or semi-finished goods, creates a finished good and sells that on to supplier B at a margin. The value added by supplier A is the difference between what the bought-in goods cost and their sale price to the customer. With perfect knowledge it would be possible to analyse an entire industry's supply chain and assess the value captured – the difference between purchase and sale prices – by all the individual players. In reality very few of us would ever lay claim to perfect knowledge, but most businesses have a fair idea of the margins made by their key suppliers and also the margins made by their customers. In fashion retail, for instance, certain norms are common. Goods sold are typically marked up by five times the cost of purchase. If that sounds like an excessively large margin, bear in mind that the retailer bears the cost of stocking and displaying the goods, plus the risk of being left with unsold and unsaleable stock!

For the business which is ambitious to grow and prosper, there are two questions to be addressed.

1. How much value are we deriving – measured, say, as net margin or value added per employee – compared with our competitors? Could we do better? (This question is also approached later from a financial perspective in this section of the book.)

2. Could we extract more value by repositioning ourselves within the industry value chain? Two BGP manufacturing businesses have transformed their fortunes by incorporating extra value in their products. Juice Technology has reinvented a traditional engineering business by patenting new inventions in

distributed electrical power. Incorporated into the product ranges of larger strategic partners, Juice's innovations enable overhead lighting to be installed in office developments faster and more cheaply than before. Since this market segment in North America alone is worth $2bn a year, the potential value to customers in terms of time and money saved is enormous, and Juice is now capturing some of that. Pro-Activ Textiles has similarly changed dramatically. No longer a sportswear manufacturer in a crowded commodity marketplace, the business has moved up the value chain through developing a range of patented 'intelligent' fabrics which can repel mosquitoes without the need for skin creams and sprays. The business is also perfecting other applications for this technology that will soothe eczema and inhibit the growth of MRSA.

Reinvention can also be incremental and progressive. Dairyborn Foods built value by constantly extending its offer as a supplier to the prepared foods industry. Finding that there was no future as a commodity distributor of cheese in blocks, founder and BGP participant Robert Segesser began to produce the grated cheese that customers needed to add to pre-cooked ready meals. Customers stopped doing this themselves and paid Dairyborn for the added convenience. From there, Dairyborn progressed to meal components, for which customers were prepared to pay an ever higher premium. In simple terms, Dairyborn was able to take for itself a bigger piece of the value, ultimately paid for by the supermarket shopper, by offering more value to others in the supply chain.

Table 1.2 offers a framework for assessing how your business sits within its supply/value chain.

The concept of a value chain applies also to service-based industries. BGP participant Raz Khan is the founder of Cobalt-Sky, a specialist in the processing of market research data. His business has expanded through increasing the value-added element in his offer to customers. This is what he has to say about repositioning the business:

> Following BGP we realized we needed to make sure we were differentiated from our competition. We were already doing this well without realizing, in that we provided a customer-focused service, but there was a danger our competition would catch up.
>
> We had dabbled in low-price 'cheap 'n' cheerful', but decided this was not us, and we would pursue a premium-priced service. Obviously, we had to make sure people would pay us! This is where key account management came in, we started talking more to our clients. We would set aside time to see the key accounts regularly and LISTEN to what they were trying to do. We found various ways where we could very simply help them to do their work better, so they gained value from working with us. Sometimes it was us training them in certain aspects of the business to help them to be more efficient. Sometimes it was doing something extra on a project, or providing additional

TABLE 1.2 Assessing the Value Chain Across an Industry

Our customer		Us		Our supplier	
Gross margin % =	Gross margin per employee % =	Gross margin % =	Gross margin per employee % =	Gross margin % =	Gross margin per employee % =
Net margin % =	Net margin per employee % =	Net margin % =	Net margin per employee % =	Net margin % =	Net margin per employee % =
		Competitor A			
		Gross margin % =	Gross margin per employee % =		
		Net margin % =	Net margin per employee % =		
		Competitor B			
		Gross margin % =	Gross margin per employee % =		
		Net margin % =	Net margin per employee % =		

Notes

Gross margin/employee is calculated by dividing the reported gross margin by the total number of people employed. A similar calculation is made for net margin/employee. This provides a common yardstick for looking at relative financial performance.

For this exercise, you need to choose a representative customer, supplier and competitors, or an average of the main businesses you deal with or compete against.

You will find the concepts of financial ratios and their application developed in Chapter 3.

information to help them. We are now proud of the fact that if you speak to almost anyone in the market research industry they will know Cobalt-Sky and say 'they're very expensive, but when you need them they're brilliant'. I'm quite happy with that.

It's especially important in the current climate of off-shoring, where the easier jobs are being run much more cheaply in India. We will stay ahead of this by concentrating on the complex projects. Of course there is still the danger they'll catch up, so we need to keep sharp!

Assignment 1.3: Your Industry and the Industry Value Chain

1. Are you clear about which industry you are a part of? If not, does this matter?
2. Using the framework supplied in Table 1.2, do you consider that at the moment you are extracting 'fair value' from your piece of the chain? Are there opportunities to capture more value for your business by repositioning yourself?

Note that this exercise is dependent on the financial data you are able to obtain. If you cannot provide the information at this stage, come back to this exercise when you have read the guidance for assembling the data required in chapter 3.

Like the questions we posed earlier about your business model, the questions about your position in your industry, and potential opportunities to improve your slice of the value, are intended to challenge and stimulate you, to get you into the mode of taking stock of where your business stands.

What is Changing in Your Business Environment?

If you started the business you currently run, when you first scanned the business environment your primary concern back then was to prove that there was a market opportunity for your idea. Subsequently, as the business has grown, feedback from customers is the prime means used to ensure your products and services are in tune with the requirements of the customers you have and the ones you would like to acquire. Markets and customers change, however, and today the rate of change in most markets is faster than ever. It follows that businesses which do not or cannot change to meet new demands will not thrive in the long term.

Let us begin the process of analysis with a review of the environment, so that your customers' needs are seen in the context of wider developments in the outside world. That review, or scanning process, should give you a clear understanding of:

- Whether you should be thinking about incremental or radical change, as you plan 'a new business for a new tomorrow'.
- How to use environmental scanning tools, to identify factors of importance likely to impact on your business.
- How to translate those conclusions into action planning.
- It will also provide you with a suitable context in which to think about your marketing aspirations and operations, topics covered in the next chapter.

Incremental or Radical Change?

As far back as the 1960s, the late, great management guru, Peter Drucker, observed that top management had three basic tasks to perform:

- to run today's business;
- to improve today's business;
- and to create 'a new business for a new tomorrow'.

Most owner-managers devote most of their time to the first task. The ambitious business is always thinking about the second and third tasks.

Task two, improving today's business, is generally a matter of making incremental changes, of de-listing old products for example, or upgrading information systems to enhance employee productivity. In well-managed businesses, incremental changes take place all the time. Some are driven by senior management, other changes arise because employees see an opportunity to make improvements, and have the discretion to do so.

Task three, creating 'a new business for a new tomorrow', implies deeper and far-reaching changes, as witnessed by the examples of Juice Technology and Pro-Activ Textiles, featured previously. In some cases, the changes are the result of careful planning over a sustained period. Thus, a conventional retail business might decide to develop both a direct sales catalogue and a web site as new channels to market. (Hotel Chocolat in fact went the other way: the founders started by selling direct through a catalogue, incorporated a website and are now selling through their own retail outlets!) Both the catalogue and the website will require the business to introduce new systems and processes, as well as requiring significant investment in sales, marketing, logistics and technology management. The business will need to acquire and embed not just 'hard' assets – warehousing, say, or computing power – but also the knowledge and skills to build new capabilities.

Radical change can also come about not because it has been planned, but because the business faces a crisis, the emergence of an unforeseen substitute technology, or an unexpected new player in the market, or the business failure of a key supplier. Pacific Direct had no intention of manufacturing the toiletries it sells until a key supplier got into difficulty. Now the company owns its own production plant and has redesigned its business structures accordingly.

Whether radical changes are planned or not, they always take place within the broader business environment. As a business grows and matures, so it becomes increasingly important to build regular environmental scanning into the planning process, so that you audit where you currently are, to be able to create a new business for a new tomorrow.

Environmental Scanning

The purpose of environment analysis for the growing business is, therefore, to determine what elements are changing in the outside world, and what the implications of these changes are for the future growth and direction of the company. As any business moves out of the start-up phase and into the growth phase, regular environmental scanning should become part of the planning process.

PESTEL Analysis

One useful approach which ensures thoroughness and consistency is to consider trends under each of the following headings:

- *Political:* Factors affecting the business and/or its market which are the result of political changes or trends (for example, changes of government policy, creation of regional bodies).
- *Economic:* Factors affecting the business and/or its market which are driven by the economy (such as whether the national economy is growing, flat or in recession, likely changes in the price of key commodities).
- *Social:* Factors affecting the business and/or its market which are driven by social changes (typically major demographic changes or changes in consumers' lifestyles).
- *Technological:* Factors affecting the business and/or its market which are caused by technological developments. These are likely to be very specific to a particular market and are typically dependent on the rate of innovation within that market (such as new technologies to enable more oil to be extracted from wells).
- *Environmental:* Factors affecting the business and/or its market arising from environmental changes (such as global warming) or ecological concerns (such as the need to conserve fish stocks).
- *Legal:* Factors affecting the business and/or its market arising from new or planned legislation (a good example being tighter data protection laws in many countries).

The first four of these factors form a PEST analysis, which has been a standard tool in strategic planning for many years. Recently, the last two factors, environmental and legal, have been added, to create the more comprehensive PESTEL analysis.

For the typical growing business, it is a straightforward process to identify and list environmental factors using this framework. Here are some guidelines on how to go about this:

1. Conduct this exercise with the senior management team, not just the boss in isolation, to ensure a broad spread of views. It may also be useful to feed into the process contributions from any advisers to the business whose opinions you respect.
2. It is more important to identify a significant environmental factor than to spend time debating whether it is, say, a political or an economic factor.
3. Do not worry if you cannot identify a significant factor under a particular heading. It could just be the case that there is no planned legislation, or change in consumer lifestyle, for example, which is going to impact on your business.

4. At the end of the listing, determine which are the key factors (probably no more than six) that are really going to affect your business. Make sure that these are clear in everyone's mind, and that they are taken account of in the planning process.

5. Do not spend too much time over this exercise (you will risk losing focus on what is important). A small to medium-sized business can complete the task comfortably in less than half a day.

Preparation: Sources of Information

Before you get into this you will be well advised to do some background research. Some of the information you need is in people's heads, but information on social and economic data most likely is not. Much of the macroeconomic and market information that you will need in order to complete a PESTEL analysis is publicly available. Thanks to the Internet, it has never been easier to access huge amounts of research on a bewildering range of product, service and geographic markets. And much of it is free!

In advanced economies, governments increasingly make available online statistics on the economy, the population, patterns of expenditure, trends in consumption and so on, all accessible through key-word searches. If the data are published in hard-copy form, they are normally available in public libraries or at government offices. Information collected by governments (or supranational bodies, such as the European Union) which is useful for this purpose includes:

- *Macroeconomic cycles:* Comparing the performance of the economy as a whole with different industrial sectors.
- *Trends in population growth or decline:* For instance, currently most western economies face a common set of demographic problems in the form of an ageing population, a fall in the numbers of those of working age and a long-term decline in the birth rate.
- *Regional economic performance:* Which regions are most and least affluent, which qualify for assisted status (and thus grants to aid business expansion!).
- *Patterns of household and personal consumption:* Where consumers are spending their money, and which sectors are declining or booming as a result of changes in lifestyle.

Official statistics are usefully complemented by market research reports produced by specialists, such as the Economist Intelligence Unit, Datamonitor and Mintel (to cite three of the best-known European providers). Their reports are typically more focused on commercial issues, and will go into greater depth on a particular industry. Market research reports can supplement official statistics by giving you a perspective on how socioeconomic, technological or legislative changes are impacting on your industry.

Are consumers spending less because of an uncertain economic outlook? Is the 'grey' market of people over 60 looking more attractive because of increased longevity and spending power?

Market research providers divide into those specializing in business-to-business, and those who deal with consumer markets. A little research on the web will soon highlight the experts in the area in which you are interested. As a rule of thumb, if the industry sector is significant – that is, involving turnover in the hundreds of millions or billions of euros – it will attract the attention of market research specialists. The downside, as you might expect, is that, since these are commercial organizations, they sell their information!

However, an important customer segment for market research is the commercially focused library. These can be found in a business school, for example, and sometimes also in a government department or agency. Before you part with your hard-earned money, check which libraries you have access to already, or are eligible to use free or for an annual subscription. Then, find out which market research services the library subscribes to; you could save yourself a significant outlay.

You could also save money by checking what is available from your trade or industry association, assuming one exists. Some interpret their remit as information providers quite widely, and can be a very useful source of hard data.

Outcome of the PESTEL Analysis

The outcome of the analysis should be a shortlist of broader environmental factors which you have reason to believe will have an important impact on your industry within the next five years. Below is an example for the global hotel industry, supplied by toiletries specialist Pacific Direct.

- *Political:* Nothing significant, since politics is mostly transacted at national levels and this is a global market.
- *Economic:* The industry is sensitive to the world economy and responds fast to both slowdowns and booms. Experience shows that the premium sector is less affected by recession. Provided there is not a worldwide slump, some regions will always perform well. Emerging hotspots are the Middle East and East Asia-Pacific Rim.
- *Social:* In advanced economies there is a growing trend for people to take more, shorter holidays, such as long weekends. This will steadily boost the premium market. In the next five years the 'silver surfer' segment – affluent 60+ consumers – will increase by 5–10 per cent across the board.
- *Technological:* Does not really affect toiletries, except incrementally. IT advances will help in making our global supply chain more flexible, allowing us to switch production between factories.

- *Environmental:* Huge concerns over packaging and recycling. Our product lines are in good shape, but we will want to stay ahead of the game, ensuring our customers and their customers perceive that we are a responsible company.
- *Legal:* Product testing requirements will become ever more stringent, as will the ability to audit the supply chain, to trace products right back to raw materials suppliers. Corporate social responsibility is the name of the game.
- *Summary:* The overall picture is good, but this is a market that can be badly affected by random, unpredictable events such as terrorism attacks. We have to be nimble and highly responsive, making sure that we are not overstocked or overcommitted to suppliers. We must also invest care, attention and cash in behaving, and being seen to behave, as a socially responsible organization.

Assignment 1.4: PESTEL Analysis

Conduct a PESTEL analysis using this tool. Can you answer the following questions?

1. How would you expect the latest forecast for the national economy to impact on your business over the next 18 months to three years?
2. Can you foresee changes in the local economy that may affect your business?
3. Do you foresee legislative changes at either national or governmental level that could affect your business? Consider consumer protection, health and safety, employee protection and other relevant areas.
4. Are there any significant, predictable technological changes that could affect how you and your competitors do business?
5. Will demographic changes affect your business?
6. And are there any developing social changes that could affect your business?

How Do You Implement a PESTEL Analysis?

As we said earlier, the ability of any business, even a large corporation, to influence external forces is limited. Bill Gates is famously on record as saying that the best way to predict the future is to invent it. But not even a business the size of Microsoft can afford to ignore in its strategic thinking what is happening in the wider world. In reality, large companies devote huge resources to scanning the environment and to planning for 'what if?' scenarios.

For the smaller business, the primary purpose of this exercise is to provide a reality check, that future plans have taken full account of the big, foreseeable trends that affect not just business but everyone's lives. If we revert to the previous example, it is reasonable to predict that there will be future shocks to the global travel industry, in the form perhaps of a terrorist attack or a natural disaster such as the Boxing Day 2004

East Asian tsunami. Of course, we cannot predict when such an event will happen, but we can have a contingency plan in place. Similarly, corporate social responsibility is not an altered state of being which a company can assume overnight, and its importance in determining future customer buying behaviour is hard to estimate. But it is a destination which can be mapped and for which specific policies and systems can be developed and applied. The PESTEL analysis provides, if you like, the frame within which strategic thinking about the future takes place. It sets boundaries and expectations. To use an analogy favoured by many BGP participants, it is a key element of the map-making process, which charts the journey of the business into the future.

As a result of environmental scanning, many businesses identify threats and opportunities. We will look at these more closely in the chapter that follows, so be ready to revisit your conclusions.

two
Your Customers and Competitors

We finished the last chapter by examining how your business priorities are going to be framed by the conclusions you draw about the wider environment. In this chapter we narrow the focus to the relationship between your business and your customers and consider how you fare against your competitors.

We will start by reviewing the market segments you serve and the way in which you meet your customers' needs. What do you offer them that is distinctive or compelling? Can you describe the life cycle of the relationship that you enjoy with your customers? And while – in theory at any rate – the customer is always right, are you doing business with the right customers?

We will turn then to look at who your competitors are and how you win against them. How do you define your competitors and how much do you know about them? What should you know about them? Where do you find the necessary information about them? And what should be the success factors which you track, to make sure that you are staying ahead?

The final section explores your overall marketing strategy. What does your current marketing mix consist of? How do you price, promote, distribute and sell your existing range of products and services? If you operate a retail business, what do your premises say about you? Lastly, we ask you to bring together your thinking so far into an overall assessment of your business's present position in the market.

The Market Segments You Serve

Market segmentation is the name given to the process whereby customers and potential customers are organized into clusters or groups of 'similar' types. At a simple level, a shop or a restaurant has both regular customers and passing trade. The more passing trade that can be converted to regular customers, the better the business is likely to do. Similarly, the revenues of a business services firm such as a graphic design agency may well be split between retained and one-off or project work. The more business that can be converted to retained, the easier it is to plan both workloads and cashflow.

As implied, these are simple examples of segmenting a customer base. Those readers who already operate with the concept of segmentation in their markets will know that there is much more sophistication possible in how you can target and classify your customers. If you do not use segmentation in the way you think about your customers, it is worth our stating briefly why this concept is useful and important:

- No business can service all customers equally.
- There are some customers whom you are naturally better suited to serve.
- Even if you operate within a narrowly defined industrial sector, there will be some customers with whom you have a better fit.
- Defining your target customers allows you to focus limited resources more effectively.
- And just as there are customers you do want, so there are some that you do not!

The approach you take to segmentation fundamentally depends on whether you sell to consumers (albeit indirectly) or to other businesses.

Consumer Segmentation

Traditionally, consumer segmentation has been based on what marketers call a priori attributes, such as income, occupation and social status. The basis for this was the belief that these characteristics were what determined how and why consumers made their purchasing decisions. In essence, wealthier people bought better-quality products, poorer consumers bought mass-market goods. Both groups, so the thinking went, were strongly influenced by their social and economic peer groups. Marketers operated with a classification scheme that categorized the population accordingly. Table 2.1 shows a recent version of this for the UK population.

In the days when consumer marketing was largely about mass-market advertising, businesses specified their target population by reference to these socioeconomic groups, typically qualified by gender and age cohorts. Advertisers trying to reach younger, more affluent female consumers (for example, ABC1 25- to 45-year-old women) would advertise in glossy upmarket publications; conversely, those targeting older consumers on a limited budget would use a different set of media.

Sociodemographics remain the basis of much consumer marketing. But in recent years this rather crude approach has been supplemented by more finely calibrated

TABLE 2.1 Socioeconomic Classification, UK Population

Social grade	Social status	Occupation	As percentage of 15+ population
A	Upper middle class	Higher managerial, administrative or professional	3.4
B	Middle class	Intermediate managerial, administrative or professional	21.6
C1	Lower middle class	Supervisory or clerical, junior managerial, administrative or professional	29.1
C2	Skilled working class	Skilled manual workers	21
D	Working class	Semi- and unskilled manual workers	16.2
E	Those at lowest level of subsistence	State pensioners or widows (no other earner), casual or lowest grade workers	8.8

Source: National Readership Survey, January–December 2004. With acknowledgments to NRS Ltd. Reproduced with permission.

methods, in response to major changes in the environment. For one thing, increasing social mobility means that today's consumers are less likely to conform to a narrow range of stereotypes. They are less likely to be conditioned by their upbringing and more likely to be promiscuous in their loyalty to different brands. For another, there has been a massive fragmentation in media channels, with two effects, good and bad: it is increasingly difficult to reach a mass audience in one 'hit', and at the same time it is easier to reach special interest groups or minority audiences through media that cater specifically for them. This last point is particularly worth noting for the smaller business, because it makes targeted consumer marketing more viable than it has ever been.

A major step forward has been the 'clustering' of consumer households by reference to location. The CACI organization combines demographic with geographic information to create A Classification of Residential Neighbourhoods (ACORN). It includes every street in the UK, comprising 17 distinct clusters of households and a total of 54 ACORN neighbourhood types. Those businesses that target consumers through direct mail are able to pinpoint exactly where in the UK to direct their marketing campaigns. The Mosaic service offered by CACI's competitor Experian combines locational information with a classification of consumers by lifestyle, that is to say what it is they value and choose to spend their money on. See www.business-strategies.co.uk for more information on Mosaic. Mosaic has developed lifestyle clusters specifically for the UK and a global group of clusters which apply internationally. They are reproduced in Table 2.2, for comparison.

Some of these clusters are self-explanatory. Suburban comfort, for example, neatly describes some well-heeled residential areas. More information about the classification is given on the website already referred to.

TABLE 2.2 Mosaic Classification of Consumers by Lifestyle

United Kingdom		Global	
A	Symbols of success	A	Sophisticated singles
B	Happy families	B	Bourgeois prosperity
C	Suburban comfort	C	Career and family
D	Ties of community	D	Comfortable retirement
E	Urban intelligence	E	Routine service workers
F	Welfare borderline	F	Hard-working blue collar
G	Municipal dependency	G	Metropolitan strugglers
H	Blue-collar enterprise	H	Low-income elders
I	Twilight subsistence	I	Post-industrial survivors
J	Grey perspectives	J	Rural inheritance
K	Rural isolation		

To appeal to different consumer categories in different locations, the Accor Hotel Group has developed a set of brands across national European markets, among them:

- *Sofitel*: Five-star luxury at the top of the market, in downtown locations.
- *Novotel*: Three-star hotels typically close to airports and major railway stations.
- *Ibis*: A two-star brand aimed at families needing an overnight stop.
- *Formula 1*: A basic motel operation.

The same individual could, in theory, stay in each type of Accor hotel at different times. It depends on the capacity in which they are travelling, and who is picking up the bill!

The capacity in which customers are buying is a fundamental consideration for consumer brand-focused businesses. Sales to consumers account for the majority of Hotel Chocolat's business and the company has spent years building a highly detailed profile of its core customer base. Much of this information is, of course, commercially sensitive, but it is no secret that both the giver of their products and the recipient are likely to be female. In growing their business, the founders found it useful to segment by occasion. Initially they sold to customers who were looking at buying gifts to send to others, typically as an alternative to sending flowers. After a while it became clear there was an opportunity to sell chocolates to the same customer group for their own enjoyment. And so the Chocolate Tasting Club was born, which has grown to become one of the most important parts of the business.

In 2004, the partners decided that the next phase of expansion should be into their own retail outlets. Over several months they reviewed their customer profile and looked carefully at different locations throughout the UK which would fit that profile. In the end they decided to open the first shop in the Harlequin mall in Watford, just north of London, on the grounds that this seemed a suitable match. Their choice proved right and eight months later Hotel Chocolat launched its second store, in Milton Keynes, 30 miles further north. That too has performed well. Five more opened during 2005 and a dozen more in 2006. However, the dynamic duo have resisted the siren calls of property agents to accelerate the pace of development too rapidly. It is better to be sure the location is right than rush in, says joint manager director Angus Thirlwell.

Business-to-Business Segmentation

As we observed in the previous chapter, the majority of businesses sell to other businesses. For them, segmentation starts with the industry or industries into which they sell. Like other advanced economies, the UK has a system of industrial classification (SIC) which aggregates and disaggregates the businesses that constitute the national economy. Since 1992 the SIC has been organized in the following way (extracted from http://www.statistics.gov.uk/methods_quality/sic/default.asp).

UK SIC is divided into 17 sections, each denoted by a single letter from A to Q. Some sections are, in turn, divided into subsections (each denoted by the addition of a second letter). The letters of the sections or subsections can be uniquely defined by the next breakdown, the divisions (denoted by two digits).

There are 17 sections, 16 subsections, 60 divisions, 222 groups, 503 classes and 253 subclasses. An example is shown in Table 2.3.

Business-to-business segmentation is performed largely on the basis of need and usage. If we revert to the example quoted in Table 2.3, we can envisage that within manufacturing of textiles alone there will be a range of subclasses: between those who produce apparel and those who do not, and within those who produce apparel those who use natural as opposed to artificial fibres, and so on and so forth. If you supply this industry you will want to be able to define as closely as possible which companies might be in the market for your product, i.e. whether they need it or not.

Having identified those who need your products, you will consider whether you are able to supply them physically. Should you segment the market geographically, restricting yourself to a local area, or are you a national or international supplier? Cambridge Regulatory Services, which we referred to earlier, is by definition an international business, since its clients are drawn from the ranks of multinational pharmaceuticals, one

TABLE 2.3 Example of Standard Industrial Classification

Section D	Manufacturing (comprising divisions 15 to 37)
Subsection DB	Manufacture of textiles and textile products (comprising divisions 17 and 18)
Division 17	Manufacture of textiles
Group 17.4	Manufacture of made-up textile articles, except apparel
Class 17.40	Manufacture of made-up textile articles, except apparel
Subclass 17.40/1	Manufacture of soft furnishings

To see the full structure of the current UK SIC visit http://www.statistics.gov.uk/methods_quality/sic/default.asp, pages 5–30.

of the most 'global' of industries. This is an unusual case, since most owner-managers who have a service business tend to supply a limited geographical area. However, as international markets open up ever more widely, we can expect to see services traded increasingly in the way that products are.

After geography, next on the list of segmentation criteria comes usage, which many businesses will split into size of customer and size of order. Often these are linked. Depending on the nature of your business, it may be uneconomic to supply orders below a certain size, or indeed orders above a certain size. Many people use the price mechanism to discourage buyers from placing disproportionately small orders: you can buy from us, but at a price that encourages you to shop elsewhere (a useful means of discouraging any type of unwanted buyer).

ABC (or Pareto) Analysis

Whether your business sells to consumers or other businesses, you may also have a system that segments size of customer by aggregated orders through the year. This is often referred to as an ABC or Pareto analysis, after the economist who first observed that about 80 per cent of a firm's sales (and profits) derive from 20 per cent of its customers. Of course, 80/20 is an approximation rather an iron rule, but the basic trading pattern is true of most businesses. The ABC analysis does just as it implies, ranking customers by top, medium and bottom performers in terms of both sales and profitability (beware: they may not be the same). Sales-focused businesses make heavy use of this tool. BGP participant Jerry Sandys has grown the electronics business he founded, TDC, through careful and consistent application of ABC analysis, identifying at an early stage B customers who through careful nurturing have the potential to enter the A cohort. At the same time, TDC has been ruthless about pruning C accounts that will never amount to much and which are unprofitable to service.

Where exactly you determine the boundaries of the ABC analysis depends on the nature of the business you run. Most A and C customers are self-evident, but setting the exact thresholds at which B customers become A customers and C customers become B customers is not always clear-cut. Our experience of working with BGP participants suggests it is an iterative process which gets better through trial and error. The benefit derives from application and subsequent refinement, not through agonizing over exact demarcations.

As a rule of thumb, for most businesses the A cohort will vary between 60 per cent and 80 per cent of sales or profit, B between 10 per cent and 20 per cent, C the rest. Often the easiest way is to start with your largest customer and work down. Some companies select their top, say, 20 customers and stick with that as the prime measure.

Do You Have a Unique Selling Point or Proposition?

From a customer's point of view, the strongest possible point of differentiation is a supplier whom they cannot live without! In a few cases that is because the supplier has a unique technology or enjoys a monopoly advantage. BGP business Hunters & Frankau is in the happy position of being the only company authorized to import and distribute cigars directly from Cuba within the UK, Ireland and the Channel Isles. If you want one of the world's finest cigars, you have to obtain it via Hunters & Frankau!

If the same applies to you, congratulations. But it is no accident that we entitle the marketing and strategy sessions on BGP 'The Battle for the Customer', because that is the everyday reality for most of us. The vast majority of businesses have to find other ways in which they can create a unique selling point or proposition, to capture the customer's attention and business. Mars famously promoted the Mars Bar for many years under the slogan 'A Mars a day helps you work, rest and play', which neatly packaged a set of benefits and made it difficult for any competitor to imitate without being an obvious 'me-too' copycat. Are you able in your business to identify a unique point of difference, or set of differences, which translates into a unique set of benefits for the target customer?

Assignment 2.1: Segmentation and Differentiation

1. If you sell to consumers, which of these segmentation criteria do you employ:

    - socioeconomic grouping
    - lifestyle type
    - occasion or need
    - location
    - other.

    Do you have a clear profile of your target segment(s)? If so, what is this/are they?

2. If you sell to other businesses, which of these segmentation criteria do you employ:

    - SIC code (at what level of aggregation)
    - location
    - usage
    - other buying behaviour
    - size of customer/order/ABC analysis.

    Do you have a clear profile of your target segment(s)? If so, what is this/are they?

3. Do you have a unique selling point, or proposition, that translates into a unique – or at any rate highly differentiated – set of benefits for the customer?

The Customer Life Cycle

Pointing out that customers and competitors change over time may seem like a state-ment of the obvious – but we have seen too many firms go out of business because they left it too late to react to changes in their market. A firm's relationship with individual customers changes over time (Table 2.4).

The relationship with someone who becomes a significant customer is in some respects like a marriage. At first, a potential customer's attitude to your company is likely to be cautious, if not suspicious. If you convince the customer to place a first order, that caution or suspicion will reduce. It is unlikely to change immediately to an attitude of complete trust until you have successfully satisfied a number of repeat orders. There then follows a period of 'honeymoon', when the relationship works well for both parties: if problems occur, they are quickly resolved, with good will on both sides. Unfortunately, that state of contentment cannot be taken for granted. Over time the relationship can slip into boredom or disenchantment, just as couples who cannot make their marriage work fall out of love.

If you think this analogy is a little fanciful, stop for a moment and reflect on your own behaviour as a consumer. How many brands of goods and services do you remain consistently loyal to over a long period of time? If you are a typical consumer, the answer is precious few. Most of us like a balance in our lives between the familiar and the new, and the attachment to what we already know can often be supplanted by what we see as a better or more interesting alternative.

You will see that there is an obvious parallel between the customer life cycle concept and the ABC analysis we introduced earlier. A customers will invariably be those who are in, or approaching, the wedlock stage, C customers have never progressed much beyond a first date and B customers are somewhere along the continuum!

A famous McKinsey study of the early 1990s identified that the prime reason why seven out of ten industrial buyers changed supplier had nothing to do with the product supplied or performance, but was rather the result of indifference on the part of the incumbent supplier! The most likely causes of commercial disenchantment are failure to communicate – through visits, newsletters, telephone calls, e-mails and so forth – or inadequate improvements to products and services as they age. The British motorcycle industry of the 1960s saw its business melt away as consumers turned instead to Japanese and continental European imports. British producers 'knew' that 'real' motorbikes were big, noisy and oily, and that is what they carried on making. Most British motorbike users knew that they wanted a quiet, clean, reliable mode of transport. American car manufacturers suffered a similar shock in the 1980s. America, after all, invented mass automobile production, and the big car companies had always taken their domestic market for granted. But brand loyalty fast disappeared when consumers were presented with the alternative of cheap, efficient, Japanese models that better fitted their life-style, and the US auto industry has never fully recovered its pre-eminence in its own backyard.

TABLE 2.4 Customer Life Cycle

	Courtship	Engagement	Honeymoon	Wedlock	Either deadlock	Or rekindled relationship
Customer attitude	Suspicious	Moderately suspicious	Trusting	Boring	Disenchanted	Newly interested
Supplier objective	Get first order	Get repeat order	Increase sales volume	Maintain sales	Sell in new products	Rebuild commitment

Adapted from *Strategic Customer Planning* by Alan Melkman, Thorogood Publishing, 2001. See www.thorogoodpublishing.co.uk

For your business, it may be a stimulus to action to categorize your major customers broadly by the stages presented in Table 2.4. The quickest way to rekindle sales may be through relaunching the relationship, by researching and reanalysing customer needs in the wedlock and deadlock stages, before you lose the business to competitive suppliers. When too many people in your firm begin to think primarily of your established customers as 'debtors', rather than the reason why you are in business, take this as a warning sign! Actions to pre-empt the loss of mature customers include:

- finding reasons to revisit;
- sharing market information;
- developing joint promotional activities with key customers;
- initiating or strengthening electronic buy/sell links.

If taken in good time, these initiatives can head customers off from seeking alternative suppliers.

Assignment 2.2: ABC Analysis and Customer Life Cycle

1. Apply the ABC analysis to your business, using customer sales and, if possible, profitability. What does the pattern look like? If you are unable to use profitability per customer as a measure, is this a shortcoming in your information base?
2. Classify your existing customer base using the customer life cycle concept shown in Table 2.4. Do you consider that you have a good flow-through from courtship to wedlock? If not, where are the blockages and what should you be doing about these?
3. Consider any recent cases where you have lost customers that you would like to have retained. Could you have taken active measures to ensure their loyalty and, if so, what would these have been?

Who Are Your Competitors?

As a general rule, a business faces two types of competition: direct and indirect. Direct competitors are those businesses who compete for the same slice of the customer's expenditure that you target. You can name them almost without thinking and, if you track them carefully, you may also be able to recite from memory their product range, distinctiveness and annual sales! Indirect competitors are more typically alternative or substitute solutions to the same customer need: perhaps a different technology, or a different service. They may represent a more subtle threat to your competitive position, since these are not usually in your sights. The environmental scanning process described in the previous chapter should alert you to early signs that an alternative technology or a different solution to the customer needs you meet could risk supplanting you.

In the first 10 years after starting up, defining his direct competitors was a relatively straightforward task for Cobra Beer founder Karan Bilimoria. Cobra targeted the Indian restaurant sector in the UK. Since this comprised several thousand outlets and was growing rapidly through the 1990s, it represented a big enough opportunity to satisfy even an entrepreneur as ambitious as Karan. The direct competition consisted of mainstream beers such as Carlsberg, and specialist brands such as Kingfisher. The indirect competition battling for the customer's wallet were other beverages: wine, fruit juices, mineral waters and so on.

Although annual sales of the curry restaurant market run into billions of pounds, in terms of beverages it is something of a niche market. By the end of the 1990s Cobra had established a very strong position against a relatively narrow set of competitors. The opportunity presented itself to diversify into new channels, and now Cobra is to be found on the shelves of off-licences and major supermarkets, competing against dozens of other beer brands. Cobra is also exported to dozens of markets and is brewed in Poland, the Netherlands, Belgium and India as well as the UK. Far from raising the business's anxiety levels, the new situation is relished by Karan and his team. 'We love a challenge', is their response. But they are also the first to acknowledge that expansion has presented a vastly different set of competitive issues.

How Do You Track Your Competitors?

This raises the next question of how you track information about your competitors. In the previous chapter we referred to the market research specialists such as Euromonitor and Mintel, who issue regular reports on different industries. If you do not already know who specializes in your industry, it will not be difficult to find out. If you are a retailer or sell through retailers to consumers, you will be well served by a plethora of data gatherers, from giants like Nielsen, who audit retail sales across the board, to agencies like BGP company Acuigen (www.acuigen.co.uk), which undertakes bespoke market research in real time. BGP past participant business Canadean (www.canadean. com) is another specialist, which focuses exclusively on tracking the global beverages market for major organizations like Coca-Cola and Unilever.

These suppliers will sell you information that allows you to identify important benchmarking data, such as competitor market share and market penetration, and to track these over time. You may already belong to a service that undertakes omnibus research, that is to say pooled research on a behalf of a number of subscribers – sometimes competitors, sometimes not – addressing questions which all are interested in. Most smaller businesses, however, do not have the wherewithal to commission bespoke research on the competition or to pay large sums for comprehensive market surveys. So how do successful owner-managed businesses keep abreast of the competition?

Trade Press

We have not yet encountered an industry which lacks a dedicated trade press. Depending on the market, publications can range from little more than gossip-sheets to authoritative titles that command industry-wide respect. You will know your own sector. If you do not already do so, allocate to a specific person the task of skimming your trade press every week to cull competitor information: new product launches, customer accounts gained and company profiles are all pieces that help to make up the competitive jigsaw puzzle. Many journalists are expert at teasing out more information from a subject than that person intended to give! Most of the larger publications will also put news items online and include a search facility, which is an easy way to search for information.

Websites and the Internet in General

It is nearly always informative to review your competitors' websites. Some will tell you nothing very much; others provide an astonishing depth and breadth of information that could include details of past and current customers, price lists, job vacancies (from which strategic intentions can sometimes be inferred), and so forth. Often the style and tone of the site will by themselves tell you a lot about whom they are targeting as their prime customers, and what they are representing as their point of difference. If they transact business over the web you can even – subject to ethical considerations – buy from them, to find out just how good or bad they are!

Competitor Marketing Literature

Any competitor of any size and substance is likely to employ sales and marketing literature. Do you systematically gather, file and record this? More importantly, does your sales force do this? Sales and marketing literature are key documents in establishing your rivals' position in the marketplace. Periodically this changes, through acquisition, disposal or even a rebranding exercise. Just as good businesses plot the development of key customers over time, so they tend to chart the progress of key competitors on a regular basis, so they know what they are facing in the marketplace.

Competitor Reports and Accounts

If your competitors are above a certain size, then this is a relatively straightforward exercise, since they are required by law to produce publicly available accounts. As a general rule, the larger the business, the more reporting is required, and the depth and detail of the information is that much greater for businesses listed on a public stock exchange.

Trade Fairs

These can be an excellent source of market intelligence, and often the quickest and simplest means of updating your file of competitors' sales and marketing literature. You do not even need to take a stand, but can register to attend as a visitor in most cases.

Your Sales Force and/or Intermediaries/Suppliers

These points of contact should be feeding back market intelligence on a continuing basis. Do you have someone in your organization who has the specific remit of collating information gathered informally from these sources? If not, perhaps now is the time to do so.

The process does not necessarily have to be purely formal. The respected British design guru and serial entrepreneur Sir Terence Conran has claimed that he undertakes no market research at all. On closer questioning, he confesses to spending nearly half of his time visiting competitors' restaurants and inspecting new and rival products.

Periodically we encounter businesses whose bosses tell us they did not get where they are by studying the competition. We do not suggest that studying the competition is a substitute for developing a distinctive business proposition of your own, but the dangers of ignoring what the competition is doing are obvious. A recent survey undertaken by Cranfield in association with accountants Kingston Smith showed a clear relationship between high-performing businesses and the monitoring of the competition.

Assignment 2.3: Tracking Competitors

1. List your direct and indirect competitors.
2. Which of these do you actively monitor?
3. If you do actively monitor them, which things do you track?
4. How is information on competitors communicated to people in your organization?
5. Do you consider this is adequate?
6. If not, what steps should you take to improve this activity?

Do You Know How You Win Business?

It seems a strange question to ask, but many smaller firms, including high-growth ones, do not really know the answer. They have an idea, or perhaps several ideas, but no one in the business is truly certain why customers buy from them rather than the competition. 'We're better' or 'we're different' may be true, but if that is the extent of the response it is a shaky edifice on which to construct a robust marketing strategy. In fact, being better and different is a message we continually drive home on BGP but it is of little use as a tool for growth unless you understand how you are better and why you are different, or how you could become more so.

Key Success Factors from the Customer's Point of View

The one person to whom this really matters is, of course, the customer. Over the years we have found that the best way to approach the question of how you win business is by identifying the key factors for success in the customer's eyes. In any market there are a limited and identifiable number of reasons why the customer will buy from the available suppliers. Some of those reasons will be, in sales force jargon, order qualifiers: unless the price quoted is within certain boundaries, for example, no supplier is likely to get the order. Other reasons will be order winners (ability to respond within a certain time-frame, for example, or to service a defined geography) that swing the buying decision one way or another. While order qualifiers will in general be common across a market, or at least a homogeneous section of the market, order winners tend to be more specific to the individual customer.

As the business grows, and the number of customers and products offered increases, management needs to check that the 'key success factors' which helped establish the business are still the most important from the customers' point of view.

One way to do this is shown in Table 2.5, a disguised key success factor (KSF) analysis presented by a BGP participant. You can list the main success factors in your market, and rank their importance as shown in the example. Then attempt to do the same for two or three nearest competitors. What customers require should then be translated into the internal tasks necessary for the company to satisfy these requirements and to monitor how well you are doing.

There are several important points to bear in mind when using this approach.

1. Most small(er) businesses start by making a subjective assessment, that is they complete the table using the opinion of the management team. That is no bad thing, since this tool can be used to make explicit the assumptions about competitors held by different people in the business. When using this on management development programmes, we have often found that managers in the same company have very different perceptions about (a) who their competitors are; and (b) the strengths and weaknesses of different competitors. The resulting discussion usually sharpens the focus on competitors dramatically!

2. If it is possible to feed into this exercise the perceptions of customers (because you have, for example, the results of a recent customer survey), then do so: you will have a much more robust set of conclusions. If you have no such data, a good proxy is usually the opinion of either your sales force, if they sell direct, or any intermediaries who sell through to the end users. These are, after all, the people who are closest to the customer. You will need, however, to conduct

TABLE 2.5 An Example of Using the Key Success Factors Approach

Competitive position		Score out of 10: yourself and your main competitors							
		Your business		Competitor A		Competitor B		Competitor C	
KSF	Rank importance of KSF (%)	Score	WA	Score	WA	Score	WA	Score	WA
KSF1: an affordable price	50	9	4.5	9	4.5	5	2.5	5	2.5
KSF2: rapid response	25	7	1.75	6	1.5	7	1.75	8	2.0
KSF3: broad product range	15	7	1.05	6	0.9	6	0.9	7	1.05
KSF4: innovation in the market	10	5	0.5	7	0.7	7	0.7	6	0.6
Total (WA, %, × score)* rounded	100		7.8		7.6		5.9		6.2

KSY, key success factor; WA, weighted average.

*To calculate weighted average, multiply each score by KSF %, thus:

Your business KSF1 is 50% × 9 = 4.50.

Your business KSF2 is 25% × 7 = 1.75.

Your business KSF3 is 15% × 7 = 1.05.

Your business KSF4 is 10% × 5 = 0.5.

Total weighted average = 7.80.

Note: the factors, rankings and scores are examples only and are used simply to demonstrate how this technique works. In order to apply this to your business, you will have to identify the factors which are key in your market, their relative importance to the customers and how you rate against the competition. The choice of weighting is yours. In most markets there is usually one dominant success factor which accounts for 50 per cent or more of the buying decision.

some kind of customer survey to have real confidence in the conclusions (or to modify them if your customers challenge your assumptions!).

3. If you have a business which competes in different markets or different market segments, where the buying criteria are clearly not the same, you are best to do this exercise separately for each market or segment. Trying to do something at too general a level will not produce useful conclusions and you will not be able to turn these conclusions into action.

4. Beware the inevitable temptation to flatter yourself about how good your business is versus the competition. In surveys of car drivers, most respondents consistently rate themselves as above average drivers (although women are less inclined to do so than men!). This is another reason why your conclusions should be confirmed by what the market thinks.

Go back and review the example above. What might you conclude from this analysis, and how might that be usefully turned into action?

Assignment 2.4: Key Success Factors Analysis

For your business/market, complete the framework in Table 2.6.

Key Performance Indicators

Monitoring the achievement of the company on key success factors is, we believe, one of the key requirements for the growing company. Monthly financial accounts are an essential indicator of the overall health of the company, but they do not pinpoint in the same way the areas where remedial action should be taken. Key success factors can frequently be measured and monitored through key performance indicators. These vary from one industry to another. Retailers, for example, traditionally measure their performance by stock turnover, sales per square metre and profit per square metre. Big operators will monitor these figures store by store and weekly, if not daily. Airlines measure their load factor (filled passenger capacity per flight) and yield (income per head per flight), hotels their occupancy rates. There are also 'softer' performance indicators, such as staff perceptions or customer satisfaction scores, which may be no less important in measuring how your business is performing over time. Your choice of key performance indicators will depend on several factors:

- What are the norms in your industry?
- What are the key success factors (typically closely related to the norms)?
- What else is important for you to measure, in that it tracks the ways that you are different from or better than the competition?
- What can be measured and will yield useful information at an affordable cost?

TABLE 2.6 Key Success Factors Analysis

Competitive position		Score out of 10: yourself and your main competitors								
		Your business		Competitor A		Competitor B		Competitor C		
KSFs	Rank importance of KSFs	Score	WA	Score	WA	Score	WA	Score	WA	
KSF1 (this is typically accorded 50% of the weight)										
KSF2										
KSF3										
KSF4										
Total (WA, %, × score) rounded	100%									

Large companies are notorious for collecting huge amounts of data which are filed and forgotten. The growing business cannot afford this luxury. Information is worth collecting only if it can be gathered (relatively) cheaply and efficiently and can be turned into action that will benefit the business.

SWOT Analysis

The topics and assignments which you have worked through in this chapter so far should have prepared you for this last section, the SWOT analysis. Many of you will already be familiar with the concept of reviewing your business's internal strengths and weaknesses and setting them against the external opportunities and threats in the market. Some people consider this approach a bit passé, but over the years BGP participants keep telling us that it is one of the best tools in the box. Karan Bilimoria makes a point of starting all his strategy reviews with a SWOT analysis, and it does not seem to have done Cobra Beer any harm!

If you are not familiar with the exercise, it is straightforward enough.

- *Strengths* are those features of the organization that help sustain your business in its market – position in your segment, product or service quality, reputation, proprietary technology, distribution agreements, a loyal customer base, research and development capability – all these are examples of sources of competitive advantage.
- *Weaknesses* are the flipside of your strengths, and are often directly related. For example, a strong supplier relationship with a small group of customers makes the business vulnerable if one or two accounts are lost. Equally, if you are tied to one key supplier, and that gives you a clear advantage in the market, there is a risk posed by the potential loss of that agreement.
- Both strengths and weaknesses are internal to the business. Opportunities and threats are identified by looking outside the business, at the market you are operating in.
- What *opportunities* exist to capture new business or market segments which you are not currently exploiting? Opportunities most commonly arise out of changes: in technology, in market structure (for example, the crumbs that fall from the table when a big company divests itself of a particular activity) or through new entrants. Sometimes opportunities arise because you have acquired new capabilities in your business: a new product line or the key skills of a newly recruited individual or team.
- Finally, just as weaknesses often mirror strengths, so *threats* to the business frequently go hand in hand with opportunities. If the opportunities you have identified are captured by a competitor, that in itself could pose a problem.

Alternatively, you may see threats, such as a new entrant into the market, which you cannot actively prevent, but which you can do some planning for.

Assignment 2.5: SWOT Analysis

1. Create a SWOT analysis for your business as it currently stands.
2. From that list, identify what you consider the priorities for action.
3. Allocate responsibility in the business for particular individuals to create the steps to address these priorities, and a timetable for implementation.

As you will see, this exercise will play an important role in shaping the forward strategy of the business. We recommend that (a) you involve your senior team in this review; (b) you restrict the number of priorities to six at most (a smaller firm cannot fight effectively on every front); and (c) you revisit this exercise as your thinking develops.

three
Are You in Good Financial Health?

Before you even start your growth plan you really should take stock of what financial shape your business is in now. You may well remember those classic lines in the TV series *Star Trek* when Captain Kirk would ask his engineer for more power to help them get out of trouble. 'Give me warp factor 10' he would ask, to which he would often get the reply 'It canna take it captain!' Your business might be a bit like the damage-stricken starship *Enterprise* – a sudden violent burst of growth might well kill it off or at least create severe cash flow difficulties. So perhaps some analysis of the current state of health should be a precursor of any growth plan to find out if your business is ready for growth.

An analysis of the financial performance of your business, or 'financial position audit', will help you to reveal:

- How the business is currently performing and which areas need improving.
- How you are performing compared with the past and compared with your competitors and your industry/sector.
- The key levers that you need to pull in order to deliver growth.
- The main areas of risk.
- Whether there are untapped sources of internal funds to help finance the growth (see chapter 12 for more on this).
- Some of the means by which you will measure growth.
- The breakeven point for you business so you can establish what you have to do to achieve and improve business profits (see the end of this chapter for more on this).

At the heart of all financial position audits is an appraisal of the profit-and-loss account, the balance sheet and ratios that can be derived from the information contained. The case for this is simple. Typically, the figures are readily available and they are comparatively easy to handle. Similar information about other companies (for example, your competitors) will be publicly available and, therefore, meaningful comparisons can be made.

The main way in which the financial position audit is established, and in which comparisons are made, is through the use of ratios. A ratio is simply one number expressed as a proportion of another. For example, travelling 150 kilometres may not sound too impressive, until you realize it was done in 1 hour. The ratio here is 150 kilometres per hour. If you knew that the vehicle in question had a top speed of 170 kilometres per hour, you would have some means of comparing it with other vehicles, at least in respect of speed. In finance too, ratios can turn sterile data into valuable information in a wide range of different ways, thus helping you make choices.

Of course there are potentially hundreds of ratios that you could calculate, but not all of them are necessarily applicable or useful for your business. Here, we will concentrate on explaining the key ratios for a growing business. Most you can calculate yourself; some you may need your bookkeeper or accountant to organize for you. All take a little time and may cost a little money to have prepared, but they do tell you a lot about what is going on.

Perhaps the main benefit of the position audit using ratios is that it points to questions that need answers. A big difference between what actually happened and what was expected suggests that something may be wrong. The tools of analysis (the ratios) allow managers to choose, from the hundreds of questions that might be asked, the handful that are really worth answering. In a small and/or expanding business, where time is at a premium, this quick pre-selection of key questions is vital.

Financial ratios can be clustered under a number of headings, each of which probes a different aspect of business performance (Table 3.1). By the end of this chapter, you should be able to calculate the key ratios under each of the following headings:

- growth
- profitability
- liquidity (and working capital)
- solvency.

In order to illustrate the calculation of the ratios, we will use a simple business, Ashcroft Deli Limited. The accounts for Ashcroft Deli for the last two years are presented at the end of this chapter (Table 3.3). These are much simplified accounts and not everything you would expect to see in a full set of accounts has been included – just enough to illustrate the use of the key ratios.

TABLE 3.1 Worksheet for Ratio Analysis

Ratio	Three years ago	Two years ago	Last year	This year	Average growth (%)	Main Competitors	Difference from our performance (%)	Action required
1. Percentage sales growth								
2. Percentage profit growth								
3. Headcount growth								
4. Sales per employee								
5. Profit per employee								
6. Value added per employee								
7. Return on capital employed (ROCE)								
8. Return on shareholders' capital (ROSC)								
9. Gearing								
10. Interest cover								
11. Gross profit								
12. Operating profit (%)								
13. Net profit (%)								
14. Current ratio								
15. Quick ratio or acid test								
16. Average collection period								
17. Average payment period								
18. Stock days								
19. Working capital circulation								
20. Breakeven point								
21. Other key ratios								

Measuring Growth

If growth is the aim, then we must have measures for growth. Growth is most commonly expressed as the improvement in some measure expressed as a percentage of the previous period's equivalent measure. So, sales growth of 20 per cent per annum would mean that the increase in this year's sales was 20 per cent of last year's total sales.

Sales growth = (this year's sales − last year's sales/last year's sales) × 100

Similarly, for any other measure of growth such as profit or number of employees (headcount), which are calculated in a similar manner.

The most common measures of growth are sales and number of employees. The former is often used by entrepreneurs as a type of virility test. The latter is popular with governments. Neither of these measures is particularly useful unless profit is also taken into account.

Many businesses fall in to the trap of becoming 'busy fools', growing turnover with little regard to profitability. However, healthy growth requires both sales turnover and profits being grown in proportion.

Growing businesses can be classified in to one of five types of growth. Only two of these types have particular merit, two are potentially dangerous, and one seems to make being in business for yourself something of a pointless exercise (Figure 3.1).

Champions is a term that describes businesses which grow both their profits and sales turnover by at least 25 per cent each year. This is a fairly small proportion of businesses, less than 6 per cent at the last count. This type of growth gives you a very strong position

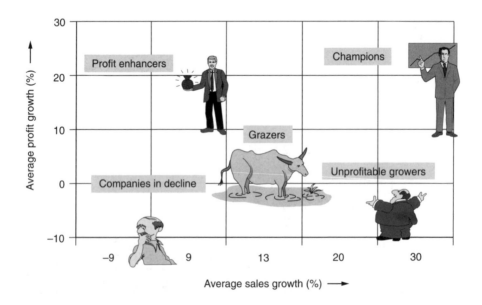

FIGURE 3.1 Typical Growth Profiles of SMEs.

in the market with a growing sales presence and the profit to develop new products and services without recourse to borrowing.

Profit enhancers, also a very small proportion of the total population, are those businesses which concentrate on growing profits but not sales. While this can be a useful position to be in, particularly since it means that you are making more money without producing more, these businesses can become vulnerable as they are typically building on a fairly static customer base. This can be a good first step to growth for a recovering business.

Grazers move forward steadily at a pace much the same as for their markets in general, rather like a boat being swept along with the tide. The danger here is that the tide may turn.

Unprofitable growers are businesses whose sales move forward sharply while their profits are either fairly static or even going down. This is a particularly dangerous course to follow. With sales growth come all sorts of additional costs. More stock, more equipment, more staff and so forth. And these have all to be supported from a static profit base. Often just one bad debt or quality problem, causing delays in payments, is enough to sink an unprofitable grower.

Businesses in decline are going backwards by both measures. Their market positions are getting weaker, with a smaller sales base. And they are not making enough profit to do anything new. They are dying slowly.

Ashcroft Deli is an example of a champion. Profits are growing at 48 per cent, while sales are growing at 30 per cent. It may be useful to position your business and your competitors on this growth chart to see how you compare.

Measuring Profitability

Profitability is clearly important for nearly all businesses. At the simplest level, profit is one of the essential reasons that a business exists. Moreover, a business needs to make sufficient profit, or return, in order to

- give a good return to shareholders bearing in mind the risk they are taking. If the returns are less than bank interest rates, for example, then your shareholders (including, of course, yourself as the entrepreneur!), will not be happy;
- allow the business to grow;
- keep the real value of the original capital intact after allowing for inflation.

There are two main ways to measure profitability of a business: profit margins and return on capital employed (ROCE). They are both important, but they reveal different things about the performance, and perhaps even the strategy, of the business. To fully understand what is happening in the business, you need information in both areas.

Gross Profit and Gross Profit Percentage

Gross profit and gross profit percentage are measures of the value added to the products/services being produced. To put it another way, they measure the power of the 'money-making engine' of the business. The higher the percentage, the greater the value being added. If your gross profits are not large enough, then it is very difficult to generate sufficient profits in order to grow the business.

To calculate gross profit, deduct the cost of sales from the sales.

Gross profit = sales − cost of sales

To calculate gross profit percentage (%), express the result as a percentage of sales.

Gross profit % = (gross profit/sales) × 100

In the case of Ashcroft Deli, the gross profit percentage in year 1 is

Gross profit % = (£50,000/100,000) × 100 = 50%

For year 2, the figure has moved down slightly to 48 per cent. Some possible causes of this reduction include lower selling prices, higher material or labour costs, wastage, theft and a change in the mix of products or services being sold.

Operating Profit and Operating Profit Percentage

Operating profit measures how well the management is running the business. To put it crudely, it shows how much (or little) of the gross profit remains after the rest of the business overheads (except financing costs) are taken into account

To calculate the operating profit, we not only deduct cost of sales from sales, but we also take off expenses (other than financing charges such as interest and taxation).

Operating profit = sales − cost of sales − expenses

It is assumed that financing decisions are taken by the owners (as opposed to the management, although in many entrepreneurial businesses these are the same people) and that the interest rates and taxation are set by the government and economic authorities of the day and therefore are not within management control and accountability.

Once again, we then express the result as a percentage of sales.

Operating profit % = (operating profit/sales) × 100

In the case of Ashcroft Deli, the operating profit percentage in year 1 is:

Operating profit % = (£17,000/£100,000) × 100 = 17%

In year 2, this percentage is up slightly to 18.5 per cent, which is for the most part the result of total expenses being only £5,000 higher (£38,000 compared with £33,000), while sales were £30,000 higher.

Net Profit and Net Profit Percentage

Net profit is the 'bottom line', i.e. sales less all costs. The figure can be shown before tax, often called profit before interest and tax (PBIT), or after tax. Although this may appear to be the ultimate measure of business performance, in owner-managed businesses, real performance can often be obscured by the way in which costs are recorded.

In its after-tax form, which we will show here, net profit also represents the sum available to be either distributed as dividends or retained by the business to invest in its future.

Net profit % = (net profit/sales) × 100

In the case of Ashcroft Deli, the net profit percentage in year 1 is:

Net profit % = (£11,880/£100,000) × 100 = 11.88%

This would generally be considered a respectable figure, the range being anything between 5 per cent and 25 per cent for most businesses.

In year 2, it is up to 13.51 per cent, which is largely brought about by the same reasons that led to the increase in operating profit. The fact that the cost of borrowing did not go up, because the growth was financed by retained profits, also helped.

Return on Capital Employed (ROCE)

The financial resources employed in a business are called capital. Capital can come in to a business from a number of different sources including the owner's capital, other investors' capital, loans and retained profits (also known as reserves). All of these sources are commonly looking for a return on the money they invest. This return is similar to the interest that you would receive if you invested your capital in a bank account.

If, for example, you had £10,000 invested in a bank and, at the end of the year, the bank gave you £500 interest, then the return on your capital employed (ROCE) would be

ROCE = (profit/capital employed) × 100
= (£500/£10,000) × 100 = 5%

For this reason, ROCE is one of the primary measures of performance for most businesses, and certainly for most investors. In a business, ROCE is calculated by expressing the operating profit as a percentage of the total capital employed.

ROCE = (operating profit/total capital employed) × 100

All the different elements of capital in the business will be found on the balance sheet in the 'financed by' section and the 'creditors over one year' (i.e. long-term loans) section. Adding all the balance sheet entries in these two sections together will give you the total capital employed. Given that a balance sheet must balance, it follows that the figure for total capital employed will be equal to the sum of the balance sheet entries for fixed assets and net current assets. Net current assets is also sometimes called working capital since this is the capital which is used on a day-to-day basis to finance the working of the business.

In year 1 of our Ashcroft Deli example, the ROCE is:

$$ROCE = [17,000/(10,000 + 8,910 + 10,000)] \times 100$$
$$= 59\%$$

In the second year, it has fallen slightly to 52 per cent. By any standards, both are excellent results.

The great strength of this ratio lies in the overall view it takes of the financial health of the whole business. The ratio gives no clue as to why there is a small change in the second year, it simply provides a starting point for any analysis and an overall yardstick against which to compare absolute performance.

Return on Shareholders' Capital

Shareholders are usually most interested in the net return on their capital, i.e. the return on shareholders' capital (ROSC). So, here the return would be the net profit after interest has been paid on any loans and after the taxman has had his slice, i.e. net profit after tax and interest. The shareholders' capital is not only their initial stake, but also any retained profits in the business since, although not distributed, these also belong to the shareholders.

$$ROSC = (\text{net profit after tax and interest/total shareholders' capital}) \times 100$$

In our example, in year 1 the calculation is:

$$ROSC = [£11,880/(£10,000 + £8,910)] \times 100$$
$$= 63\%$$

Once again, this is an excellent result. For owner-managed businesses in general, this ratio can be anywhere between a few percentage points and upwards of 35 per cent. Results such as those in this example would be in the top 10 per cent.

Profit per Employee

If, as in most cases, your principal 'assets' are people, and not just capital assets such as equipment, then you will need to monitor what value employees are contributing. A good ratio to use for this purpose is profit per employee:

$$\text{Profit per employee} = \text{net profit before tax/number of employees}$$

In the case of Ashcroft Deli, the ratio for year 1 is:

$$\text{Profit per employee} = £14,850/2 = £7,425$$

The figure drops sharply the following year to £5,487. This would not be unusual, as growing businesses tend to move forward in a lumpy fashion. For a business employing, say, 30 people, taking on two more employees would be a relatively small step. But for this business it represents a doubling of the workforce.

It can also be useful to calculate the sales per employee, to give you a feel for activity levels. This is calculated in a similar manner to profit per employee but you just need to substitute sales for the profit figure. As you can see, things at Ashcroft Deli are slowing down.

There is just one final profitability ratio that you should look at, which again measures the efficient use of probably your most scarce and valuable resource – people.

Value Added per Employee

Although profit per employee and sales per employee are useful measures, neither really shows how efficiently your people work. Value added per employee attempts to measure how much financial contribution, or value added, each employee contributes. The value added figure is essentially the same as gross profit (which we calculated earlier). However, we need to look a bit closer at the gross profit figure to add back any wages figures that may be included in this calculation. By wages we mean any employees of the business that you have attributed to cost of sales, e.g. production wages:

Value added = gross profit + direct wages

We can then calculate value added per employee in much the same way that we calculated profit per employee and sales per employee above.

If we look at Ashcroft Deli using this measure we can see that value added per employee has fallen dramatically from £35,000 to £21,750 – a sure sign that there are too many people now employed in the business and this is dragging down efficiency. Crudely it would appear that the business is carrying about 1.5 extra people for the current level of business!

If we bring all these ratios together, we could produce a table such as the 'Profitability at a glance at Ashcroft Deli' in Table 3.2.

TABLE 3.2 Profitability at a Glance at Ashcroft Deli

	Year 1	Year 2
Gross margin	50%	48%
Operating margin	17%	18.5%
Net margin	11.88%	13.51%
Return on capital employed (ROCE)	59%	52%
Return on shareholders' capital (ROSC)	63%	55%
Profit per employee	£7,425	£5,487
Sales per employee	£50,000	£32,500
Value added per employee	£35,000	£21,750

We could then go on to benchmark Ashcroft Deli against others in the industry. As a result, we may conclude that our sales per employee is lower than it should be and we need to improve in this area.

However, our ROCE performance is above average. The message here is perhaps that our capital investment is paying off, using good new equipment, but we need to get a better result from our people.

Measuring Liquidity

Liquidity is a measure of a business's ability to meet its current financial obligations (i.e. creditors and short-term loans such as overdrafts), known as current liabilities, as and when they fall due. These liabilities will need to be met from cash in hand and any other resources which can quickly be converted in to cash, such as debtors and stock. These are known as current assets (as opposed to fixed assets, which are items in which the business has invested for the longer term and cannot easily be converted into cash).

The two key measures of liquidity are the current ratio and the quick ratio (or acid test).

Current Ratio

The current ratio for a business is the relationship between the current assets and current liabilities and is calculated by dividing the former by the latter:

Current ratio = current assets/current liabilities

where current assets is the sum of stock, debtors and cash; and current liabilities is the sum of creditors, overdrafts and any other short-term loans. It is clear that liquidity is closely related to working capital since

Working capital = current assets − current liabilities

In the accounts for Ashcroft Deli, the first year's picture on the balance sheet shows current assets at £23,100 and current liabilities at £6,690. Therefore, the current ratio for Ashcroft Deli is

Current ratio = £23,100/£6,690 = 3.4

This shows current liabilities to be covered 3.4 times, and the ratio is usually expressed in the form 3.4:1. In the second year, this has come down to 2.2:1. The first year's ratio represents a business which is more able to meet its current liabilities. On the other hand, it is achieving this by having more working capital in the business, and this in turn will reduce the ROCE. Therefore, as with nearly everything in business, there is a tricky balance to be struck between risk (the ability to meet you financial obligations) and reward (your ROCE).

For this reason, the general rule about the current ratio is that it should be as close to 1:1 as the safe conduct of the business will allow. This will not be the same for every type of business. A shop buying in finished goods on credit and selling them for cash could run safely at 1.3:1. A manufacturer, with raw material to store and customers to finance, may need over 2:1. This is because the period between paying cash out for raw materials and receiving cash in from customers is longer in a manufacturing business than in a retail business. And, as a complete contrast, a small hotel with a bar and restaurant will typically have a current ratio of 0.25:1 because of the special nature of its business. In this case, there will be minimal stock (as food and beverages are delivered almost daily), few debtors (customers pay as they leave) and minimal cash (all used to improve the facilities). On the other hand, the overdraft is typically at its limit and there is a stack of unpaid trade creditors as long as your arm.

Quick Ratio (or Acid Test)

The quick ratio (or acid test) is really a 'belt and braces' ratio. In this ratio, only assets that can be realized quickly, such as debtors and cash in hand, are related to current liabilities. We often refer to it as the 'when the creditors come knocking on the door' ratio:

Quick ratio = (debtors + cash)/current liabilities

In the Ashcroft Deli example, in year 1, we would exclude the £10,000 stock because, before it can be realized, we would need to find customers to sell to and collect in the cash. All this might take several months. So, the quick ratio for Ashcroft Deli in year 1 would be:

Quick ratio = £13,100/£6,690 = 1.9

If anything, this quick ratio of 1.9:1 is, perhaps, too respectable since, once again, it indicates that the business is tying up working capital in debtors and cash. This might indicate that Ashcroft Deli could be collecting payment from their customers more quickly or that the cash could be being used to invest in further growth.

Once again, general rules are very difficult to make, but a ratio of 0.8:1 would be acceptable for most types of business.

Measuring Working Capital

As we have seen, liquidity is closely related to working capital where:

Working capital = current assets − current liabilities

The larger the difference between current assets and current liabilities the higher the current ratio – but also the higher the level of working capital. And, the higher the level of working capital, the higher the overall amount of capital that is being used. That in turn means that profits have to be that much higher to make the same (or better) ROCE. The converse is also clearly true, i.e. if you can make the same profit with a lower level of working capital, then you will be achieving better ROCE.

So, tight control of working capital is a good way of improving the profitability of the business and generating funds for growth (see also chapter 12). So, let us consider some of the key measures of how you are managing your working capital.

Average Collection Period (or Debtor Days)

Most businesses whose customers are other businesses give their customers credit (i.e. allow them to pay at some later date). This means that you create debtors (people who owe you money) from whom you need to collect cash. Since you will probably have already paid for the items which you have needed to buy in order to deliver to the customers, one of the effects is that you will be spending money before it comes back in. As a result, and as any growing business selling on credit knows, cash flow can quickly become a problem.

Surprisingly enough, bad debts (those which are never paid) are rarely as serious a problem as slow payers. Many businesses think nothing of taking three months' credit, and it is important to remember that even if your terms are 30 days it will be nearer 45 days on average before you are paid. To some extent, this depends on how frequently invoices are sent out and how quickly and hard you chase them. Assuming they do not go out each day and, perhaps more importantly, that your customer batches bills for payment monthly, then that is how things will work out. This is particularly true if the customers are big companies, and despite the wave of legislation in many countries to encourage prompt payment.

There are several techniques for monitoring debtors, the most well used of which is the average collection period, also known as debtor days. This ratio is calculated by expressing debtors as a proportion of credit sales, and then relating that to the days in the period in question:

Average collection period = (debtors/sales in period) × number of days in period

In our example, let us suppose that all Ashcroft Deli's sales are on credit and the periods in question are both 365-day years (i.e. no leap years). Then in year 1 the average collection period is:

Average collection period = (£13,000/£100,000) × 365 = 47 days

And, in year 2, the average collection period is 36 days. Some readers may have spotted a slight apparent inaccuracy in this calculation because our debtor figure will have included VAT and the sales figure will have excluded VAT. This is the way financial analysts calculate this figure and as long as you always do it this way then you will be able to show trends and comparisons with other businesses. You should note that the same apparent inaccuracy applies to the creditor days calculation for the same reason.

So, in year 2, Ashcroft Deli management is collecting its cash from debtors 11 days sooner than in year 1. This is obviously a better position to be in, making its relative amount of debtors lower than in year 1.

It is not making the absolute amount of debtors lower, and this illustrates another great strength of using ratios to monitor performance. Ashcroft Deli's sales have grown by 30 per cent from £100,000 to £130,000, and its debtors have remained at £13,000. At first glance then, its debtors are the same, neither better nor worse. But when you relate those debtors to the increased levels of sales, as this ratio does, then you can see that the position has improved.

This is a good control ratio, which has the great merit of being quickly translatable into a figure that any businessperson can understand, showing how much it is costing to give credit. If, for example, Ashcroft Deli is paying 10 per cent per annum for an overdraft, then giving £13,000 credit for 36 days will cost £128.22 [(10% × £13,000 × 36 ÷ 365].

Average Payment Period (or Creditor Days)

Of course, the credit world is not all one-sided. Once you have established your business, you too will be taking credit. You can usually rely on your suppliers to keep you informed on your indebtedness, but only on an individual basis. Therefore, it is prudent to calculate how many days' credit, on average, you are taking from suppliers, i.e. the average payment period or creditor days. This is a very similar calculation to average collection period. The ratio is as follows:

Average payment period = (creditors/purchases in period) × number of days in period

In our example, in year 1, the average payment period is:

Average payment period = (£1,690/£30,000) × 365

= 21 days

And, in year 2, the average payment period is 47 days.

The difference in these ratios probably reflects greater creditworthiness in year 2.

Generally speaking, the longer the credit period you can take from your suppliers the better, provided that you still meet their terms of trade.

It is also quite useful simply to relate days' credit given to days' credit taken. If they balance out then you are about even in the credit game. In year 1, Ashcroft Deli gave 47 days' credit to its customers and took only 21 days from its suppliers, so it was a loser. In the second year, it got ahead, giving only 36 days while taking 47.

However, just let us leave you with a parting warning over how you treat your suppliers. If you take credit from your suppliers you are using them to finance your business – there is nothing wrong with that. If you are taking, say, 60 days' credit they are providing quite a lot of your working capital. If, however, you grossly exceed their credit terms – often referred to as 'creditor strain' – you will lose their goodwill and two things will happen. First, they will put you on stop and all future purchases will be either pro forma or cash with order. It does not take a genius to spot that this will leave a funding gap that has to be made up – either by you or by the bank (more on this in chapter 12). And, second, if supplies become limited (e.g. in a petrol crisis) then you can be certain that you will not be first in the line to be supplied, which may cause you problems in supplying your customers.

Stock (Inventory) Control

Any manufacturing, subcontracting or assembling business will have to buy in raw materials and work on them to produce finished goods. They will have to keep track of three sorts of stock (or inventory): raw materials, work in progress and finished goods. By comparison, a retailing business will probably be concerned only with finished goods, and a service business may have no (or very little) stock at all.

Clearly, the more stock you have, the more money (working capital) you are using simply to finance that stock. A common failing of businesses of any size is to plan production levels to get the most out of the plant and equipment without taking account of the costs involved in holding stock. There will be a direct cost in terms of borrowings while obsolete items may have to be sold at a discount, and possibly even at below cost. Equally, in periods when demand falls, be wary of attempting to keep the workforce and the plant busy. If you go on building up stock, you will face a bigger cash drain.

So, good control of your stock levels is a key element of managing your working capital.

The most commonly used ratio for measuring stock is stock days. This is the average number of days' worth of stock that you are holding and can be calculated for each of raw materials, work in progress and finished goods. The calculation for finished goods is as follows:

Finished goods stock days = (finished goods stock/cost of sales in period) × number of days

Cost of sales is used because it accurately reflects the amount of stock. The overall sales figure includes other items such as profit margin and, therefore, is less accurate. Nevertheless, if you are looking at a business from the outside, it is probable that the only figure available will be that for sales and so you may have to use it as an approximation.

The same basic equation can be applied to both raw materials and work in progress stock. In the case of raw materials, you should substitute raw materials consumed for cost of sales.

If we assume that all of Ashcroft Deli's stock is in finished goods, then:

$$\text{Finished goods stock days} = (\pounds 10{,}000/\pounds 50{,}000) \times 365$$
$$= 73 \text{ days}$$

In year 2, the ratio is 64 days.

It is impossible to make any general rules about stock levels. Obviously, a business has to carry enough stock to meet demand, and a retail business must have it on display or to hand. However, if Ashcroft Deli's suppliers can always deliver within, say, 14 days it would be unnecessary to carry 73 days' stock. Once again, the strength of this ratio is that a business can quickly calculate how much it is costing to carry a given level of stock, in just the same way as customer credit costs are calculated.

Another way to look at stock control is to see how many times your stock is turned over each year. This ratio is almost the inverse of stock days and is calculated as follows:

$$\text{Stock turn} = \text{cost of sales/stock}$$

So, for Ashcroft Deli this is £50,000/£10,000, or five times a year.

Circulation of Working Capital

Although the current ratio gives an overall feel for a business's ability to pay its creditors, the manager of a business is usually more concerned with how efficiently the working capital is being used to generate sales. The most useful ratio for this is working capital circulation, calculated as follows:

$$\text{Working capital circulation} = \text{sales/working capital}$$

Remembering that working capital is equal to net current assets on the balance sheet, we can see that, for Ashcroft Deli, working capital has shrunk from £16,410 in year 1 to £14,000 in year 2. Not too dramatic. But let us now look at these figures in relation to the level of business activity (sales) in each year. In year 1:

$$\text{Working capital circulation} = \pounds 100{,}000/\pounds 16{,}410 = 6 \text{ times}$$

and in year 2

$$\text{Working capital circulation} = \pounds 130{,}000/\pounds 14{,}000 = 9 \text{ times}$$

We can see that not only has Ashcroft Deli got less money tied up in working capital in the second year, but it has also used it more efficiently. In other words, it has circulated it faster. Each pound of working capital produces £9 of sales in year 2, as opposed to only £6 in year 1. And as each pound of sales makes profit, the faster the working capital is turned around the higher the profit. Thinking ahead we can see that as a result of managing working capital better, as Ashcroft Deli continues to grow it is reducing the amount of additional financing (pro rata to sales) that it will need – this is good news.

Measuring Solvency

Just as liquidity is concerned with the short-term position, solvency is the term used to describe a business's long-term financial position. Trading while insolvent is a serious matter, and one that could strip away the protection of limited liability. The key indicators of the long-term financial position are the proportion of a business's funds that are borrowed as opposed to being put up by the shareholders, known as gearing, and how well the business is able to meet any interest costs associated with such borrowing, known as interest cover.

Gearing

The more borrowed money a business uses, as opposed to that put in by the shareholders (either through initial capital or by leaving profits in the business), the more highly geared the business is. High gearing may seem attractive in the sense that it is preferable to use someone else's money! However, borrowed money does of course need to be paid back with interest. So, highly geared businesses can be vulnerable either when sales dip sharply, as in a recession, or when interest rates rise rapidly.

Gearing is calculated as a percentage as follows:

Gearing = [creditors over 12 months/(creditors over 12 months + total shareholders' capital)] × 100

So, in our example, in year 1

Gearing = [£10,000/(£10,000 + 18,910)] × 100
= 35%

indicating that 35 per cent of the money employed in the business was borrowed. In year 2, the corresponding figure is 22 per cent.

Gearing levels for smaller businesses range on average from 60 per cent down to 30 per cent. But many businesses entering the first stages of growth are seriously over-geared, leaving them exposed. Remember, the higher your gearing, the less potential you have to borrow more.

Interest Cover

Although gearing is important, it is equally important to look at your business's ability to service the interest on the borrowing. If you were fortunate enough to inherit £0.5 million, you could borrow another £0.5 million and buy a substantial house for £1 million and still only be 50 per cent geared. What you may find a little difficult is to find the money to pay the interest on the loan each month. Similarly, a business must be able to meet the interest on its borrowings out of profit. This is known as interest cover and is calculated as follows:

Interest cover = operating profit/interest on loans

So, in our example, the interest cover in year 1 was eight times (£17,000/£2,150), and in year 2 it increased to nearly 12 times (£24,000/£2,050).

Anything upwards of four times interest cover would be viewed as respectable; below three might be worrying.

Breakeven Analysis

Breakeven is the KEY business benchmark because it identifies the level of sales a business needs just to cover all costs – that is to make neither a profit nor a loss. The *breakeven point* (BEP) is the stage when a business starts to make a profit. Identifying the breakeven point may sound simple – and indeed it should be! Nevertheless, many businesses, both early stage and more mature, fail to use this important and powerful idea.

Breakeven analysis is a tool for combining different types of costs and sales volumes so that you can calculate when you are likely to start making money. It is an important and powerful tool to be used both in preparing a business plan and in the day-to-day running of a business.

The first step in breakeven analysis is to understand the difference between two important and different types of cost.

Identifying Fixed and Variable Costs

The key point is that you cannot simply treat all costs as the same – some behave differently to others as sales grow or decline. In general, costs fall into two categories – fixed costs and variable costs – and you must be able to distinguish between them.

Fixed costs are those costs which do not change however much you sell. For example, if you are running a conventional shop, the rent and the rates are relatively constant figures, quite independent of the volume of sales. On the other hand, the cost of the products sold from the shop is completely dependent on volume. The more you sell, the more it 'costs' to buy stock. These are called variable costs.

Let us take variable costs first. For example, if you run a restaurant, and you forecast that you will sell 100 dinners, you will have to buy a fairly predicable quantity of ingredients beforehand. So, the key items of variable cost are likely to be:

- bought-in stock or raw materials;
- direct labour (note that this is only the labour that varies with the number sold);
- packaging;

- direct selling costs (e.g. a commission paid on each unit sold);
- delivery.

Fixed costs, or overheads, are likely to be of more numerous different types and might include things like

- rent and rates (or loan repayments) on premises;
- leasing (or depreciation) of major items of equipment (note that this could include equipment such as cars, commercial vehicles, computers and telephone systems as well as machinery used in production);
- heat, light and power;
- labour (which does not vary with the number sold);
- marketing and promotion;
- telephone call charges;
- postage and stationery;
- insurance;
- legal services;
- accountancy services;
- consultancy;
- bank charges and interest;
- software licences and maintenance charges;
- travel and subsistence expenses;
- training and staff development;
- memberships and subscriptions;
- fixtures, fittings, furniture.

The list is, of course, not necessarily exhaustive!

Calculating Your Breakeven Point

Let us take an elementary example: a business plans to sell only one product and has only one fixed cost, the rent. In Figure 3.2, the vertical axis shows the value of sales and costs in thousands of pounds and the horizontal shows the number of 'units' sold. The second horizontal line represents the fixed costs, those that do not change as volume increases. In this case it is the rent of £10,000. The angled line running from the top of the fixed costs line is the variable cost. In this example, we plan to buy in at £3 per unit, so every unit we sell adds that much to our costs.

Only one element is needed to calculate the breakeven point – the sales line. That is the line moving up at an angle from the bottom left-hand corner of the chart. We plan to sell at £5 per unit, so this line is calculated by multiplying the units sold by that price.

The breakeven point is the point when the sales revenue begins to exceed both the fixed and variable costs. The chart shows our example breakeven point at 5,000 units.

A formula, deduced from the chart, will save time for your own calculations.

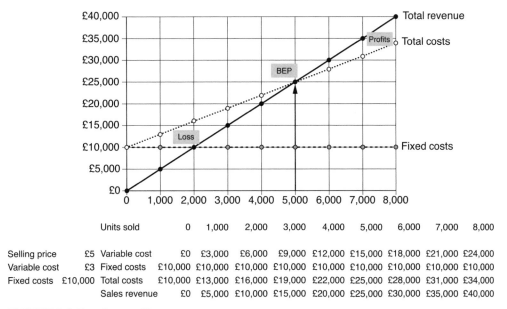

Units sold	0	1,000	2,000	3,000	4,000	5,000	6,000	7,000	8,000

Selling price	£5	Variable cost	£0	£3,000	£6,000	£9,000	£12,000	£15,000	£18,000	£21,000	£24,000
Variable cost	£3	Fixed costs	£10,000	£10,000	£10,000	£10,000	£10,000	£10,000	£10,000	£10,000	£10,000
Fixed costs	£10,000	Total costs	£10,000	£13,000	£16,000	£19,000	£22,000	£25,000	£28,000	£31,000	£34,000
		Sales revenue	£0	£5,000	£10,000	£15,000	£20,000	£25,000	£30,000	£35,000	£40,000

FIGURE 3.2 Breakeven Chart.

BEP = fixed costs/(selling price − unit variable costs)

= £10,000/(£5 − £3) = 5,000

Capital Intensive Versus 'Lean and Mean'

Consider two hypothetical new businesses. They are both making and selling identical products at the same price, £10. They plan to sell 8,000 units each in the first year.

The owner of Business A plans to get fully equipped at the start. His fixed costs will be £40,000. This is largely because, as well as his own car, he has bought such things as a delivery van, new equipment and a photocopier. Much of this will not be fully used for some time, but will save some money eventually. This extra expenditure will result in a lower unit variable cost, a typical capital-intensive result. As a result his variable cost is £1.25 per unit.

Business B's owner, on the other hand, proposes to start up on a shoestring. Only £10,000 will go into fixed costs, but, of course, the unit variable cost will be higher, at £5. The unit variable cost will be higher because, for example, the business has to pay an outside carrier to deliver, while Business A uses its own van and pays only for petrol.

So the breakeven charts will look like those in Figures 3.3 and 3.4.

From the data on each business you can see that the total costs for 8,000 units are exactly the same – £50,000. The key difference is that Business B starts making profits after 2,000 units have been sold. Business A has to wait until 4,571 units have been sold, and it may not be able to wait that long.

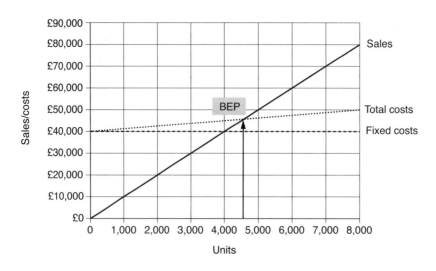

Units sold	0	1,000	2,000	3,000	4,000	5,000	6,000	7,000	8,000
Sales revenue	£0	£10,000	£20,000	£30,000	£40,000	£50,000	£60,000	£70,000	£80,000
Fixed costs	£40,000	£40,000	£40,000	£40,000	£40,000	£40,000	£40,000	£40,000	£40,000
Total costs	£40,000	£41,250	£42,500	£43,750	£45,000	£46,250	£47,500	£48,750	£50,000

FIGURE 3.3 Business A: Capital Intensive.

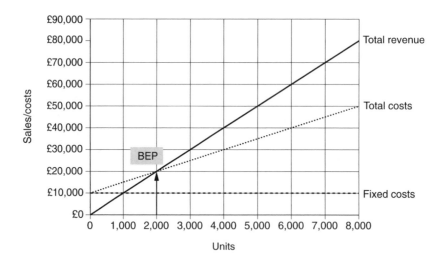

Units sold	0	1,000	2,000	3,000	4,000	5,000	6,000	7,000	8,000
Sales revenue	£0	£10,000	£20,000	£30,000	£40,000	£50,000	£60,000	£70,000	£80,000
Fixed costs	£10,000	£10,000	£10,000	£10,000	£10,000	£10,000	£10,000	£10,000	£10,000
Total costs	£10,000	£15,000	£20,000	£25,000	£30,000	£35,000	£40,000	£45,000	£50,000

FIGURE 3.4 Business B: Lean and Mean.

This is a hypothetical case; the real world is littered with the corpses of businesses that spend too much too soon. The marketplace dictates the selling price and your costs have to fall in line with that for you to have any hope of survival.

Profitable Pricing

To complete the breakeven picture, we need to add one further dimension – profit. It is a mistake to think that profit is an accident of arithmetic calculated only at the end of the year. It is a specific quantifiable target that you need at the outset.

Let us go back to the earlier example we used (Figure 3.2). This business has fixed costs of £10,000 and it wants to make a profit of £4,000. Now, let us see when it will achieve that profit target.

The new equation must include the 'desired' profit so it will look like this:

Units to achieve profit objective = (fixed costs + profit objective)/(selling price − unit variable costs)
= (£10,000 + £4,000)/(£5 − £3) = 7,000 units

We now know that to reach the target the business must sell 7,000 units at £5 each and have no more than £10,000 tied up in fixed costs. The great strength of this equation is that each element can be changed in turn on an experimental basis to arrive at a satisfactory and achievable result. For instance, suppose the owner-manager decides that it is unlikely they can sell 7,000 units, but that 6,500 is achievable. What would the new selling price (NSP) have to be to make the same profit?

Using the NSP equation you can calculate the answer:

NSP = [(fixed costs + profit objective)/estimated unit sales] + variable cost per unit
= [(£10,000 + £4,000)/6,500] + £3
= £5.15

If the market will bear a selling price of £5.15 as opposed to £5 all is well; if it will not, then ways should be found of decreasing the fixed or variable costs, or of selling more, rather than just accepting that a lower profit is inevitable.

Assignment 3.1

1. Undertake a complete financial position audit for your business by calculating all the ratios described above and your breakeven point for each of the last four years. (There is a pro forma at the end of this chapter to record this on.)
2. Are there any areas where you should take immediate action either to obtain a benefit or to reduce a risk?
3. What trends can you see? What does this tell you about what is happening in your business and its environment? What do you need to do as a result?
4. Obtain as much financial information as you can about your top three competitors and calculate the same ratios for each of them. A good place to start is to look at the published accounts information for these companies. How do your ratios

compare with theirs? In the UK, this information can be found at Companies House, and most other developed countries have similar organizations to which all companies must submit annual financial information. However, each country has different regulations about the amount of information that needs to be submitted and the thresholds (usually expressed in terms of the size of the business) at which full information must be disclosed.

5. Where competitors appear to perform better, try to find out how they are achieving this better performance.

Accounts for Ashcroft Deli for Past Two Years

Table 3.3 Accounts for Ashcroft Deli
(a) Profit and loss account

	Profit and loss account year to			
	31 March, year 1 (£)	%	31 March, year 2 (£)	%
Sales	100,000	100	130,000	100
Cost of sales				
Materials	30,000	30	43,000	33
Labour	20,000	20	25,000	19
Cost of goods sold	**50,000**		**68,000**	
Gross profit	50,000	50	62,000	48
Expenses				
Rent, rates, etc.	18,000		20,000	
Wages	12,000		13,000	
Advertising	3,000		3,000	
Depreciation			2,000	
Total expenses	**33,000**		**38,000**	
Operating or trading profit	17,000	17	24,000	18.5
Deduct interest on borrowings	2,150		2,050	
Net profit before tax	14,850	14.8	21,950	16.8
Tax paid at 20%	2,970		4,390	
Net profit after tax	11,880	11.88	17,560	13.51
Number of employees	2		4	

(b) Balance sheet

	At 31 March year 1 (£)		At 31 March year 2 (£)	
Net assets employed				
Fixed assets				
Furniture and fixtures		12,500		34,470
Less depreciation				2,000
Book value				32,470
Current assets				
Stock	10,000		12,000	
Debtors	13,000		13,000	
Cash	100		500	
Total current assets		23,100		25,500
Less current liabilities				
Overdraft	5,000		6,000	
Creditors	1,690		5,500	
Total current liabilities		6,690		11,500
Net current assets		16,410		14,000
Total assets		28,910		46,470
Less creditors over 12 months (long-term bank loan)		10,000		10,000
Net total assets		18,910		36,470
Financed by				
Share capital	10,000		10,000	
Profit retained (reserves)	8,910		26,470	
Total shareholders' capital		18,910		36,470

four

Diagnosing Your Organizational Health

In the next chapter, we will talk about **you**, your personal drivers and leadership style. Of course, you are an absolutely key factor in growing your business, but you cannot do it on your own. In fact, if you are so critical to the future success of the business, and it is not really sustainable without you, then you have a big problem. Should you want to exit or realize some capital you will not have anything to sell but yourself. This will mean the business is worth less and you will be locked in, like it or not.

So you need a strong management team and an effective organization. These will help create a sustainable high-value business and allow you to keep your options open. In this chapter, we will be answering the question 'Where are we now?' in relation to your organizational structure, systems and people. It would be nice to find that you already have in place all the capability you will need to realize your business plan. This is extremely unlikely! For example, some of the people you recruited when you started the business may not have the ability to become what you need in the future. Yet you are lumbered with them, clogging up the arteries of your organization!

Without management capability, your strategy is not worth the paper it is written on. Sure it may sound good, but how are you going to make it happen? Unfortunately, there are also in-built time lags, which mean that your window of business opportunity may have disappeared long before you have recruited and trained the right people, restructured or put in new systems. So you need to be looking at what internal capability you have right now, warts and all, in order to make provision for what you will need in the future to realize your new ambitions.

In its construction, a business organization is similar to an individual human being. Just like us, the organization has a skeleton, a nervous system and some blood and guts. The skeleton of the organization is its structure or shape – the thing which gives it form and indicates its potential to flex and grow. Just as the starfish does not have the skeleton to grow into a cheetah, so a bureaucratic business cannot be as nimble in the marketplace as a small, adaptive organization.

The nervous system of your business is represented by its processes, or systems and infrastructure, from the sales invoicing system to how people communicate with one another, from budgeting to appraisal. Systems form the linkages, the connective tissue between one part of the business and another. How often do you find that one function of the business is refusing to cooperate with one of the others? Sales insult production, one region competes with another?

The blood and guts, the messy bits of your business, are provided, as you suspected, by the people in it, who, as individuals and as teams, contribute to the unique personality of your business entity. You can have a streamlined organization, brilliant systems and infrastructure, but if you have got the wrong people with the wrong attitudes the business will go nowhere.

So, later in this chapter, we will help you assess what you have at present in terms of your people, structure and systems. Together these create the organizational capability to deliver your business strategy.

We will examine staff attitude and skills, identify your management capability and help you pinpoint your unique culture. We will look at how you are currently organized (you may even have an organization chart!) and how you go about dividing things up into separate roles and accountabilities and then getting people working together across these boundaries.

Then we will carry out a quick MOT of your processes for recruitment and selection, motivation and retention, training and development, and communications.

What Is the Right Organization for Your Business?

There are always plenty of fashion fads in management. One day it is centralization, next it is diversification. One day profit centres are beautiful, the next it is economies of scale. In trying to see whether you have got the right organization in place, there are unfortunately no absolute rules about numbers of people, or management style or reporting relationships. It all depends on the business environment in which you operate. In fact, there is no such thing as the right organization at all; there is only one which is appropriate to what you are trying to do with your business in your unique business environment. So, the starting point for getting the right organization in place is the work you did when you looked at your external environment and identified, through SWOT analysis, the chief threats and opportunities which are impacting you from outside.

What are they? Only then can you start to look inside the organization at your current strengths and weaknesses to see what delivery capability you have. As you progress through later chapters, and you begin to articulate where you are going in terms of your strategy for growth, you will be able to evaluate whether the organization is helping you or getting in the way.

Even if you get the organization right, it will not stay right for long. The concept of fit, Figure 4.1, says that your organization is right if it fits the business environment in which you are operating and helps you achieve your strategy.

You might think that as the environment changes so the organization, in one bound, shifts to accommodate the new reality. Unfortunately, this is never the case. It is amazing how long it takes organizations to recognize the unpleasant writing on the wall: that their marketplace has shifted or gone away, that their sales pipeline is non-existent. Leaders become like rabbits in the headlights – frozen into a state of shock and denial – or like boiled frogs unable to feel that their environment has hotted up. One company we know was haemorrhaging cash at the rate of £300,000 a month but it still took the directors a year before they realized there was a problem. By that time, they had almost been boiled alive and it was very nearly too late to recover. Different bits of the organization will respond at different speeds – and therefore get out of sync. For example, your structure is almost always a reflection of what you needed in the past rather than what you need now. Even when you change the structure, you will find you also need to revamp the

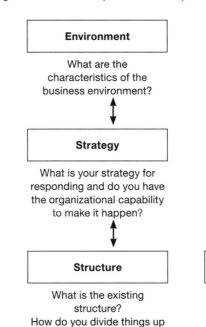

FIGURE 4.1 Organizational Fit.

appraisal system, your method of tracking performance or your management training. Running your own business is very much like the feat of the circus performer trying to keep a great many plates spinning on sticks at the same time – one plate is always in a state of terminal wobble and in need of an urgent tweak!

Assignment 4.1: Taking a Fresh Look at Your Organization

Let us grind a new pair of eyeglasses. Suspend for a minute your logical left-brain thought processes and engage the creative right brain in literally drawing a picture of how you perceive your organization as it is now. A picture is worth a thousand words and, like all the assignments in this book, the exercise can also provide a fun way of involving your team in the thinking which will eventually come together in your strategy. BGP participants have produced a rich cache of organization pictures including: islands without bridges, castaways in a stormy sea of shark competitors, ships with crew asleep and drunk downstairs, even a cosy, comfy country cottage. The messages can be strong!

Phases of Organizational Growth

Having identified the major external pressures on your business in your earlier SWOT analysis, you are in a good position to start diagnosing whether you have the right organization for your present stage of growth.

The Greiner model in Figure 4.2 shows the five phases of growth through which all businesses move and is a very good basis for diagnosing where you are in the development cycle. If you know where you are, perhaps you can do something about it! All business growth calls for change. As businesses get older and bigger, they face new challenges. The problem is that change is not always incremental. Children do not grow seamlessly from babies to adults, but pass through recognizable phases: infancy, adolescence, teenage troubles and so on. Businesses too pass through distinct phases. Each growth phase is punctuated by a crisis, a word which derives from Chinese and loosely translated means dangerous opportunity. An inability to recognize their current phase of growth and, therefore, how to manage the next transition lies at the heart of why so many owner-managed firms fail to achieve their true potential or realize the founder's dream. Each phase of growth calls for a different approach to managing the business. Just like bringing up a child, there are no arrival points in a growing business, just different problems requiring different solutions. Some phases call for more systems and procedures, some for a focus on teamwork and communication. Some demand strong leadership, others a more consultative approach to building the management team. Unfortunately, most founders try to run their business in much the same way as it gets bigger as they did when it was small. More of the same – shout louder, run around

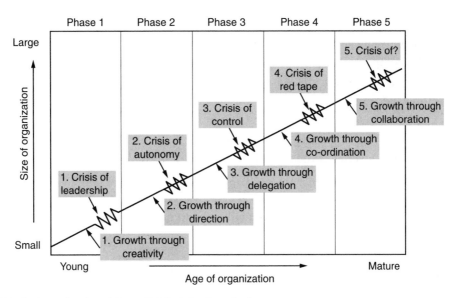

FIGURE 4.2 Organizational Growth Model, after Greiner.

harder. This approach is rather like suggesting that the transition from infancy to adulthood can be accomplished by nothing more significant than providing larger clothes!

Each growth phase brings its own organization challenge: phase 1, the start-up phase, requires ideas, energy and customers. Often, all of these are provided by the founder, who makes all the decisions and signs the cheques. There is little in the way of controls or management. Inevitably the owner-manager becomes bogged down in the day-to-day and there is a crisis of leadership. Sometimes this can be a good time for the founder to bail out. Sir Clive Sinclair liked making things but did not like the management challenge of running a bigger business. The founder of Covent Garden Soups loved the business he had created but was not temperamentally suited to take it to the next phase of growth demanded by external venture capitalists.

In phase 2, the challenge becomes putting in the infrastructure for growth: the systems and controls for tracking performance, recruiting professional managers and communicating on a more formal basis to more people. This demands management skill and inevitably leads to a crisis of autonomy when the new people you have recruited object to their lack of freedom and demand that you delegate more authority and become less autocratic. This starts to mean that it is not just the business that has to change – you have to change too!

In phase 3, the challenge is that supremely difficult one of letting go – moving from a top-down management style to delegating and creating a first-class team. But the trouble with delegation is that it can mean a crisis of control; people start to do their own thing and the owner-manager panics and pulls the plug!

During phase 4, there is more focus on coordination, addressing an increasingly fragmented organization through sophisticated controls, strategic planning and top-down corporate programmes to regulate behaviour and corporate culture. This growth phase usually ends in a crisis of red tape, when the clutter of rules and regulations which bind the company together results in missed opportunities. Bureaucracy becomes the order of the day and initiative is stifled. The crisis of collaboration leads to a more team-oriented approach, simpler re-engineered workflows and much more emphasis on management education and personal development.

It is interesting to speculate what happens next. Greiner poses this as an unanswered question. Perhaps this is the time when the business breaks into smaller units in a desperate bid to release creativity. Perhaps there is a cyclical rather than a linear dimension to Greiner's model. What the business cannot do is return to phase 1 growth. You can never be 21 again however many medallions and new spouses you collect! But you can reinvent yourself.

Let us now look more closely at each of these growth phases and see whether you can recognize which stage of evolution or revolution characterizes your business.

Phase 1: Growth Through Creativity

The founder is at the heart of everything. He or she is usually an energetic entrepreneur who has had a good idea for a product or service for which there is a demand. Success at this stage is down to a very few people, primarily the founder. Communication among employees is frequent and informal. There are usually not too many people and they can easily meet over a drink or in someone's house. Long hours of work are rewarded by an involved, happy atmosphere. The hunter–gatherer philosophy predominates; the approach to customers is action orientated. The business is sales led; everyone is crawling all over potential customers. The philosophy is to get the business and worry about how to fulfil the order later. There is a passionate attempt to avoid politics and a disdain of internal management.

This wonderful creative, exciting buzz is essential for the company to get off the ground. But therein lies the problem. As the company grows in size and age, more efficiency is needed in managing money and resources, new employees do not always know what is going on, more people make informal communication more difficult to achieve. The company finds itself burdened by unwanted management responsibilities, which it reluctantly sees as necessary but does not regard as fun. Here are some typical descriptions of how phase 1 organizations described themselves as they approached this first crisis of leadership:

- We're self-centred rather than customer centred.
- We're happy amateurs.
- We're not businessmen; totally top line sales driven.
- We're unplanned and confused.
- It's organized chaos, you sink or swim.
- We let ourselves down on detail.

Phase 2: Growth Through Direction

In the crisis of leadership, the business requires a strong leader who is able to make tough decisions about priorities and provide the single-minded direction needed to move the business forward. The ideas which the pioneer has been carrying round in his or her head need to be formalized. Systems and controls need establishing: management information systems, cost control systems, stock control systems, budgeting and forecasting, people systems such as reward structures and appraisal. Policies need to be evolved, teams built up and key people appointed with specific roles to play. The personal management style of the founder becomes secondary to making the business efficient. Sometimes the founder is not the right person to lead the business through this phase and, through either lack of management skills or personal preference, may decide to give up or sell out.

If this is not a desirable option then the key to success at this stage of growth depends on finding, motivating and keeping key staff – no easy task. As the company grows and matures, the directive top-down management style starts to become counterproductive. Others working in the organization acquire more expertise about their own particular area than the boss. Not surprisingly, they want a greater say in the future of the business and may become demotivated and leave if this does not happen. This is the crisis of autonomy and if it is not recognized and managed it will absorb so much time and energy that it will drag the company down. The loss of key employees can hugely damage the capacity to drive the business forward.

Phase 3: Growth Through Delegation

Many, many companies founder at this stage. The solution is to recognize that more responsibility has to be delegated to more people in the company. Building your management team becomes the foremost business challenge. You need them; you cannot do it all yourself, you must let go and move from meddler to strategist. The trouble is that most founders hang on to too many jobs in their firms, mostly in the mistaken belief that nobody else can do them as well. Problems arise at this stage. First, this change in role can make you personally feel extremely uncomfortable and vulnerable. If you stop doing those things, what does your role become? Second, you may also find that there is no one to let go to! Frequently, lower levels of management want power but their history has not taught them how to use it. Third, a number of the people you appointed at an earlier stage in the company's history will simply not be up to the task of accepting responsibility. Finally, the ones that do accept the authority you delegate may take your business in a different direction from the one you had in mind. The business is likely to become fragmented and uncoordinated as managers run their own shows in their own ways. This affects profit margins, causing scatter-gun development, competition between different bits of the business and loss of strategic focus. Another crisis looms: the crisis of control.

Phase 4: Growth Through Coordination

It might seem tempting to return to a centralized organization where what you say goes. But this usually fails; things have become too complicated to be effectively run from the centre. Moving ahead means finding a new solution that utilizes the strength and independence of your hard-won management team but also gets them to look beyond their own parochial interests and work within a coordinated strategy. There are lots of ways you can get a more coordinated response. Decentralized units can be merged into product groups, formal planning processes across the business can be installed and reviewed, staff and HQ personnel can be bought in to initiate group-wide programmes. Controls can be imposed on capital expenditure and incentives such as stock options and company-wide profit-sharing schemes introduced to encourage identity with the firm as a whole. Just as you might have expected, there is another crisis ahead – the crisis of red tape.

Phase 5: Growth Through Collaboration

Your business has become stodgy and bureaucratic. Line managers begin to resent heavy direction from staff functions, systems and procedures proliferate, innovation is stifled. What is worse, you have probably succeeded in creating exactly the kind of organization you set up your business to get away from in the first place! Phase 5 growth emphasizes greater spontaneity and flexibility, the skilful handling of interpersonal issues take over from rules and regulations. But the managers who created those rules can feel very threatened. The focus becomes solving problems through team action: creating temporary project teams across functional barriers, frequent conferences of key managers, educational programmes, real-time information systems and reward structures geared to team as well as individual performance. Experiments in new practices are encouraged.

It is important that you know where you are in the developmental sequence so that you recognize when the time for change has come, both for the business and for you personally. We should bear in mind that most independent businesses pursuing growth will be somewhere between phase 1 and phase 3.

Benchmarking against Best Practice

In putting your stethoscope to the heart of your business to diagnose organizational health, we have so far suggested two approaches: that you draw a picture of how you see your organization, warts and all, and that you try to identify your stage of growth.

A useful third approach is to benchmark your organization against best practice. In combination with our earlier approaches, this can give you some clues, or at least confirm that you are heading in the right direction.

There are probably as many best practice guides as there are management bestsellers. You are free to pick out your own from any airport bookstall. However, there do seem to be some common themes which over many years we have observed to be associated with successful owner-managed businesses.

McKinsey used to have a very famous Seven S model of organization. Here, we propose our own seven Ss version as a basis for a quick and dirty MOT of your organization. This will then lead you on to a more detailed analysis of your organization's people, systems and structure. The seven Ss are:

1. spot the external signals;
2. share the vision;
3. share the values;
4. share power;
5. suitable structure;
6. strong team;
7. significant rewards.

1. Spot the External Signals

Too many businesses end up as boiled frogs (see *The Age of Unreason* by Charles Handy) because they fail to pick up the signals from a changing environment: that the market has moved away, that new technology is creating new possibilities, that increasing supplier prices will decimate margins. Sometimes, when you carry out a quick radar scan of your external environment you will find that the terrifying blip on the screen turns out to be a seagull rather than a supertanker. But if it is the other way round, you had better know about it!

You may think you are closely in touch with your customers and competitive activity; is this assumption correct? Are you obsessional about asking your customers what they want or do you just assume they want what you are giving them? How regularly do you, as the boss, get out in front of key customers? Sure, your sales people will be out there, but they do not and should not own the customer relationship and they are selling today's solutions not identifying tomorrow's possibilities.

Innovex, the UK's leading CRO (clinical research organization), had three large thermometers on permanent and prominent display in their office: Bus (Business), Cus (Customers) and Us. Regular customer satisfaction surveys provided quantifiable data which were monitored and benchmarked month on month and which were as immediately visible and as important as business measures and the results of their annual internal attitude surveys.

You will be amazed at the information you personally are able to unearth. Have you thought about getting customers together for a workshop to tell them what you are up to and involve them in shaping the future? How actively do you measure customer satisfaction?

Braxxon, providing operational risk assessment and efficiency solutions to investment banks, use its non-executive directors to carry out annual customer feedback interviews with key customers. In addition to customer events, once a year an evening get-together is provided for all suppliers; this nurtures another group of key relationships, which are so easily overlooked.

2. Shared Vision

In a recent survey of more than 250 executives of British firms, only 2 per cent of bosses rated the quality of management in this country as excellent. They all agreed that the UK management teams had good technical and financial skills, but 52 per cent of them concluded that vision was the greatest weakness and that many bosses were woefully inadequate in defining the vision for the future of their enterprises.

What is this thing called vision? It is the direction in which you want the business to go. If your mission statement answers the question 'What do we do?', the vision answers 'Where are we going?'. If you do not know where you are going then you will end up somewhere else and you will not even know it – you will certainly be in no position to grow the business, except by serendipity. As the American author Faith Popcorn (really!) says: 'If the customers get to the future before you do, they will leave you behind'.

Starbucks was the inspiration of founder Howard Schultz. He believed that many of us wanted a 'third place' apart from home and office, where we could sit and talk. His vision was that there is a way to combine 'coffee, commerce and community'.

Of course, you may have a personal vision, perhaps to get filthy rich, but this is unlikely to inspire your people, your customers or potential investors! For this, you need a business vision that gets your stakeholders excited about the long-term prospects and sustainability of your business. When you started the business, you most certainly had a business vision or idea. What was it and how can you restate it to motivate others?

Many leaders have their own personal vision of their business, but it tends to stay in their heads as a kind of private daydream in the bath or while pruning the roses. Often the owner-manager assumes that this vision will transmit itself into the skulls of his or her employees by some miraculous process of osmosis. Nothing could be further from the truth. Do not assume that your staff will automatically know what your business is there for. It is your job to ensure that the business vision in your head is articulated and communicated to the whole organization. One owner-manager told us: 'Yes I have a vision – but I haven't told anyone about it.' What a wasted opportunity! Unless this particular individual can do it all on their own, how on earth are they going to inspire and engage the troops?

To have a value to the organization, the vision must be owned and lived by everyone in the organization; and for this to happen it has to be constantly stated, restated and reinforced. There is an apocryphal story of the liftman taking the chairman to his penthouse executive suite and chatting in the meantime about the business. The chairman mentions a possible diversification; the liftman immediately presses the emergency button and stops the lift – 'Mr Chairman', he said, 'this cannot happen: it is inconsistent with our vision of the business.'

The characteristics of a powerful vision are that it should be:

- Transformational – describing a future which is significantly 'better' than today.
- Inspirational – exciting people with the possibilities that the envisaged future will bring.
- Passionate – based on deeply held beliefs.
- Short and simple – easy to communicate and easy to understand.
- Shared – taken up and owned by everyone.
- Visible – the future state can be described using pictures and visual images.
- Long lasting – describing a longer-term future which remains valid, rather than something which can be achieved in the short term.
- Constantly communicated – reinforced in day-to-day work by everything you do and everything you say.

The words you use are important. How much less powerful it would have been if Kennedy had said 'I want to make a major technological breakthrough', rather than 'I want to put a man on the moon.'

The first speech of Ted Turner to employees at CNN, 'See, we're gonna take the news and put it on the satellite, and then we're gonna beam it down to Russia, and we're gonna bring world peace and we're all going to get rich in the process. Thank you very much.'

In Part 2, we will look at how to develop and articulate a vision of 'Where are we going?' For now, ask yourself the following questions

- Do I have a vision of the business in the future?
- Have I shared it with other people in the business?
- Do they believe it?

If the answer to any of these questions is 'no', then there is some work to do!

3. Shared Values

Values sum up the way we do things around here and define the unique personality, almost the fingerprint, of the organization. They form the culture of the organization, the genetic code which lets people know how to behave. Managers can act as policemen, telling people what to do and applying sanctions, but what happens when the managers are not around? Culture is what people do when and where nobody watches. If you have the right shared values, they will be doing the right things for the business. How much more powerful than relying on, at best, patchy management controls.

Culture has also been described as what you do when the chips are down. You may say that you believe in people, but if the first thing you do when life gets hard is to fire them, then this is demonstrably not one of your core values.

Johnson & Johnson has long been famed for its credo (shown in Figure 4.3). Before you attack it as being 'motherhood and apple pie', hear this proof that they really practise what they preach. Some years back, J&J had a grave crisis when its drug Tylenol was deliberately sabotaged with cyanide. At first the managers all ran around like headless chickens, until the chief executive officer (CEO) said 'hang on a minute – let's go back to our core beliefs'. They took a deep breath and then blitzed all American TV channels, explaining the size of the problem, the risks and what they proposed to do about the situation. Their honesty and calmness helped inform and reassure the public – a public relations triumph and a vindication of the company's values as expressed in its famous credo. Contrast how J&J handled its PR crisis with the behaviour of Perrier, when its product became polluted with benzene. The managers hid the facts, they blamed one another and in the end it cost the CEO his job.

We touched earlier on the need for vision and how it can be translated into something meaningful for all staff. Shared values give us the way forward because they show each individual what they must do to be successful and because they can ultimately be measured. This is particularly important as your business grows; new staff coming in often do not share or understand the vision of the original people. The culture has diluted. People will go off in the wrong direction unless you can create a framework of shared beliefs. Ericsson talks about their three musketeers: perseverance, professionalism and respect. What are your core values and how do you live them and reinforce them? You of course are the greatest role model for your corporate values. It is all about walking the talk – little signals and symbols mean a lot. Ralph Lauren literally models what he stands for in what he himself wears. Barrie Haigh, of Innovex, poured the tea at every induction programme and wowed new employees.

Federal Express translates its service values into hard measures through key performance indicators (KPIs). Every day in every Fedex office throughout the world, screens light up with KPIs of how each office did in terms of delivering what it promises – 'on time package delivery and tracking' of every parcel. Service delivery quotients are weighted in terms of the seriousness of the mistake made. For example, 'lost package' has the highest weight because it represents the most serious thing that could damage the image of Fedex. This is followed by things like 'right day – late'; 'wrong day – late', 'damaged'.

David Pointer of Point Source has a business based on five values: excellence, energy, contribution, innovation and integrity. These values are etched in the glass doors between offices. Excellence depends on engineering precision – a squeaky-clean streamlined environment is essential in manufacturing. This value is demonstrated by David's passionate attention to every detail of the office environment: the entrance area, every coffee cup, the boardroom and the executive loo.

Our Credo

We believe our first responsibility is to the doctors, nurses and patients, to mothers and fathers and all others who use our products and services.

In meeting their needs everything we do must be of high quality.

We must constantly strive to reduce our costs in order to maintain reasonable prices.

Customers' orders must be serviced promptly and accurately.

Our suppliers and distributors must have an opportunity to make a fair profit.

We are responsible to our employees, the men and women who work with us throughout the world.

Everyone must be considered as an individual. We must respect their dignity and recognize their merit.

They must have a sense of security in their jobs.

Compensation must be fair and adequate, and working conditions clean, orderly and safe.

We must be mindful of ways to help our employees fulfill their family responsibilities.

Employees must feel free to make suggestions and complaints.

There must be equal opportunity for employment, development and advancement for those qualified.

We must provide competent management, and their actions must be just and ethical.

We are responsible to the communities in which we live and work and to the world community as well.

We must be good citizens - support good works and charities and bear our fair share of taxes.

We must encourage civic improvements and better health and education.

We must maintain in good order the property we are privileged to use, protecting the environment and natural resources.

Our final responsibility is to our stockholders.

Business must make a sound profit.

We must experiment with new ideas.

Research must be carried on, innovative programmes developed and mistakes paid for.

New equipment must be purchased, new facilities provided and new products launched.

Reserves must be created to provide for adverse times.

When we operate according to these principles, the stockholders should realize a fair return.

Johnson & Johnson

FIGURE 4.3 Johnson & Johnson Credo.

Happy Computers was founded by Henry Stewart in 1991 and by 1997 had an annual turnover of £800,000 and 45 employees. Henry believes in absolute transparency and openness throughout the company, even when it comes to the details of his own salary: 'Why would you want to keep anything secret, knowledge is power, if everyone has knowledge then you have a more powerful organization?' To Henry, a strong culture provides the engine for growth –'without the clear transmission of this ethos, we have nothing'. Most staff are wildly enthusiastic about the company and express huge loyalty and ownership. One comments, 'I feel valued; I enjoy working here because you have to take more responsibility, but you never feel you are alone'. This feeling of being valued even allowed Stewart, in a time of cost cutting, to get a salary cut agreed – to be replaced by a bonus. Business boomed and the bonus far exceeded the original cuts.

4. Shared Power

One of the greatest transitions for the founder of a growing business is to move from direction to empowerment. Giving power does not mean that you lose power. Certainly you will need to learn to let go of some responsibility, but your efforts to delegate will be amply rewarded by the value you gain. If you sit in the business rather than on the business, you will hold back growth. Avoiding this means being prepared to change your personal style of leadership.

Fathoms specializes in underwater surveys. Matt French describes the challenge he faces:

> I must change. We need a complete change of attitude. It must be their company, their money, their profit. They have all got the ability to give more. It is hard work and it has completely stressed me out, but my wife has observed a massive increase in my drive and enthusiasm. All my people have customer contact, so empowering them is vital. It is a constant challenge to pull myself back, look more objectively and not fall into the temptation of saying people are bloody useless, as I used to when assessing cadets. After all, I have been there too!

It is quite difficult to find the right balance between letting go, challenging and getting results. Often people will have been used to coming to you for decisions and expecting you to pull the rabbits out of the hat. It is very hard for them and for you to change. The way to go about it is a combination of supporting your people in taking reasonable risks, training them and making sure that they have clear accountabilities. Delegation is not abdication, so it is vital to tell people what is not up for grabs and to delineate the arena in which they can take decisions.

Philip Green of the Arcadia Group has become a billionaire faster than anyone in UK history. In a rare speech to the 'Entrepreneurs' Entrepreneur' award in December 2005, he explained that he passionately believes in empowerment and training:

Are my businesses a one-man band? They are certainly not. We have got a wonderful team of people. We employ 42,000 people across 2,300 outlets. We have given people a structure in which they can operate under their own steam. People seem to come alive when they are actually allowed to make their own decisions, and can come up with ideas they can make happen.

5. Suitable Structure

The organization structure of the past was like a New York skyscraper: very tall, lots of levels of hierarchy, a great distance between boss and subordinates, vertical rather than horizontal communication.

The spoof organogram in Figure 4.4 demonstrates all the characteristics typically associated with a big company organization. There is an important person at the top, a named chairman who has a number of important people directly reporting to him; in this case a span of control of 10. Each of these has a specific role from vice president of all things beginning with H to vice president of all things not covered by other vice presidents. There are layers of hierarchy with big cheeses, head cheeses and Swiss cheeses. Inside all this formal hierarchy there is the hidden reality of how things actually happen, in this case probably a combination of political power – the owner of the negatives from last year's Christmas party – and quiet efficiency – the secretary who secretly runs the whole shooting match.

Parody though this is, there are still a lot of such organizations around: response to external change is painfully slow, everyone is looking inwards rather than outwards. Yet, as Peter Drucker explained recently, the only thing that lies inside an organization are costs – all the opportunities lie outside! So, why spend so much time being inward looking and contemplating our own navels? In the old-style hierarchical business, communication up, down and across the business is nigh on impossible. Everyone is in a distinct functional silo where communication across-wise can be limited and confrontational. With so many layers of hierarchy, messages on their way down from senior management are invariably distorted.

In a small entrepreneurial business organization, there is no excuse for such heavy, bureaucratic structures. What you want are simple, flexible and probably temporary ways of organizing your business so it can better respond to customer need and to rapid change. Let us turn the old model literally on its head – what we want is a structure which supports the most important people, the front-line troops, in selling to customers.

How you structure your organization will depend on what your key processes are and how product or services get delivered to customers. Here are some guiding principles:

■ Think about the customer first. Business process re-engineering (BPR) tells us that if you can align all your core processes towards customer needs you will have a more streamlined and effective organization. You do not always have to divide things up functionally, i.e. sales, finance, production. It might be better

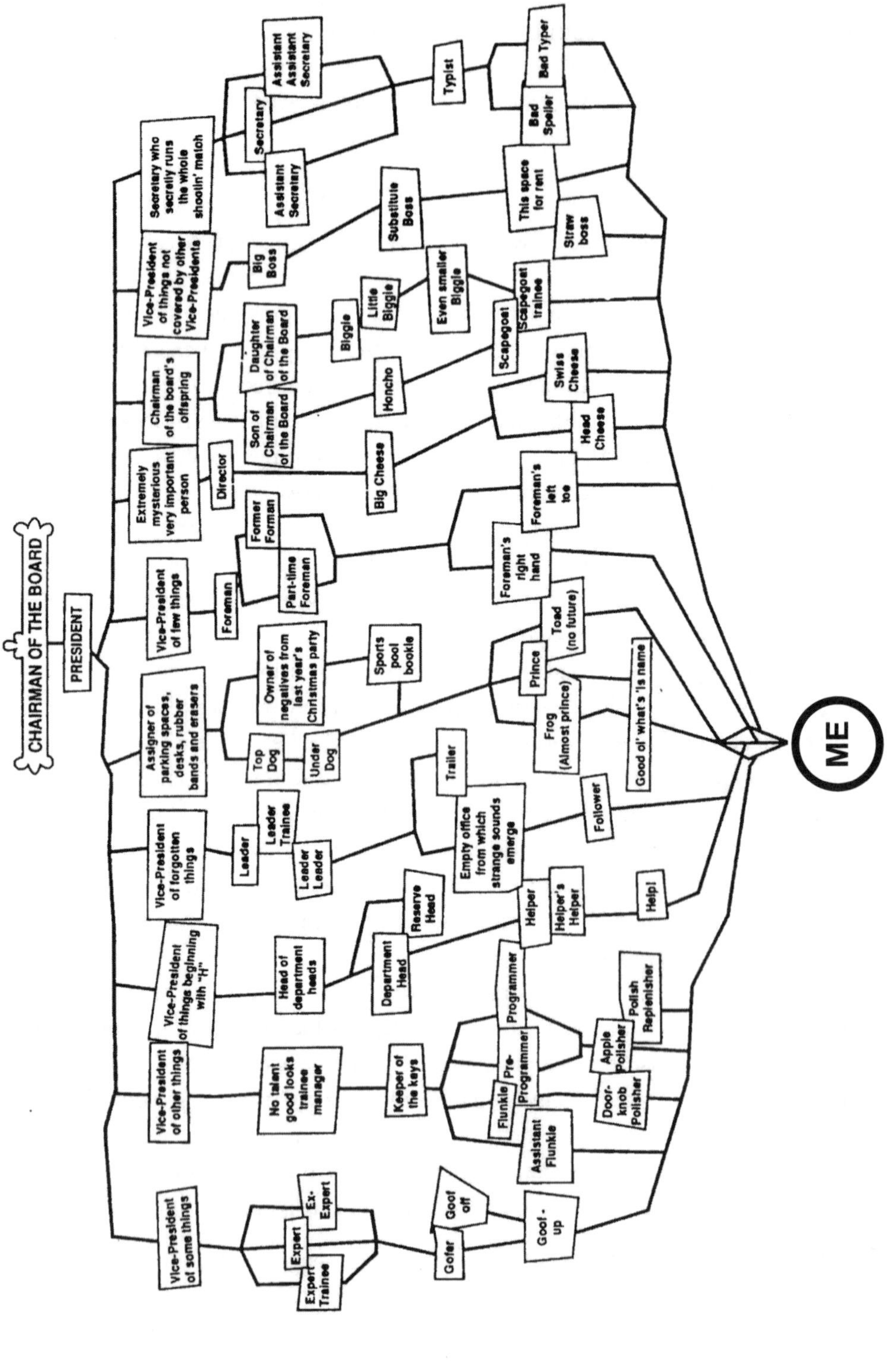

FIGURE 4.4 My Organization.

for people to take specific responsibility for a group of customers or to work in small self-sufficient business groups or in temporary project groups.

- Have as few levels of management as possible. This does, of course, have repercussions for succession opportunities, so you may have to grow people in the job they are in, rather than promoting them to a more senior position.
- Make sure that everyone has a one-page role definition. This means you too and, of course, your board members. They do not have to include everything: just the objective of the job, key deliverables, responsibility for managing others and decision-making authority.
- Emphasize teamworking. So that different functional or geographic teams pull together rather than compete internally.
- Do not get hung up on the span of control role. This rule says that a manager should only have five or six direct reports. Your job as the leader is orchestrating the team rather than directing and controlling it. A strong culture will help make the rules clear to everyone and avoid you having to spend time policing them.
- Keep things outwardly focused and flexible to change. Think of outsourcing non-core activities such as personnel and training, marketing, asset management. What about competitors with whom you can collaborate or joint supplier agreements?

6. Strong Team

Most employees tend to identify with their immediate work team rather than the organization as a whole. However, this can easily lead to internal barriers and divisiveness with sales fighting production, the northern team obstructing the southern team, one branch delighting in the failures of another. Increasingly, businesses are making attempts to create a total corporate identity, for example sending production people out to meet customers, rotating job roles, holding regular problem-solving meetings across departments, meeting up regularly with customers and suppliers. This can help create a more adaptive business where people are in touch with customers needs and therefore more open to change and to innovation.

Shared values can help here in creating a kind of umbrella culture with which everyone can identify regardless of what department they work in. So, generally, the best businesses have the strongest corporate team spirit.

Apart from the overall strength of your team, the other vital requirement is for a strong management team. Ask any aspiring investor what they look for in a potential acquisition and they will tell you 'management team, management team and management team!' As we will see later, one of the greatest challenges to the owner-manager of a growing business is to establish a strong second-tier team, freeing the owner up to create tomorrow's business.

7. Significant Rewards

There is an old axiom which says, 'What gets measured gets done. What gets rewarded gets done again'. As a business grows, it is common to find that reward systems are encouraging the behaviour needed in the past rather than the behaviour needed now. For example, salespeople may have been targeted on turnover but not profitable turnover.

As a small business moves through Greiner's phases of growth it will constantly need to change both what behaviour is rewarded and how those rewards are made. For example, in phase 1, growth through creativity, the need is for customers so the rewards are likely to be immediate, sales related and perhaps commission based. In phase 2, growth through direction, control-based systems are introduced and managers may be primarily measured against their control of costs. In phase 3, growth through delegation, the move towards profit centre responsibility necessitates rewarding not sales, not cost control, but profit performance, and the rewards may more sensibly be linked to some measure of corporate profit sharing.

Rewards do not just mean money. There are many others ways of recognizing good performance. Sometimes a simple thank you is enough. Praise given in front of other people can be very powerful, as can the publicizing of customer feedback on great performance. Any initiatives that add to the individual's sense of achievement and responsibility, for example asking a junior person to make an important external presentation, can also be very effective.

Whatever rewards you think up they will inevitably get stale. There is room for continuous ingenuity in seeking out different rewards: individual or group incentives, trips away, free tickets and gift certificates, profit sharing, promotion, excellence awards, new work assignments. One powerful reward these days may be paid time off. But remember the greatest reward of all is to do a satisfying job.

As your business grows up the Greiner growth curve, think about a reward structure which:

- encourages ownership in the business;
- provides some element of reward both for individual achievement and for team effort;
- directly relates to performance;
- encourages the kind of behaviours and outcomes you want, whether managerial, technical or sales.

Assessing Your People Capability

People are the powerhouse for growth so it is useful to look at people capability under three headings for

skills and attitudes;

management capability and style;
culture.

Skills and Attitudes

Regardless of the intentions you express in your business plan, where you put your key people is the direction in which your organization is going to move. This means getting the right number of people with the right skills and attitudes in the right jobs. It means investing today in the resources you will need for a new tomorrow. Of course, there will always be a time lag in acquiring those skills, which can be bad news if you can see a market opportunity to go for right now. Whether you train or recruit from outside, it all takes time and must be planned for. Skills mix is the first place to start. Ask yourself the question:

- Will existing skills be adequate or do these need to be built up before the business can grow?

There are several ways you can slice the skills cake: one is to look at it function by function, another is to look at the different levels of your organization and yet another is to assess how many square pegs you feel you have in round holes. If you look at the functional mix of skills it is inevitable that you will find shortages as the business grows. For example, the typical business start-up in Greiner's phase 1 is rich in sales skills. However, as it moves into phase 2, growth through direction, it will demand skills to do with accounting and setting up basic systems – very different from the entrepreneurial profile of the phase 1 employee! Again, as the business moves into phase 3, growth through delegation, it is quite probable that there will be a need for some kind of personnel function, maybe professional marketing skills and, above all, management skills needed to run small parts of the business as autonomous units.

As well as skills shortages, you may find you have the business equivalent of bed blockers, people who were great at an earlier stage of growth but are now draining away the lifeblood of the organization. It is worth being brave and confronting the possibility that even you yourself may be a blockage. What about the board of directors you set up eight years ago? Has it now got the right characteristics and calibre for future growth? As the business grows, relationships inevitably change, sometimes painfully. As one managing director explains:

I'm identifying some casualties of growth; for example, when I set up the business George was my only co-director and we enjoyed a very immediate and special relationship. Now, I have a board of directors and a young management team, George is off to one side. He does not like it and I'm not sure he can cope.

It may be better to face up to the square pegs in the round holes that are, after all, an inevitable consequence of growth. Very often people left in such positions – marooned at high tide – are uncomfortable and quite well aware that they are not performing. Facing the problem may be a relief to both parties.

As well as assessing skills mix, you will find it valuable to take a barometer to the attitudes and morale of your employees. Asking yourself the following questions may help pinpoint whether you have a problem:

- What is my employee turnover rate? How does it compare with other local businesses/last year?
- Are levels of sickness/absenteeism high or low?
- Do I know why people are leaving?

A useful diagnostic tool that will give you a direct answer to the last question is provided by the exit interview. The exit interview means arranging for anyone leaving the company to be questioned by an impartial person who can establish the real reasons why. For example, is that person leaving for more money, because of a better opportunity, or because he or she feels frustrated? Most people in these circumstances are quite happy to talk freely and you can learn a great deal. Attitude surveys, particularly if you carry them out year on year, will also help benchmark levels of employee morale and highlight problem areas.

Always recruit for attitude rather than skills. Skills can usually be grafted on, but you will never change people who have the wrong attitude. They can so easily become your traitors, people who are bad-mouthing your business, your plans and you. Do not put up with it for a minute.

Management Capability and Style

In looking at where your organization is now, ask yourself the following questions:

- Do I have the right kind of managers to run my business?
- How much growth can they handle?
- How strong is my current management team?
- What am I doing to develop a second tier of management?

Take a look not only at the management capability of yourself and your team, but also at your management style. As the old saying goes, 'It's not what you do but the way that you do it.' What typifies the style of yourself and your managers? How appropriate is this style to cope with the challenges you face?

One director described his immediate boss as 'having the charisma of a slug'. Or do you lean towards Attila the Hun style typified by Harold Geneen of ITT in his philosophy: 'Express criticism, withhold praise and instil job insecurity'. The management style of the founder can sometimes be a major block on growth in phase 2 and beyond.

The typical transition for owner-managers is from a directive autocratic style towards a more consultative, empowering one.

Culture

When you put together all the day-to-day ways in which you and your managers behave you get culture. How the receptionist greets a visitor, whether managers are visible to staff, where managers eat and with whom, who goes or does not go to the pub, what people wear; all these things and many more provide the signals which people read as: the way we do things round here. What is your culture? Will it help or hinder you from achieving your plans for growth?

In order to diagnose your culture, ask yourself the following questions:

- What do I spend time on?
- What is first on the agenda of management meetings?
- Who attends and where are they?
- What stories do I tell about the business?
- What questions do I ask of my employees?
- What ceremonies and symbols do we have?
- What behaviours do we reward?
- How do we use office space?

Your answers to these questions will tell you a lot about your values and culture. For example, if you say that you are passionate about customers but we see that you spend all your time behind your office door then we know what to believe! If the first item on the agenda of your management meetings is always the financials, then this is what you care about. Why not put quality, or people or culture first? If that is what you believe.

What stories are told in the business. Are they about how you won your first order? Are they about your heroes – the guys in production or the warehouse who went the extra mile to get the job out? What are you always passionately questioning? Is it about how people treat customers, about product quality or tidiness in the plant? What ceremonies and symbols do you use? For example, do you have wall of fame letters from customers? What pictures do you have in reception? Do you have a logo like the WWF panda, which is found on all their publicity material and a huge stuffed toy version of which sits in their reception? What sort of people do you reward and promote? Are they good people managers, ace salespeople or yes people? How do you use your physical office space? Do you have the biggest office with all the windows? Is it open plan? Are there reserved car parking spaces? All these are powerful messages about your culture.

The sum of your culture can provide a nutritious jelly, as in the case of one small company, which describes itself as 'demonstrably different from our competitors – we have a real enthusiasm, great atmosphere, are dynamic and are professionally run', or the culture can be treacle, the inertia which will stop your business from changing and growing – because 'We've always done things that way.' Years after the death of Walt Disney, for example, his top management apparently met every new proposal with the comment, 'Walt wouldn't like it'.

Assessing Your Structure

Structure is the skeleton of organization. It tells you how work is divided up, who does what, and how the different roles relate one to another. Structure is more than the organization chart of today! While your business can increase in size without changing its structure, Greiner suggests that the structure of your business will necessarily change at different stages of development. Is your structure a straitjacket for the people who work within it? Does your structure reflect the problems you are trying to solve now or is it an inappropriate inheritance from the past? Those managers in search of the ideal organization structure – the Holy Grail – will be disappointed. In answer to the question, 'What is the right structure?' comes the reply, 'it all depends'. It all depends on the business environment you are operating in and how uncertain it is. It all depends on what kind of business you were historically and what kind of people you now employ. The only statement we can make with any certainty of being right is that, whatever structure you have in place now, it will not be the one you need in the future! So, before we start examining matrix structures, business centres or centralized structures, it is worth asking the following questions:

- At what stage of development is my business now?
- What are the key controls? (i.e. profit centres/budgets/corporate plans)
- How would I describe my present structure?'

We will start to address these questions under subheadings for:

- How to divide things up;
- Types of structure – advantages/disadvantages;
- How to pull things together again.

How to Divide Things Up

The minute your business is more than a one-man band you will have to start defining specific roles and allocating them to specific individuals. Typically, in a smaller business, you may not have the luxury of one role to one person; rather people have bits of jobs. In a consultancy, for example, an individual may have some responsibility for delivery of client work, alongside some responsibility for generating new business and some for corporate practice development. You will need role specifications, partly because it is nigh on impossible to recruit without them and partly because this tells the individual what is expected from him and how his responsibilities relate to others.

- Does everyone have a job description explaining exactly what is expected of them?

No roles should escape this process, including those of chairman, manager director and non-executive directors.

As the business grows, it becomes convenient to group activities into teams either by geography, by function or by product group:

- How far do these groupings really help us deliver what the customer wants?

To answer this fundamental question, you may need to take a hard look at your core business processes and how they align to the customer. The concept of straight through processing in banking, or BPR (business processing re-engineering), is a useful one. Stripped of all its accretions, what is the input/output line in your business? For example, in an IT consultancy like Braxxon, which sells to UK-based investment banks, there are really only two important dimensions along which to organize: sales and delivery. In the case of MMR, which delivers an IT service to apparently the same market, it makes sense to organize the business in terms of the two main customer groups: legal and banking. If you look at a business like Point Source, which provides flexible laser technology to leading edge manufacturers of scientific instrumentation, then the business is organized to focus on engineering quality and bespoke customer service.

The most commonly used dimensions along which to organize a business are probably to divide it up by function, by geography, by market or by product. The traditional principle is to group together like activities. Unfortunately, these groupings tend not to stay static as new market requirements force new kinds of response. What therefore results is a complicated overlay of different types of structure. This can be very messy and can also involve making some difficult decisions, for example:

- Should quality control be centralized or put into specific business units?
- Should the sales function remain centralized?
- Do geographical groups have full autonomy?
- How should business units relate one with another?
- What should the role of the head office be?
- How do line functions relate to staff functions?

Finally, there are the old chestnuts – the rules to do with span of control. Urwick has a lot to answer for! In the 1920s, he established a rule of thumb which said that no manager should have more than a maximum of five or six direct reports. This reinforces the one man–one boss principle and allows for clarity and strong control by the manager. However, there is a very big price tag. Obviously, the narrower the span of control, the more levels of hierarchy must exist. The more levels of hierarchy there are, the more difficult it is to get sensible communication up and down the organization: 'Send reinforcements we're going to advance' very soon becomes 'Send three and fourpence we're going to a dance'.

It is said that, if an organization has five levels of management and the president communicates a message from the top, then the percentage of information recalled will be as follows:

- Level 1: 63 per cent
- Level 3: 40 per cent
- Level 5: 20 per cent.

Small wonder that an engineering firm of 250 employees, with seven levels of hierarchy, reported communication problems!

The answer is to keep your organization structure as flat as possible, even though this may mean that you have quite a large number of direct reports. This will be a problem only if you have a command and control style of management. But if you have a strong culture, committed people and clear accountabilities, people will manage themselves with little interference from you and the communications up and down the organization will be that much better.

Types of Structure: Advantages/Disadvantages

Greiner's model is a useful way of reminding ourselves that there is no one right answer – it is a case of horses for courses. The summary chart in Table 4.1 is intended only to be used to check that the structure you are about to introduce is not going to create more problems than it will solve. There is plenty of room for creative thinking in devising new and flexible structures which work for you (project teams, quality circles, temporary groupings, etc.)

How to Put Things Together Again

The problem with organizations is that they are like Humpty Dumpty; having divided them up, it is often very difficult to put them together again in such a way that they will actually work. So, for differentiation gone mad, read this delightful spoof McKinsey report on the organization of a concert:

> The four horn players are seriously underemployed and their number should be reduced. In fact, if their workload was shared out among the other players they could be dispensed with altogether. The 12 first and second violins were observed to be all playing the same notes. This duplication of effort should not be tolerated and the group could be cut drastically. If the sound becomes too thin it could easily be amplified electronically to whatever level is desired. The playing of semiquavers was seen to be a considerable, and in our view unwarranted, effort. It could even lead to a demand for payment at piece-work rates. If short notes such as quavers and semiquavers were

TABLE 4.1 Types of Structure

Type of structure	Features	Advantages	Disadvantages
Informal	Business start-up Few people Highly committed Little need for structure	Fun Market orientated Responsive	Can be disorganized Attention to detail lacking Few systems in place
Functional/centralized	Functions are separated one from the other Vertical hierarchy Clear accountabilities Strong HQ Cost centres	Clarity of role Specialization by function Systematic	Unresponsive to business/market change Communications up/down and across suffer Compartmentalization and empire building
Decentralized business units	Focus on business accountability Unique business mission Business manager calls the shots HQ manages by exception	Motivates managers Responsive to customers Flexible	'Robber Barons' may go out of control Problems of integration of different strategies Problems of HQ control
Product groups	Daily operating decisions remain decentralized HQ takes a more active and special-ist role in co-ordinating plans and investment strategy	HQ people are more comfortable A global response to markets and competition may be more possible Strategies are integrated	Cumbersome red tape 'Us' and 'Them' builds up between field and HQ Conflicts arise
Matrix	Dual chain of command: two bosses (everyone had a mother and a father) 'Business results' manager on one axis and a 'resource manager' on the other hold equal power	New and exciting; can build in flexibility Allows organization to respond to two sectors simultaneously (i.e. market and technology) Suited to uncertainty and complexity	Difficult for managers to get used to Tendency towards anarchy Power struggles inevitable Severe 'groupitis' can occur Role ambiguity inevitable

grouped together, by rationalizing the score, into more economic units, a less qualified workforce, and even students, could be engaged without the loss of efficiency. In some passages, there is far too much repetition, and we recommend a thorough reprocessing of the material; for example, it serves no useful purpose for the oboe to repeat passages which have already been fully dealt with by the violins. If all such superfluous passages were eliminated, the concert, which at present lasts up to 2 hours, could be adequately completed in approximately 20 minutes. The unproductive interval could then be dispensed with.

The conductor does not fully grasp today's concepts of management science as applied to orchestral activities, and he is apprehensive that artistic standards might decline. In this unlikely event, there would be compensating financial savings, since audiences, who are only, after all, a major distraction to the smooth functioning of the operation, would decline. Although improbable, this would merely call for parts of the concert hall to be shut off, thereby bringing added cost savings in electricity, personnel, ticket printing, etc, on the one hand, and an essential improvement of acoustics by reduction of the background noises.

At the worst, the whole enterprise could be shut down, with consequent major economies in artist fees ... and we could then all retire to the bar.

Every time you reorganize you create another potential set of barriers between different parts of the organization; barriers between the first and the second floor, between secretaries and managers, between line and staff, between field and head office, between sales and marketing, between UK and European. No wonder we all need as much help as we can get in coordinating activities. Ask yourself:

■ How is integration achieved at present?

Traditionally, integration was achieved through the manager at the top of the hierarchy personally coordinating and controlling. As the business grows more complex and diverse, this becomes more and more difficult. The solutions lie somewhere in the area of formal communications, teamwork and strong culture and values.

There are some clues. A corporate vision that is shared by everyone (as in the consultancy group McKinsey) integrates. A strong set of shared values or culture (like McDonald's) integrates. Informal networks help to integrate (Tandem Computers hold regular beer-busts – get-togethers everywhere in the world at 4 pm every Friday afternoon). Project teams across disciplines build integration; job rotation and mobility across functions also help to integrate. The other key integration strategy is to overdose on communications. As the business grows, it will start to pull apart and splinter. The original values will be diluted by new people. You just cannot communicate too much!

Every attitude survey that has ever existed will show that even in the best-run businesses there is an insatiable demand for more communications. The essence of the challenge is to create team identity at both a local level and also at a corporate level. Teamworking across boundaries is the key to innovation and is the shape of the future.

Assessing Your Systems

Systems are the nerves of the organization, the processes and connections which can switch the organization on – or stop anything happening at all. Organization systems are generally considered boring, but the truth is they can be very powerful levers for change. Systems can be sexy! We will briefly consider people systems, just to get you thinking about what you have in the way of people processes and what you might need to put in place. These aspects are explored in much more detail in chapter 10. For now let us touch on:

- recruitment and selection processes;
- motivation and retention processes;
- training and development processes;
- communications processes.

Recruitment and Selection Processes

Recruitment is perhaps the biggest worry for growing businesses. It can prove to be a major constraint on development plans. A Cranfield survey (Table 4.2) identified the recruitment of key staff as the overwhelming worry of most small businesses, ahead even of concerns about customers or raising finance.

Getting the right people is a difficult, time-consuming and costly business. Most capital investment decisions pale into insignificance against the cost of recruitment (think four times salary!) Getting it wrong is even more expensive and can be extremely painful. Few growing businesses can claim not to have fallen into this trap. However, you can increase the odds on success by assessing whether you have in place suitable processes and disciplines. These are likely to include:

TABLE 4.2 The Key Problems of Small Business

Key priorities	Percentage of respondents
Recruiting key staff	83
Finding customers	59
Raising new finance	31
High interest rates	27
Red tape	21

- Deciding on the numbers and skills mix you are going to need over the next 1–3 years to meet your business plan for growth.
- Writing role specifications as a guide to recruitment. These should cover job title and purpose, to whom responsible, for whom, limits of accountability and main tasks.
- Preparing a person specification, outlining the characteristics of the sort of person you think is likely to be effective in the job.
- Sourcing your requirements creatively, not just through your personal contacts and your website but possibly also using staff referrals, local radio, head hunters and recruitment agencies.
- Using psychometric tests to supplement your interview process. A huge range of tests covering aptitude or ability are available: tests of general intelligence, tests of attainment and personality inventories.
- Giving some thought to designing a systematic programme of interviews.
- Taking up references before people start with you.

We will look at getting your recruitment and selection processes right in more detail in chapter 10.

Motivation and Retention Processes

Having recruited the right people you need to ensure that you have the right processes for recognizing, rewarding and retaining them. If morale and levels of job satisfaction are low, then performance will suffer, the team will be affected and often people (usually those you want to keep) will leave.

- How do I handle the 'hygiene' factors?

Certainly financial rewards are important. But one of the biggest mistakes you can make is to assume that money alone is the way to motivate staff. In his seminal work in the Pittsburgh Iron and Steel Company, Frederick Herzberg discovered that money is actually not a motivator at all. It is a hygiene factor. Just as removing rubbish does not produce good health but may prevent bad health, so getting the hygiene factors right removes dissatisfaction and gets people to a basic level of survival, but that is all!

Hygiene factors include: company policy, supervision, administration, working conditions, interpersonal relations and salary. So, getting salary levels right is important as a baseline requirement but makes very little difference to morale or their job performance. In his hierarchy of needs, Maslow makes a similar point, that our basic needs are for survival and safety, but once these are up to an adequate level, people look for other factors in their life and giving them more food and more safety has no effect. So, do not waste your time on the hygiene factors if you want to make a difference to staff morale!

- How do you build in the motivators?

In order to motivate people we have to look at an entirely different set of factors – the motivators. These include achievement, recognition, responsibility, advancement and growth and work itself. In other words, if you want to increase job satisfaction and really get people performing with gusto, increase the opportunity in the work for people to find these factors. You may be able to do this by making the job itself intrinsically more interesting, by delegating more responsibility or by just by saying thank you now and then. In fact, the problem is not so much motivating people as avoiding demotivating them!

- What are the levels of morale in your business?

There are some key measures and processes that you can use to benchmark the morale of your people; we will explore some of them in more detail in chapter 10. They are:

- Monitor labour turnover regularly against industry norms.
- Carry out exit interviews when people leave.
- Benchmark morale by putting in place a regular attitude survey.

Earlier on, we rather crudely stated that 'What gets measured, gets done. What gets rewarded gets done again.' Getting your reward systems right will be crucial to moving your business in the direction you want. Unfortunately, it is not a case of plugging in to one sort of reward system (for example, bonuses or share options) and expecting that to work forever. As you go through different phases of growth, the behaviour you will be looking for will change and so must the way you reward it. This is an area requiring constant monitoring.

- How do you currently reward people for achieving goals?

As you test out your reward systems, ask yourself what it is that you are expecting from people, and is this what is being produced and being rewarded? It is very easy to find that you are expecting one thing (i.e. quality) and rewarding another (i.e. throughput). Do not be frightened of discriminating between good and bad performance; accountability for results must go with growth. Do you provide bonuses alongside basic pay? Does the company operate a profit-related pay scheme (PRP)? Do you reward team or individual performance?

- How much of a sense of ownership do your people feel?

You can tell when everyone has a sense of ownership in the business by what they say about the company in the pub. Pump a driver or a secretary for information. If you cannot get them to say a bad word about the business, then you have got ownership

– people who think about the company as a whole and are prepared to go the extra mile. Ownership is a hot topic in entrepreneurial firms; everyone wants to know how to instil this spirit. Have you thought about giving employees an equity stake in the business? A lot of owner-managers have. According to ProShare, the organization that encourages wide share ownership, 1 million people in 859 companies are covered by Inland Revenue-approved share schemes; a further 1.25 million people in 1,201 companies take part in 'Save As You Earn' share-saving schemes; and 300,000 people in 3,769 companies participate in the government's share option plan. All in all, that means there are 2.5 million British people working in share-ownership schemes.

Training and Development Processes

As the business grows you are bound to find that you need more people with different skill sets. You can, of course, recruit them from outside, but this is costly and time-consuming and can destroy the team spirit and positive attitudes you have built up internally. Clearly, some will have to be recruited, but a preferable option is to keep training and developing your existing people, so that you grow your own from inside the organization. This way you are motivating staff by offering them the chance of growth and advancement and you are not risking diluting your culture. There are several reasons for training: there may be a gap between current performance and what is required, or you may find that people's skills need to be developed for the future of the business.

Even those who have been recruited with the skills they need require training to do things your way, which may not be the way they have been taught in the past. Positive attitude is so vital that it is worth being prepared to recruit people who have the right attitude and whom you will then train.

■ How many days training per year do you give every employee?

As we will see in chapter 10, there is a crystal clear link between investing in training and having a profitable business! Yet small businesses are notoriously bad at training their staff, over 40 per cent devote less than one day a year to staff training. What is the point in paying a fortune to recruit people and then not making the most of them?

Think about giving each employee 10 days a year training; yes, that seems a lot, but watch what it does for staff performance, motivation and retention. By adding value to your employees you add value to the business.

■ What percentage of your revenue do you reinvest in developing your people?

You depreciate your computers and machinery so that you can reinvest in new ones, so think of constantly investing at least 2 per cent of your turnover into staff development. People, after all, are far more important to the future of the business. You will need to have systems for identifying training needs and then meeting them. Unfortunately, when asked what training they need, most people find it difficult to answer. It is therefore essential to spend time identifying training needs for your team, for each key individual and also for yourself.

If you are going to be serious about training and developing your staff, then you need an appraisal system, as this is a first-rate way of identifying individual training needs.

■ Do you have an adequate appraisal system in place?

The appraisal discussion provides a good opportunity for an open discussion about performance and for identifying training needs. Another approach is to carry out a training needs analysis. This analysis depends on interviewing members of staff to determine key issues such as their background, role, skills needed in the job, strengths and weaknesses, career aspirations. So you need to:

■ have a training budget;
■ set up an appraisal system;
■ carry out a training needs analysis;
■ prepare a training and development programme;
■ source suppliers of training (see chapter 10);
■ follow up with those being trained.

Communications Processes

Finally, a seemingly innocuous question:

■ How good are your internal communications?

Once you are past the euphoria of phase 1 growth, we suspect that your answer is likely to be, 'not very'. Communication problems are a classic consequence of growth. In the early days you do not need anything very formal, you are probably a small team, openly involved in sharing information and playing bar billiards together.

The troubles come as you get bigger and people no longer come together on a regular basis, new people have joined who do not have the same shared history and none of you has time for meetings. Cracks begin to appear in the communication downwards, in communications across from one department to another and in the extent to which anyone listens to the ideas coming up through the organization.

The state of your communications is a good barometer of your corporate health. Once this goes, look out for fragmentation: us and them type behaviour, lack of team identify, frustration about goals, patchy information flow, politicking and cliques. It is a paradox that even informal communications (once you are past a certain size) need formalizing. Communications never happen unless there are the disciplines and mechanisms to make them happen.

■ What communication mechanisms do you have in place?

Are you satisfied that you have in place at least some of the following, very simple, mechanisms:

- staff briefings
- regular management meetings
- management by walking about (MBWA) carried out by you!
- social get-togethers
- one-to-ones with your key reports
- occasional get-togethers of the whole company
- presentations by one department to another
- somewhere to eat where people can relax and mix.

So, now is a good time to start assessing your recruitment, motivational, reward, training and communication processes. You may frighten yourself with the amount of work to be done in getting the basics in place but do not be! You do not have to do it all yourself, nor do you necessarily need to recruit an HR manager. Find someone who is young and keen to take on the role internally and then use outsiders to help. There are many one-man bands who will be able to look at your systems for you, advise on improving them and not charge you an arm and a leg. Alternatively, if you have not done so already you can think about applying for Investors in People accreditation: (www.investorsinpeople.co.uk.). The main benefits are not so much the piece of paper you may get at the end, but the fact that you are provided with a discipline, focus and framework for getting your people systems right.

Assignment 4.2 Diagnosing Your Organization

Use the framework set out in Table 4.3 to summarize your assessment of your organizational capability based on the questions posed in this chapter.

TABLE 4.3 Framework For Diagnosing Organizational Capability

People	Skills and attitudes	Will existing skills be adequate or do these need to be built up before the business can grow? What is the labour turnover rate compared with competitors/last year? Are levels of sickness/absenteeism high or low? Do I know why my people are leaving?
	Management capability and style	Do I have sufficient managers to run my business well? How much growth could they handle without becoming overstretched? Is there anyone who can run the business in my absence? If a key manager left is there someone to fill his or her place? How much can I delegate? What is my personal management style and that of my managers?
	Culture	How would my managers and myself describe the organization culture?
Structure	What kind of structure exists?	At what stage of growth (Greiner) is my business? How is my business currently controlled? How would I describe my present structure?
	How to divide things up	Does everyone have a job description and know what is expected of them? Are the various tasks divided up and grouped in the best way?
	How to integrate	How is integration achieved at present? Do people work individually or in teams?
Systems	Recruitment	Role specifications? Sourcing appropriately? Selection procedures?
	Motivation and retention	How do I recognize and reward staff? What is morale like?
	Training and development	What are our training needs? How much development do we provide?
	Communications	How good are internal communications?

five
Now Let Us Talk About You

We have looked at organization and management capability, now let us take stock of the me factor, that is your personal drivers and motivations, your leadership style, your leadership strengths and weaknesses and your current role. In chapter 13, we will look at reinventing yourself, possibly changing your role and the way you allocate time and adapting your leadership style to handle the transitions of growth.

The start point is to look at where you are now and help you to develop greater awareness about yourself. As the owner-manager of your company you are of paramount importance. You are likely to be both the best news and the worst news about your business. You are the best news because it is your drive, energy and ideas which fire progress, the worst because you yourself may be part of the problem, an obstruction to growth rather than an enabler.

Entrepreneurs, by definition, tend to be strong characters who tend to push to make things happen. These very characteristics can impede the growth of a more mature business that depends upon having a management team. You are also the most visible person in the company so that, like it or not, every detail of your behaviour will be watched for the signals it contains. By the end of this chapter, you should be able to carry out a personal SWOT of your own strengths, weaknesses, opportunities and threats. So, let us think about you!

Personal Drivers and Motivation

The more you are aware of your, perhaps hidden, personal drivers, the more likely you are to arrive where you want in life. However, it is astonishing how little time and effort most owner-managers spend on trying to understand themselves. You will remember that in chapter 4 we touched on Herzberg's hygiene factors and motivators. You will recall that the hygiene factors are things like working conditions, money and security. If they are not there, they act as demotivators, but putting more and more effort into improving the hygiene factors does not actually create positive motivation. The motivators come from a different list of factors – things like a sense of achievement, recognition, responsibility, job growth and the intrinsic interest of the work itself. Everything about you as an owner-manager says that you are a highly motivated individual with powerful drivers and a strong desire for success.

But there are some fundamental questions to ask:

- Why did I set up the business?
- What have I achieved so far?
- How much satisfaction do I currently get from my business life?
- What is my home/work balance like?
- What would happen if I did nothing to change my business?
- What type of things am I worrying about now?
- How far have I progressed towards achieving my personal goals?
- Am I getting bored?

It really pays to revisit your drivers and get back in touch with why you set up the business in the first place and where your passion came from.

Sophos is a well-known anti-virus and anti-spam software company. It has huge sales, a global customer base and a state-of-the-art £32 million headquarters in Abingdon, UK. The building was paid for in cash! Yet it was started only 20 or so years ago in a two-up two-down house on a 1960s housing estate outside Oxford. Its charismatic CEOs, Dr Peter Lammer and Dr Jan Hruska, first met in Oxford while studying doctorates in medical science. They were both full of ideas and they both wanted to do their own thing, so they hit it off immediately. While studying, they started building computer hardware devices. Then, with £100,000 funding, they started a laptop computer company (this was in 1982). This went bust, they wound down the business, Hruska went back to his native Croatia to do his military service and Lammer finished his PhD. But the seeds had been sown and when they met up again in 1985, they decided to try again: 'And in the same breath', says Hruska, 'we said it must be a software company. That way we could be a two-man operation, self-sufficient and not reliant on big manufacturers.' So the new Sophos was born.

Before the company flotation, Hrsuka and Lammer were asked if they would move on? 'We do not have anything better to do. We very much enjoy our work. It would be very difficult to muster enthusiasm amongst the staff today without being enthusiastic ourselves.'

Recent research by YouGov for Intuit shows that one in ten small business owners are more passionate about their business than about their partner, and more than 10 per cent actually put business before their partners! Sixty per cent of entrepreneurs set up their businesses to gain autonomy and flexibility and almost half of the entrepreneurs aged 18–30 translated a hobby into their business idea.

Edgar H. Schein (*Career Anchors: Discovering Your Real Values,* 1990, University Associates) maintains that we are all motivated by our own unique combination of eight career anchors. If you take a look at these, they may help you pinpoint what very specifically motivates you.

Technical/Functional Competence

What turns you on is the content of work, things like graphic design, running complex manufacturing plant, engineering or film special effects. Your technical expertise in a particular area gives you most job satisfaction and the degree to which you gain recognition from your peer group is important to you. Many owner-managers at least originate with this career anchor strongly in their mind, whether it be a passion for printing, designing manhole covers or writing leading-edge software.

Fathoms was set up by Matt French after he left the Royal Navy, where he had been a surveyor/mapmaker for 23 years. Because of his expertise, Matt found that even in the Navy he could do things differently from the standard Navy way. He initially wanted to run a business with himself and his wife. He described himself as 'a positive, pragmatic ex-mapmaker'.

Managerial Competence

What interests you is making major policy decisions, leading others, high earnings and rising to the top. You probably have experience of more than one functional area; you are stimulated by interpersonal issues and crises rather than exhausted or debilitated by them. You tend to be motivated by money and status – large offices and large cars may be important measures of your success.

Independence and Autonomy

You cannot stand to be bound by other people's rules. You do things your way, thinking outside the box and creating new rules. Others will tell you that the bee should not be able to fly because it is too heavy, you will prove them wrong. You must be master of your own ship. Freedom is important to you. You hate red tape. You want to be a leader in your industry and you want this recognized. Winning prizes, testimonials and awards is more important to you than making money.

David Pointer, a PhD physicist, set up Point Source in 1991. The company is a pioneer and world leader in flexible laser technology. The first sentence of its vision states 'we want to be recognized internationally for our commercial, technological and organizational success'. The entrepreneurial flair of Point Source has won it many awards, and

David's boardroom is full of high-status trophies. David and his business thrive in a creative environment where they are always pushing the boundaries. He likes being a maverick.

Security and Stability

You like stable predictable work and like to work within an organization. You want to be recognized as a loyal and steady performer. You are very unlikely to be an entrepreneur if this is your entire motivation!

Entrepreneurial Creativity

You have an overriding need to create new businesses of your own. You probably had small money-making schemes at school. Your motivation often derives from your own family, who may themselves have been successful entrepreneurs. You have both talent and a huge motivation to prove to the world that you can succeed. You are unlikely to be happy in a traditional organization. You are motivated by wealth as the means of showing the world what you have accomplished. You get bored easily. You want ownership and control. You want to build a fortune and a sizeable enterprise and may well seek personal visibility and public recognition.

Virgin's Richard Branson provides a good example of a classic entrepreneurial motivation. He started his money-making schemes when he was a schoolboy at Stowe, he enjoys proving to the world that you name it and he can run it better – and particularly better than British Airways! He used to appal the business establishment by turning up in woolly jumpers and a beard. He does things his way, even when putting a friendly arm around a royal shoulder may be misinterpreted! And he loves being in the limelight.

Service/Dedication to a Cause

You want to make a difference, to improve the world. You want to be able to exert influence and to feel that your contribution is recognized.

The Body Shop, under Anita Roddick, prided itself on its passion for making a difference in the world. She was always on the campaign trail, from opposing animal testing to campaigning on 'trade not aid' and 'saving the rainforest'. She once said:

> I am still looking for the equivalent of those Quakers who ran successful businesses, made money because they offered honest products and treated their people decently, worked hard, spent honestly, gave honest value for money, put back more than they took out and told no lies. This business creed, sadly, seems forgotten.

Pure Challenge

You are competitive and seek ever tougher challenges. You believe you can conquer anything or anybody. You define success as overcoming obstacles, solving unsolvable problems, winning over tough opponents. You are single-minded and highly motivated. You are a warrior and this may affect home/work balance:

Charles Rigby is the owner-manager of World Challenge Expeditions, which provides challenging trips for schoolchildren in out-of-the-way places. He is a former army officer; you can see it in his bearing and hear it in his lively and innovative means of expressing himself! He loves the challenges of building a highly successful business and is happy to describe the many obstacles he has met and overcome. Handling crisis comes naturally to him and a business combining the words 'children', ' adventure' and 'overseas' provides plenty of opportunity to constantly test himself against new problems.

Lifestyle

This may seem like a contradiction in terms: that your lifestyle is more important than any career. But many highly motivated people reach a point when career must be integrated within total lifestyle. You seek flexibility and control and are keen that travelling and work commitments are compatible with family arrangements.

Chris Renardson, chairman and founder of Braxxon, has a grown-up family, a lovely wife and some gorgeous grandchildren. He has houses in Spain and Wales, as well as Henley. He is a golfer and cyclist with a heap of outside interests. He says that he has as much money as he needs to live the life he does. He says he would not know what to do with another £10 million. It just is not a motivator. Time with his family, enjoying his life and building a sustainable business for all Braxxon employees are his motivators. Oh and also, though his wife wishes this was not the case, he loves the involvement in Braxxon!

So think hard about yourself and your job. Are you enjoying life? What did you expect to have achieved by this stage in your life? What is holding you back? What are your sources of dissatisfaction? It is all too easy to get stale or to find that the role you are now in is not the one that really suits you. Challenge some of your assumptions. Do you want to exit the business in the next four years with shed-loads of dosh, or do you actually like doing what you are doing and want to stay on to build a bigger business?

MMR founders Moira Pollard and Doug Brown founded the company some 15 years ago because they were sick of corporate life and felt they could do things a lot better! They wanted to control their own destiny and very much enjoyed working together. They say that money was never the chief motivator. They had a passion for the business and loved the client contact and the challenges of growth. There was a buzz which constantly motivated them. But over the last five years things have changed. Moira is coping with a long-term illness, so she cannot get around to clients the way she used to and she and Doug do not have the long, stimulating conversations on the way back from an exciting meeting. Doug has a million other business ideas he wants to pursue. They are getting just a bit older, the buzz has gone and it is time to hand over to a younger team. In fact, they are now getting a new buzz from mentoring the management team and seeing it rise to the challenge!

What is really important to you? That you find more time for the family, that you secure their future financially, that you have the freedom to do a million other things on your wish list? Is it high income that you want? Do you want a chunk of capital out? When? Why? Who are you doing all this for? Is it to prove something to yourself? To your father? To the peers who you want to exceed?

Also ask yourself about home/work balance and whether this suits you.

Dan Harnett is manager director of Martec, his father's business before him. His aim is to create a business which will survive him as the key person. In his Christmas letter to friends, he realized Martec was the centre of his life – he had no family news to transmit. He got his family together with a flipchart to brainstorm what was going wrong. That crystallized his transition issue in terms of home–work balance. He gets bored with the day-to-day issues – it can work well without him being there all the time. As a leader in the past, he was hesitant about taking control, feeling he was not quite ready. He still feels this, but times have changed, his young family is forcing the issue, external forces are pushing him harder. Longer term, he wants to sell out, enjoy life a bit more, have more holiday. Perhaps float at £10 million.

His drivers? His father once hit £1 million profit, now he has achieved this. He wants external recognition. He fills in all the surveys, entered an environmental award in Kent, later he wants the Martec team recognized as the best. Dan maintains that this year he has taken two weeks' holiday without taking his mobile and laptop with him!

If you want to know whether or not you are a workaholic, then see how many of the following you say yes to! If you are up to ten, then you are an extreme and probably hopeless case!

Are You a Workaholic?

1. Does work dominate your life?
2. Do your children need to make an appointment to see you?
3. Do you like to work at a frantic pace?
4. In the last year, have you not read a book unconnected with work?
5. Do you make excuses to justify your pattern of work?
6. Are you afraid to delegate for fear that others will not do it as well as you?
7. Do you judge people by their value to you in business?
8. Do your family accuse you of not taking enough holiday?
9. Do thoughts of work intrude on your leisure time?
10. Have you ever forgotten a social engagement because of work?

What Kind of Leader Are You?

Taking Stock of Your Leadership Philosophy

Leadership is the art of mobilizing others to want to struggle for shared aspirations. Leadership is absolutely fundamental to growing a business because leaders do two things: first, they set the vision or direction and, second, they energize and inspire willing and motivated followers. Clearly, leaders need followers, but perhaps followers need leaders too?

It is worth asking yourself:

- Why should anyone be led by me?

When you find the answer you will have your own leadership formula. Leadership is different from management. Managers maintain today's business, think short term, rely on control and are obsessed with efficiency. Leaders, on the other hand, challenge the status quo, create change, think long term and are obsessed with doing the right things for tomorrow's business. It is worth taking a few moments to take stock of your personal assumptions and beliefs about leadership and how they were built up. Where did you learn leadership? Was it at school, in the forces, or by following a role model, such as a successful entrepreneurial father? Role models can be very powerful, as these comments from earlier participants of the Business Growth and Development Programme (BGP) show:

> I've seen good and bad leadership in the Royal Navy.

> I had a good Commander who pushed me.

> My Dad was an entrepreneur; as a small child, I always knew I would be one too. He was a useful mentoring figure; we had a fabulous three years. I was really up for it. I emptied his hard drive.

In some cases leadership is thrust upon a new generation of entrepreneurs, by the death of a co-founder or because of family pressures. It seems that having an entrepreneurial father can be a mixed blessing and a hard act to follow for any leader who is trying to carve out his own way:

> When my father stepped aside as MD, I thought I would miss sheltering behind him, but it is like the sun came out, I feel confident!

> My father's model of leadership is different, he does not delegate.

> Without me the business would not have changed from authoritarian to consultative, without that the business would not have grown. I knew employees were good, once I gave them their heads they produced astounding results,

to the surprise of my father who didn't think they had the capability. Father is an engineer, I am a people person, I am evolving as a leader.

So, where are you now in terms of your leadership beliefs? You might like to check them against some other owner-managers personal models of leadership:

My model is relaxed military, there is always an end result, everyone knows who is in charge, not too rigid, all teamwork.

I care passionately about people, if I take out a stakeholder pension, the same should be available to others.

I think we should resort to the truth, play it straight. I have the highest respect for the quality of the job, even if it means losing money.

I like to lead, to forge people into groups. I'm happy to facilitate things and blend into the background.

I am a great believer that you collect as much information as you can and then make a decision and stick to it. You will never know if it is the right decision.

I feel I am responsible for 160 families.

I see myself as building team spirit, being a catalyst, coach and nurturer. I would not be comfortable being more dictatorial.

I had no management training until the last year or so. I had no time before, but it was not working. Now I can delegate, and it works.

I would love to be charismatic and inspire people.

I cannot see myself running a £150 million turnover business.

Should I be the MD, will I change enough to be the leader?

Growing into Leadership

After taking stock of your mindset for leadership, then consider the kind of leadership transition you face. Where are you on your personal leadership journey and what might you have to learn to do differently? Typical owner-manager transitions are:

- assuming a sole leadership role on the death of co-founders;
- moving from a strong technical/doing orientation to leading others;
- managing people not things or numbers;
- bringing in help rather than doing everything oneself;
- leading people as strong as oneself or not on the same wavelength as oneself;
- assessing honestly one's own best future role in the business;
- assessing whether to bring in someone else as leader;
- transferring a personal vision to become everyone's vision;

- shifts in the home–work balance;
- fundamental shifts in styles of influencing.

Leadership transitions like these can demand fundamental shifts in style which any owner-manager will find difficult:

From Direction to Empowerment

> I have to learn to sit on the company not in it otherwise it will hold back growth. Until recently I was doing a lot, not trusting people, not empowering people, now I have started to delegate.

> I have learnt not to shout at people, but to train them and find jobs where they can be capable.

> One of the things I have learnt is hold the hands of staff, but do not interfere. I have had to work very hard not to make the decisions for people as they have traditionally come to me.

From My Vision to Our Vision

> I have struggled with vision, I find it difficult to articulate.

> Trying to get a common vision is a challenge, I need real clarity on it first.

> The most critical action I have taken is to put time into selling my vision, that is the greatest challenge of any MD.

> I will be satisfied when the last person in the chain sees the message.

From Managing Things to Managing People

> My greatest weakness is that I back off from confrontation. I will sacrifice my own interests and lack assertiveness. When I was faced with getting rid of someone it caused me so much angst it ruined a holiday.

> I am an engineer, people can be irritating, I prefer to deal with how things work.

> The three-year plan will pose a leadership challenge, I will need to get better at people motivation, I get too irritated.

> It is interpersonal things that worry me.

> A problem for me is assessing who will not make the grade, what do I do with them yet they are good guys.

So are YOU the Barrier to Growth?

Often it is the case that entrepreneurs are the biggest barrier to growth, but if you can learn to stop meddling and start leading, then both you and the business can start to take off. Cranfield School of Management has been studying the behaviour of owner-managers, and their relationship with their staff, in nearly 1,000 growing UK companies. We have concluded that owner-managers can be clustered into four dominant types of relationship with their staff: heroes, meddlers, artisans or most desirably strategists.

Other research has uncovered the alarming fact that 60 per cent of senior staff in small firms leave within two years of their appointment. Some of these premature departures can be put down to poor recruitment. For example: half of all key staff in small firms are recruited via personal contacts, a notoriously variable method at the best of times – but the largest part is down to the relationships formed between the owner-manager and their key managers, which are often not conducive to achieving growth.

The researchers studied two key elements of this relationship. First, how much time the owner-manager spent on routine management tasks such as marketing, selling, analysing figures, reviewing budgets or arbitrating between managers. On average, with the exception of the group of entrepreneurs who were still preoccupied with basic non-management functions such as delivering their service or making their product (e.g. architects, small builders, retailers, etc.), over 85 per cent of an entrepreneur's working day was spent on these routine management tasks. The owner's behaviour can be more easily understood by showing this graphically, as set out in Figure 5.1. A low score on the vertical axis indicates either that most time is spent on basic non-management functions or that most time is spent on strategic issues such as new product or market development, improving market share, acquisitions and divestments or diversification. A high score indicates that the owner-manager is still largely preoccupied with routine management tasks.

The second element examines how well the owner-manager has developed his or her team, and this is plotted on the horizontal axis of the graph. Here a low score would

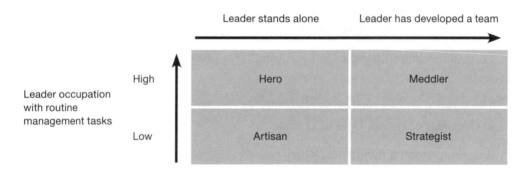

FIGURE 5.1 From Meddler to Strategist.

be where most of the management team were relatively new to their tasks or largely untrained for their current job or where the owner-manager still has difficulty letting go. An example (true, believe it or not) of this would be an unqualified bookkeeper trying to produce the management accounts for a £5 million business. A high score would be where the team were mostly either specifically qualified or trained for their current job and the owner-manager is allowing them to perform.

The Four Types

The artisan is typified by low occupation with routine management tasks – because most of his or her time is spent producing a product or delivering a service. The level of business skills in the company is also low as most of the artisan's staff are employed helping in production or carrying out primary tasks such as bookkeeping or selling. The owner-manager is still very much one of the boys. Artisans can encompass professional firms such as architects and surveyors, manufacturers, subcontractors or small building firms; as well as owners of small retail chains such as chemists or video stores and proprietors of hotels and restaurants. A company run by an artisan has low growth prospects relative to its market. Artisans' training and development needs will be to raise awareness of the importance of management as a business task of equal importance with daily revenue earning.

Heroes, by contrast, probably heads up one management function such as sales or production. But if, for example, they head up sales they will do little selling except for handling some key accounts. Time is now spent on managing the business. As the level of business skill throughout the employees is still relatively low, they will take the lead in initiating routine management procedures. Typically, they will read up or attend one-off courses on ideas such as accounting, business ratios, market segmentation, sales management and staff appraisal systems. They will introduce these ideas to the firm, and be the only person who really understands them. To their managerially illiterate team they will consequently be seen as a hero. Unfortunately, the hero has a Herculean task on his or her hands. Shedding the doing tasks is relatively simple as the working skills in most businesses are either readily available in the local community or people can be trained up without too much difficulty. But passing out routine management tasks will almost invariably require that the owner-manager trains up his or her own management team. But this team will be starting from scratch. For one thing, team members will have received little training; for another they will be used to the boss making the decisions and will depend on his or her continuing to work miracles. Heroes breed dependency, and this makes them dangerous for a growing business. Heroes have a high capacity for improving the performance of their firm, but it still has low growth prospects relative to their market. They have no time for strategic thinking and no depth of management to handle growth effectively. Their training and development needs are to help them raise the general level of management skills in the business, while at the same time increasing their own grasp of motivation, leadership and of strategic management issues in general. If they fail to do this, as most do, they become a meddler.

The meddler raises the level of management skill, either by training or by recruitment, but then fails to let go of routine management tasks. At this stage the owner-manager probably has no functional responsibilities and has assumed the role of managing director. Typically, meddlers spend much time second-guessing subordinates, introducing more refined (but largely unnecessary) management systems. They also go on courses or read books that make them even more knowledgeable and sometimes better at routine management tasks than their own subordinates, who anyway are by now doing a perfectly satisfactory job of managing today's business. They get in early, and leave late and, because they delve into the detail of everything, are, not surprisingly, constantly finding problems. One owner-manager in the study still arrives each morning in time to let in the cleaning staff and leaves at 8.00 pm 'when the neighbouring car park closes'. Meddlers' problem is that they cannot let go of routine management tasks, because their day will feel empty. They have been used to a 70- to 90-hour week, with only 10 days' holiday each year. Once their management team is in place and trained, they are out of a job. Until they reduce their involvement with routine management tasks, they will limit the growth capacity of the firm for two reasons. First, their management team will not take on more responsibility if the reward for taking on the last lot of responsibility is being nagged and criticized. Second, they are too busy checking on people to develop sound strategies for growth.

The strategist is the most desirable type of entrepreneur to develop a growing business. Strategists develop the management skills of the team to the highest appropriate level and in depth. They may introduce a staff function to help line managers in such areas as personnel and market research. This will free up the key managers to think strategically too. They will devote roughly a third of their time to management tasks such as monitoring performance, coordinating activities, resolving conflict and helping to manage today's business. A third of their time will be spent motivating, counselling, developing their management team and helping them to manage change. This activity is aimed at improving the existing business. The final third of their time will be spent developing strategic opportunities to form the shape of the future business. Their training needs will be to constantly update core leadership and motivation skills and to increase their depth of knowledge on strategic issues, acquisition or divestment activity, financing sources and the City. The natural path of development for the relationship between the owner-manager and his or her team is to pass from artisan to hero to meddler and – for the lucky few – on to become strategist.

Assessing Your Leadership Capabilities

If you get the chance, complete a leadership self-assessment such as the visionary leader questionnaire (VLQ) by Marshall Sashkin (VLQ distributed in Europe by MLR, PO

Box 28, Carmarthen, SA31 IDT, www.mlruk.com). You will get a good picture of where you are now on your leadership journey. Using the VLQ, you can literally plot your progress on the mountain of leadership from 'On the trail' up to 'On the final ascent'. You will also be able to plot your scores on a triangle consisting of three dimensions:

- Your leadership behaviours – what you do.
- Your leadership characteristics – what you are.
- Your impact on culture building – the situation.

The bigger the triangle the more visionary a leader you are (size matters here!). The skew of your triangle will also tell you whether you are a charismatic individual, a visionary thinker or an organizational tinker.

The questionnaire plots you against ten factors which research shows are associated with visionary leaders. These are shown in Table 5.1.

Because a table of norms is provided you will be able to benchmark your own personal scores against a large database. Typically, owner-managers are confident and creative (see scales 5 and 6), but tend to fall down on scale 2 (communicative leadership), scale 7 (empowered leadership) and sometimes scale 8 (visionary leadership).

Of course, the VLQ is based on what you say about yourself! If you are really keen to learn more about yourself as a leader, then you need to get feedback by soliciting the views of your colleagues, employees, shareholders. Why not your partner too? This will

TABLE 5.1 Ten Scales of Visionary Leadership

1.	Clear leadership	Effective leaders focus themselves and others on a few key goals and priorities
2.	Communicative leadership	The ability to get one's message across, interpersonal skills, listening skills and rapport
3.	Consistent leadership	Outstanding CEOs exhibit consistent behaviour. It's clear where they stand and they do what they say they will do
4.	Caring leadership	The leader displays self-respect but also respect for others, boosting people's sense of self-worth by paying attention to them, trusting them and sharing ideas
5.	Creative leadership	The leader is willing to take risks and doesn't spend time in 'cover-your-ass' type activities
6.	Confident leadership	Effective leaders have a sense of self-assurance and a belief that they can make a difference
7.	Empowered leadership	Effective leaders have a strong need for power and influence but use this power to empower others
8.	Visionary leadership	Effective leaders are able to think over relatively long time spans of at least a few years. They have a clear vision communicating and involving others so that it becomes a shared vision
9.	Organizational leadership	Effective leaders help the organization to change and adapt to new challenges
10.	Cultural leadership	Effective leaders articulate and inculcate values which support the vision and strengthen the organization

enable you to see yourself as others see you. You can buy copies of the VLQ to give to others. Their feedback will be invaluable.

Assignment 5.1: Your Leadership SWOT

1. Complete a leadership self-assessment questionnaire such as the VLQ.
2. Based on the questionnaire and all that we have looked at so far in this chapter, identify your very personal leadership strengths, weaknesses, opportunities and threats. Summarize them in a table like that shown in Figure 5.2.
3. What will you need to do differently and what opportunities are open to you to enhance your natural strengths and compensate for the weaknesses which may well make you the biggest barrier to growth in your business?

What Is Your Current Role?

So how do you spend your time?

Most owner-managers are so busy rushing around that they never get round to actually working out what they spend their time on! You will find it useful to keep a diary of where your time is going so that in chapter 13 you can decide whether this needs to change. Typically, you may find that as much as 25 per cent of your time goes under general headings such as in-house activities or administration. Is this really a valuable use of your time? You can also look at the percentage of time you spend *in* the business as opposed to *on* the business (internal versus external). Remember that you should be looking to spend at least 30 per cent of your time *on* the business as the strategist, building tomorrow's business and nurturing key customers and external relationships. Otherwise the risk is that you will spend 100 per cent of your time in today's business meddling. The best owner-managers generally spend a third of their time monitoring internal performance, a third motivating, counselling and developing the management team, and a third on the future business.

Strengths	Weaknesses
• Set the vision and values • Confident leadership • Long-term focus	• Don't communicate • Don't empower others • Lose my temper too often
Opportunities	Threats
• Celebrate success, praise more • Let people get on with it • Express confidence in people	• If I don't let go I won't build a management team • People are too dependent on me • Key people may leave

FIGURE 5.2 Your Leadership SWOT.

Assignment 5.2: How Do You Spend Your Time?

Complete the pro forma given in Table 5.2 and assess how you spend your time.

Are You the CEO or the Office Boy?

In growing businesses, it is all too easy to spend time tidying the loose ends dropped by others – as a sort of meddler/artisan. You might also like to benchmark how you currently spend your time against this nine-point template of what an effective CEO should be doing:

TABLE 5.2 Your Current Use of Time

Major activity and breakdown	Total % this activity
Strategy planning and forward thinking Business plans Acquisition/disposal Management development Other	
Board meetings Planning Actual Follow-up	
Meetings with management In groups One to ones Visits/travel together Other	
Review of business performance Regular sales/income/costs/cash data Monthly accounts Other	
Other in-house activities	
Meetings off site Suppliers Customers Trade organizations Other	
Trade/travel (not holidays) Conferences/trade shows/exhibitions Market research tours Foreign business development Other	
Other (please specify)	
Total	100%

1. Ensure Survival

You are ultimately responsible for the survival of the enterprise. Avoid complacency in the organization, anticipate change and understand the changing external environment.

2. Establish and Communicate the Vision

Be clear about what you want to be, what you want to do and what you want to have. Engage your whole team in making this vision their own.

3. Know your numbers; this is not an option

Make sure you are personally aware of the numbers that matter to the business, including the indicators of where you are going, not just where you have been. Make sure your team is aware of the importance of them knowing what they each have to do to contribute to making the numbers.

4. Identify the Secret of the Business

Identify what makes it distinctive and unique, what is the core, then defend and develop this jealously.

5. Identify the Rivers of Cash

Which of your product lines provides your rivers of cash, how are you going to ride it, when do you need to get off and find another river?

6. Be the Chief Deal Maker

Be involved in the critical deals that affect your future, customers, employees, funders and banks. These are fundamental to your success and should not be delegated.

7. Lead – Let Others Manage

Set the priorities, communicate like mad, one to one and in groups, then let them manage the business within clear parameters. Find people with passion and stand back. Get the right people on the bus in the right seats facing the right direction.

8. Get Rid of Deadwood

It is always a mistake to delay. If they are either a non-contributor or a major disruptive force in the business you can do without them, however valuable they may have been in the past.

9. Be yourself

Be like Frank Sinatra, do it your way!

Are YOU Holding the Business Back?

Are you actually enjoying what you currently do or have you promoted yourself to your level of incompetence? Are you still having fun? Not everyone can make the jump from energetic entrepreneur to professional manager. So why try? What you want is to enjoy yourself and grow the business. Some of the challenges which owner-managers frequently pose for themselves are:

- Do I bite the bullet and bring in an MD?
- I left it too long to manage the business while I was out on the road selling.
- I am open to the fact that I may not be the best person to take the business forward.
- I am excellent at working with customers, I can always see more opportunities to improve their businesses, I get frustrated because I am too busy to do this.
- I am spending too much time on the day-to-day running of the business.
- I do not have to do it myself, my strength is not sales and marketing.
- Do I continue doing something I do not want to do, or bring in a strong general manager?
- I am trying to work out what I want to do. It is frenetic going from struggling with no management team to a new management team who are rushing on.

There is a cruel paradox awaiting at least some owner-managers. You may have put your life, soul, health and personal life into the business but at the end of the day it may only succeed without you.

Luke Hughes runs a business selling high-quality wooden furniture. Over the years he successfully negotiated the rapids of some Greiner-like crises: a recession, the market practically disappearing, the hunt for profitable business, then the push for revenue growth. 'It was a bit like being at sea in a sieve with some Blu-Tack to patch up the holes. But I was good at surviving by the seat of my pants', says Luke. He continues, 'It was passion that made me start this business. My main assets are architectural knowledge; I am a good designer and very good at solving technical problems. But a couple of years ago I realized that I didn't enjoy and was not particularly good at selling. So I recruited a professional sales and marketing director.' He found the experience so liberating that last November he took the unusual step of demoting himself from managing director to design and production director (while remaining the largest single shareholder) – and bringing in an expensive but top-flight professional managing director over his own head, to pilot his company to greater things. 'I was, am, short of a host of serious business skills – marketing, finance, negotiating, team-building and strategic thinking, to name but five. My shortage of skills was holding the business back', he admits.

Luke's honesty may surprise you. In chapter 13, we will examine in more detail the dilemmas of succession, letting go to grow and possibly even replacing yourself.

part two
Where Are We Going?

Having worked through Part 1, Where Are We Now?, you should now have a good feel for your business's current position in terms of markets, money and measures, management and me. You are now in a great position to start thinking about the future by moving on to Part 2, Where Are We Going?

Most conventional approaches to strategic planning will consider a range of ideas with regard to the external market, the competition and the internal resources of the business (i.e. money and management). In the owner-managed business this is not enough. In the owner-managed business, it is simply not possible to disentangle the business – its goals and strategies, its challenges and issues – from the owner-manager and his or her personal goals and drivers. The two sets of goals and drivers and inextricably linked.

Therefore, in the owner-managed business, it is also necessary to consider the personal goals, drivers and motivations, and the leadership and management capability, of the owner-manager themselves, in addition to the more conventional areas of strategic planning.

Indeed, we would argue that, in the owner-managed business, the future of the business starts with the owner-manager – personal drivers drive everything.

We like to describe this part of the process as 'articulating the future that you want to bring about for yourself and for the business'.

Two interesting points emerge from this. First, strangely enough, if you can articulate the future you want, then it is more likely to happen. The act of saying it, sharing it with others and committing yourself to it means that you are more likely to move towards it in all your actions and decisions.

Second, many of us find it difficult to articulate the future and set goals. For many of us it is very much a case of 'I will not know what I want until I get it!' For these people, we introduce some imaginative techniques for envisaging the future in a way which hopefully helps them to feels as if they have 'got it' already so that it can then be described.

The chapters and assignments in Part 2 are intended to help you to articulate the future you want to bring about.

six

What Do You Want?

Personal Goals and Drivers

As you have probably realized by now, being an entrepreneur can be tough. It can also be tough for an entrepreneur's spouse. We asked one partner to tell us what life had been like over the past three years as her beloved negotiated and implemented a major deal. Living with an entrepreneur – the true story.

It's 8.30 on Saturday night. I'm waiting for Jack to come home from the office. He said he'd be done by 6 pm but I learnt long ago to add at least an hour to his deadlines. Still, it's been a hectic week. Two new restaurants opening in the next 10 days and he's exhausted. Oh yes, it's exciting, all this battling with the builders, negotiating for sites, hiring staff, it's creating something, isn't it? It's growth. It's what they call 'rolling-out-the-concept.' It's what he went through all the hell of money-raising for. It's what being an entrepreneur is all about. Isn't it?

The phone goes. It's Jack. He's sitting on the floor of the ladies loo of one of the new restaurants in the West End. He's got one hand on his mobile, the other stuck over a pipe that's burst a leak. It's been running for two hours, he says, and the place is flooded out. For despite all you may read and all you may hear about the glamorous life of the entrepreneur, this is really what it's all about. It's not about black tie dinners at the Grosvenor House Hotel on Park Lane and being voted Entrepreneur of the Year; it's not about smiling press pictures on the front of the Financial Times when the business reaches the stock market, it's not even about making money. It's about sitting like a boy with your finger in the dyke on a Saturday night because that is what needs to be done. I would tell myself: 'Once he's raised the next round of finance ..., once he's opened these next restaurants ..., once he's found a new office ..., once he's hired the operations director ..., then all will be well. Then we can have friends round for supper and book holidays. How could I have been so stupid?

The life of an entrepreneur can become a daily grind: another day, another problem and no end in sight. People depend on you, which can mean anxiety and sleepless nights. Your enthusiasm can wane, you can end up feeling you are the only one carrying the business while employees consistently disappoint. You are stressed and your partner gets the flak. As Mark Catlin of Music Box said 'I feel like a bird, like a bird with ten suitcases strapped to me.' As the business grows your problems increase and this can leave you at a crossroads. Where should you go now? Do you hang in and battle on? Do you pack it in and move on? Running your own company can be a very lonely business.

Blishen & Co

In the 12 years since Chris Blishen took over the family business from his father he has only recently sat down together with his co-directors and asked: 'What next?' What motivated him to do this was the sense of being alone and uncertain about the future and the difficulty of constantly finding new inspiration. After all those years of running a tight ship, of spotting new product opportunities, of being the figurehead for his dozen-odd employees there were some real questions about exactly where the company was going. He needed to talk. Blishen's industry has changed and so has he. And, of course, he's 12 years older – 45 in fact. He is comfortably off with two teenage kids and a liking for skiing. For many years, he has been the heartbeat of his little business. But now he faces the trickiest decisions of his business life: Do we launch afresh into new product areas? Do we stick with what we know? What about the Internet? What next for John Blishen & Co?

So Make It Worth It

If being an entrepreneur can be lonely, stressful and confusing, then at least make it worthwhile! What do you really want out of the business? What future reality do you see? Is the business running you or are you running the business?

In starting to answer the question where you go next, give yourself the opportunity to articulate your own goals, aspirations and dreams. It is only when you start surfacing and talking about your dreams and sharing them with others that you find out what really matters to you. It is very much a case of 'How do I know what I think until I hear myself say it?' As you start to give shape to your business goals and personal drivers, you will find that you go through an iterative process: refining your goals as you reflect upon them and share them with more people.

Aspirations and Outcomes

The future of your business starts with YOU – personal drivers drive everything. In chapter 5, you took stock of what motivates you now and you carried out a personal SWOT of your leadership strengths and weaknesses. Now is the time to look forward and articulate your aspirations and driving forces.

Mrs Steve Shirley is one of Europe's outstanding businesswomen. She arrived in Britain as an unaccompanied child refugee and grew up to become Founder Director of FI Group. She set up the FI Group (now Xansa) with £5 in the 1960s, an innovative business venture which became one of Britain's leading information technology groups. She played an active role in the management and development of FI Group, sometimes being entitled 'The Keeper of the Corporate Culture'. She officially retired in September 1993 but remains its Life President.

Her action-oriented management style, and emphasis on ethics and professional standards, led to her being awarded the OBE for services to industry in 1980 and the Freedom of the City of London in 1987. She was President of the British Computer Society from 1989 to 1990 and in 1985 was awarded a special RITA (Recognition of Information Technology Award).

There have been three driving forces in Steve Shirley's business life: a desire to build a successful and lasting company whose management and ownership could be passed on to the staff, a growing interest in the philosophy and ethics of the private enterprise system within a world whose values were changing, and a determination to make things happen rather than just talk about them.

What do you want to do with the rest of your life? Have the goals and objectives you set when you started the business changed? How satisfied are you with what you have achieved to date, is it all about the material trappings of life or are you looking to make a difference in other areas as well?

Paul Barry-Walsh, after selling his business Safetynet for a very sizeable sum, founded Netstore Plc, offering online back-up principally over the Internet. In 1998, it went public, raising 60 million dollars. He is aggressively growing the business through acquisition and expects to achieve a turnover of £150 million in the next 3–5 years (this was back in 2003!). Pretty heady stuff; but business is not the only, or even the primary, thing that turns him on. He is passionate about the Fredericks Foundation, which he founded three years ago to help disadvantaged people set up their own businesses. 'Freds' has so far invested in over 300 small businesses.

You might think that all you want to do is to make your millions and spend the rest of your life on a golf course in the Bahamas. Is this really true, would you not get bored to death? Would it not be hell if your golf handicap still did not go down and you had no excuses? On the whole, entrepreneurs are not the sort of people who can just sit around and chill out. Barrie Haigh, owner-founder of Innovex, made several hundred million from the sale of the company to Quintiles in the States, enough to live comfortably off the interest. What he has done since is what he always wanted to do – be a farmer. Of course, this is not just any farm, but a state-of-the-art dairy farm producing milk with natural melatonin from cows milked at night, but probably not by Barrie!

Sir Peter Lampl made his career in leveraged buy-outs in the States. In 1995, he founded the Sutton Trust, which provides educational opportunities for able young people from non-privileged backgrounds. Sir Peter campaigns tirelessly for a cause he feels passionate about and is probably working harder now than when he was in his 20s! The difference is, he calls the shots.

The difference is making a difference, and these people want to. It is a fallacy to think that business has an arrival point called exit and that you are slogging your guts out so that you thereafter live in perpetual sunshine! Certainly, exit is a perfectly respectable outcome. But have you really thought about what it will mean for you personally, as well as for your family and for the business? It will be a traumatic and exhausting process, you will get about half as much for the business as you had anticipated and it will take twice as long to get it all sewn up. You will drive your family to distraction. Your employees may feel that you have sold them down the river, you will not be welcome in the business you started up, you may have to watch it being mismanaged and not be able to do anything about it. For every owner-manager who, after exit, goes off joyfully backpacking round the world, there are two who feel genuine grief and sadness and wonder what to do with the rest of their lives. Sure, you may make serious millions by exit, but might you actually be happier staying on in a role you choose, making a good income every year and living the way you want?

The way to start addressing your future aspirations is to think about the business and personal outcomes you seek by using the framework illustrated in Table 6.1.

Business Outcomes

What do you want for the business, regardless of your self-interest? What does success look like and how will you know when you get there? Do you care about the long-term survival of the business after you exit? Do you want to create a bigger business and is that measured by revenue, profit or number of people? Do you want to become a global player, diversify or stick to what you are good at? Do you want the people in the business to make money from its growth?

Leadership Outcomes

In chapter 5, you took stock of yourself as a leader, your strengths and weaknesses and the sort of transitions you might have to make. How will your leadership role change and develop over the next few years? How much fun are you having? What will you

TABLE 6.1 Refining Your Desired Outcomes

Business outcomes	Leadership outcomes	Personal business outcomes	Personal life outcomes
What you want for your business as a whole over the next five years irrespective of your role	How you want to develop as a leader over the next five years	What you personally want to achieve in your business life over the next five years Position, financial, key achievements, etc.	What you want to achieve in your personal life over the next five years
Global player	Work outside the organization more	Sell the business	Getting better home/work balance
Stay in business	Create a strong management team	Smaller share of larger business	Reason to get up in the morning
Focus on core business	Find new ideas	Six million in bank	Eliminate stress
Motivated people	Gain industry respect	Have more fun	Backpack round the world
Bigger business			Get a mentor
Outperform competitors	Create a sense of purpose		

need to stop doing and what will you want to do more of? Do you see a leadership role for yourself outside the company as well, e.g. industry leadership, leadership in the community?

Personal Business Outcomes

What do you want for yourself from the business? Are you looking to take out a chunk of money? By when? Do you prefer to stay in the business securing a long-term income stream? What, if any, family interests do you want to achieve?

Personal Life Outcomes

What specific goals in your life do you want to achieve, or not lose, as a result of your business activities? What about your key relationships? Taking that walking trip to the Himalayas? Coaching the local football team or entering politics? Indulging your passion for golf or fast cars? Spending six months a year in the Caribbean?

In chapter 5, we introduced David Pointer, the owner-manager of Point Source, experts in laser technology. We saw that his prime motivator was the desire for independence and autonomy and how important recognition was to him in the form of things like company awards. But in the process of examining what he thought were his key drivers, David is changing his views! He has built an extremely successful business but has started to question why he is doing it, what he would most like to change and how he wants to spend his time in future. In conversation with his mentor, he started the process of articulating his goals and drivers. This is what he said in January.

His business goals are to build a £20 million turnover business within five years with a fully integrated US acquisition, at least 20 per cent revenue from the Far East and 20 per cent from new products. He will maintain 20 per cent net margins and continue to achieve 40 per cent ROCE. He expects manufacturing to be outsourced to the Far East. This he will do with no external funding.

His leadership goals are to spend 20 per cent time outside the UK, developing the US and Far East businesses. He anticipates becoming chairman in three years' time. He already has a boardroom full of awards and citations including at least two Queens Awards and one for world-class manufacturing. He wants to achieve more awards both for himself and for the business. His prestige in the industry is something he wants to continue enhancing and he wants to continue investing in and making a difference to local technology start-ups.

His personal business goals are to take a chunk of capital out by 2009 and exit the business in 2012, leaving his management team with tangible ownership. He aims to build a management team that does not need him within this time frame.

His personal life goals are to get his two boys through university, secure the family's financial future, buy a property in the Rockies and build a technology business portfolio.

Once David had started to articulate his ideas, he could begin to hear what he was thinking! Talking to others, in particular sharing thoughts with his wife Jan, further refined what he really wants from his future.

By March, the conversation had moved on. His wife made it clear that she did not want David out of the country for the equivalent of one day a week – and by the way, she had enough to do running a home and looking after two active teenage boys without taking on another house in the Rockies! A reality check showed that it would be impossible to achieve a stand-alone US acquisition within a three-year time span without recruiting additional US resource.

By April, things had moved on again. A conversation with KPMG opened David's eyes to some much greater opportunities for his business. He started to question why he wanted out anyway. Why not change his personal goals and aim to take out £6 million by 2006, but stay with the business, possibly float and go for a £100 million business by 2010? With these objectives, it would become paramount to build a strong management team for a big future.

No doubt David's personal goals and drivers have moved on again; but the point is that, until you start to think about them, talk about them and share them, you will remain in a position where the business is driving you, not you the business. Start to engage yourself in the debate! See how robust your aspirations are!

It is salutary to summarize just how significantly in the space of only a few months, David started to challenge his original thinking about what he really really wanted.

Business Outcomes

Why £20 million in five years?

> To be honest, £20 million in five years is a number I created for a staff presentation last year. I'm very comfortable working without targets, but I know most people aren't. So if I got up and said 'I don't know what the targets are, we'll figure it out as we go along, and by the way, work really really hard', then I don't think I would be credible. What I want is for us to be the BEST to achieve GREAT THINGS and to be MAVERICKS i.e. stick two fingers up to conventional business ideas.

Leadership Outcomes

> I've been rethinking. I wouldn't like to be on the receiving end of my management style. I'm not sure I really do enjoy this role (working with other high-tech start-ups) even though I keep saying it! Perhaps I need to spend my time and money on my own business. ... Yes I am quite passionate about this (being a good neighbour in the community). My role will be to work more outside the organization, I will need to have an effective team back at base. My role will

also be to find new ideas and enthusiastic external advisors and introduce them into the organization.

Personal Business Outcomes

This is the link between the two areas I guess? Do I want to sell the business? No! If someone came along and offered me a lot of money for it then would I think about it or bite their hand off?

Personal Life Outcomes

I also need something to get me up in the morning, something to energize me and to totally absorb me at times. I'm energized by building and creating things – whether it's sand castles on the beach or a high-tech business. That's why business growth is so important. This is what the business does for me. I don't dream of not working but I do dream of getting balance, not coming home torn up by the anguish of personal issues at work and ignoring my family, or worse, taking it out on them. I need to eliminate this stress from my life otherwise the first bit won't happen. I believe the problem is that I am totally absorbed in the business. I take it very personally when something goes wrong with an employee or an employee takes us for a ride. It sometimes feels that I have a limited amount of emotional energy and a little bit is sucked out every day and very little emotional energy gets deposited back in.

Assignment 6.1 Your Personal Goals and Drivers

Using the questions and example given above, and the template in Table 6.1, set out your personal goals and outcomes. Now, discuss them with other key stakeholders in your life and your business and be prepared to adapt them!

Assignment 6.2 Postcard from Your Future

Usually, forward planning is a dry and rather depressing exercise involving identifying long action plans to get over a series of obstacles. With the postcard from the future approach, instead of starting from where you are now and then outlining the steps towards where you want to be, you put yourself in your ideal future and then look back to see how you got here. The benchmarks along the way are now achievements rather than obstacles, a much more motivating thought!

This is how it works. Remember that everything is in the present tense because you have placed yourself in the future!

Stage 1

Put yourself in an imaginary future on a specific date when your ideal outcome has been achieved. Let us say 10 June 2012. So, it is the future right now and you are savouring your success!

Stage 2

Now describe the nature of your achievements under headings such as:

- *Personal relationships*, e.g. the management team is really developing, I am proud of them; my managing director and me as chairman are a great partnership.
- *Time with the family*, e.g. I am building a Lotus Esprit with my elder son, we get away for a long weekend to our cottage very regularly.
- *Financial*, e.g. I have taken £6 million out to secure our family future and I have raised more capital to grow the business.
- *Leisure*, e.g. the family is back from two weeks' walking in Patagonia and I am coaching the local football team.
- *Business growth*, e.g. we have grown to ten million turnover with a 40 per cent gross margin and acquired a new business with enormous potential.
- *Market share*, e.g. we have a 30 per cent market share in this global niche.
- *Innovation*, e.g. we are regarded as the industry leader and my management team give papers at all the big international conferences.
- *Company culture*, e.g. our distinct culture no longer depends on me, there's a real buzz and excitement and 'can do' attitude about the place.

Stage 3

Now write a postcard to yourself from your own future that includes single words or short phrases describing your achievements. Describe what you see and hear and how you feel about them. You should be able to feel and hear and see your success! The evidence might be laughter, energy, pride in the team, excitement at a new deal:

> *Dear John,*
>
> *You should be here! You can hear the Bolly corks popping and we all feel in party mood! We have taken over a chateau outside Paris for our celebrations in reaching twenty million and successfully floating on the Alternative Investment Market (AIM). All the senior team are millionaires and as you can imagine I've done a lot more than OK! You will remember Joe, a very young nervous engineer, I don't think you rated him when he worked for you, well he runs the whole of our San Diego plant, you should hear what the others now say about him! Little Manisha heads up our subsidiary in Singapore I feel really proud of both of them. There is a new team and they are going places. Mary and I are spending a lot of snow-time at our chalet in Gstaad looking out onto the wonderful mountains and we've also opened a little winery in Beaune, just for fun. I will send you a bottle or two; we've*

just had a glowing write-up in Decanter and it really tastes great! You probably saw our company write-up in the Financial Times – looks like we had better get used to the publicity! Anyway, wish you were here!

Stage 4

Stay in the future but look back. What were the key events or decisions which you took, without which your achievements could not have been made? Remember to phrase them in the past tense and just concentrate on the big ones such as:

- We recruited an MD in January 2008.
- We hit a million profit that summer!
- We successfully moved to new premises in March 2009.
- We acquired Company X in June 2010.
- We floated in April 2012.

Building a clear sense of what the future holds will help you guide the enterprise and yourself through the rough passages ahead and give you the best possible chance of meeting your aspirations and having fun in the process.

seven
Articulating Your Future (or What Does the Business Have To Do To Enable You To Achieve What You Want?)

Having set out your own personal goals and drivers, it may come as something of a shock to discover that everyone else in the business does not necessarily share them! You are going to need to persuade the other key people in the business to follow your lead and to help you bring about the future you have described.

This requires you to be able to

- clearly articulate what the business needs to do and needs to look like in order to achieve what you want;
- inspire the other people in the business so that they help you to achieve the future you want.

Business Objectives

The most common way of articulating a future state for a business is in terms of a set of business objectives. In establishing business objectives, always try to be SMART

- Specific   Precise, specific outcomes
- Measurable   Can be measured and targeted
- Achievable   Challenging but do-able
- Relevant   To the people concerned
- Time-based   Have an end-date

Financial Objectives

The most usual type of business objectives are those relating to the financial measures of the business such as turnover and profit. This is partly because these factors are already measured by every business. It is also because, as we saw in chapter 3, the financial measures are a great way of indicating the health of a business.

Remarkably, nearly two-thirds of European SMEs do not set a profit objective. This seems very odd given that one of the main purposes of business is to generate a profit! It is also dangerous in that, if objectives are set only in terms of turnover, then there is a risk that the business slips in to the 'busy fool' mode where there is more and more activity, which creates more and more costs, for the same, or even less, return. The template in Table 7.1 presents a useful framework for setting financial objectives.

A couple of points are worthy of note. First, the precise measures in the left-hand column depend on the type of business. Although profit, gross margin, sales and some measure of return (e.g. return on capital employed) are probably applicable in every business, other measures will vary from business to business and from industry to industry. For instance, in a retail business, sales per square metre is usually a key indicator, whereas in a consultancy business average daily fee achieved and utilization (i.e. the percentage of people's time which is charged to a client) are vitally important measures.

Second, this template includes the historical performance. This is to provide a reality check so as to avoid the overoptimistic 'hockey stick' curve situation.

Third, the template also suggests breaking longer-term objectives down in to interim targets rather than simply having three- or five-year goals. This again provides a reality check on whether the end objectives are achievable from where you are now and also helps in focusing the mind on the shorter-term actions which will be required in order to start the journey to the achievement of the objectives.

Market Objectives

It is also very common to see objectives expressed in relation to markets, for instance

TABLE 7.1 A Template for Financial Objectives

	History			Objectives		
	Year –2	Year –1	Year 0	Year +1	Year +2	Year +3
Net profit						
Gross margin (%)						
Sales						
ROCE						
Profit per employee						
etc.						

a market share objective. You may also have market-related objectives regarding such areas as

- your market distinctiveness (e.g. to move away from winning business based on price);
- customers (e.g. customer retention, the total number of customers, the reliance on a small number of large customers, sales and profitability per customer);
- new products/services to be developed and introduced;
- new markets to be researched and entered.

Market-related objectives can be set out in a similar template as shown in Table 7.2.

People and Management Objectives

Oddly, it is far less common to see objectives related to people and management of the business, for instance how big the organization needs to be in order to achieve the other objectives – or, alternatively, how big an organization you want to be running! Other people and management-related areas in which you might consider setting some objectives include:

- staff satisfaction and morale;
- development of a management team and/or specific roles within the management team;
- recruitment of key individuals;
- staff retention targets;
- introduction or improvement of processes for appraisal, retention and motivation of people;
- introduction or improvement of reward mechanisms;
- improvement of communication mechanisms;
- succession plans for key roles, most importantly, your own!

TABLE 7.2 A Template for Market-related Objectives

	History			Objectives		
	Year –2	Year –1	Year 0	Year +1	Year +2	Year +3
Market share						
Number of customers						
Customer retention						
Average sales/margin per customer						
Per cent sales from new products						
etc.						

Assignment 7.1: Business Objectives

1. Using the templates provided in Table 7.1 and 7.2, set out your business objectives under each of the three following headings:
    - money and measures;
    - markets;
    - management and people.
2. Check that these objectives will enable you to achieve your personal goals and that they are consistent with one another and with your personal goals.
3. Share the full set of business objectives and personal goals with key stakeholders and be prepared to adapt them, if necessary.

Vision

Despite the prevalence of business objectives as the most common way of articulating the desired future state of the business, they tend not to be particularly inspiring. Often the most inspiring way to describe the future is by offering the other people in the business a vision of that future that they can buy in to. In fact, today, many commentators believe that creating and communicating the vision is the single most important job of the leader.

Visions are about dreams, the 'promised land', a desirable destination shared by everyone, and an inspiration to all. A perfect example of this is Martin Luther King's 'I have a dream' speech, which powerfully, emotively and inspirationally painted a picture of a future which every person in his large audience could see would be better than their current situation.

> One day, on the red hills of Georgia, the sons of former slaves, and the sons of former slave-owners, will sit down together at the table of brotherhood!

King's dream was so powerful that some people laid down their lives in pursuit of it.

Although not suggesting that your employees should be prepared to die for your vision, the most successful businesses are those whose leaders can see and articulate to others the exciting possibilities of the future in the way that King did. There is nothing Sir Terence Conran hates more than unfinished dreams. An article describing Sheila Pickles, the woman who transformed Penhaligon's from an ailing perfumery business into an international empire, compared her to Laura Ashley, founder of 'another company built on the nostalgic vision of one woman'.

Hotel Chocolat is passionate about chocolate! The business is 'totally dedicated to good chocolate and committed to excellent service either through delivery of chocolate gifts or through its recently opened chain of 'chocolate boutiques'. As co-founder and managing director, Angus Thirlwell, says, 'It's been a lot of fun dreaming up ideas and seeing them become products. We like to think that by doing this we can keep people in touch with the power of chocolate'. Like many successful entrepreneurs, Thirlwell is a powerhouse of ideas. Hotel Chocolat's brochures, retail outlets and website are not just about getting orders: they also entice chocolate lovers everywhere to become part of the Hotel Chocolat community by participating in tastings, providing feedback on new chocolate creations and new chocolatiers, and helping to design new products. Who could then resist becoming a member of the Chocolate Tasting Club or fail to order the 'chocolate labrador looking for a home and willing to share chocolate bones'?

And beyond the power of chocolate, Angus has an even wider vision. Hotel Chocolat has recently bought a cocoa plantation on the West Indian island of St Lucia and is also offering to buy cocoa from other producers on the island at higher prices than could be achieved on the cocoa exchanges. Hotel Chocolat will ship the St Lucian cocoa to the UK, where it will be made into chocolate which can then be traced back to a specific plantation much in the way that a wine comes from a specific vineyard. In so doing, Thirlwell intends to help the growers create their own brands, thus preserving the endangered cocoa-growing industry in St Lucia and, in essence, transforming the island's economy!

The spur for Karan Bilimoria to set up Cobra Beer in 1990 was that he could not find the right kind of beer to eat with Indian food. Despite the UK being the most competitive and crowded beer market in the world, Karan decided to brew the perfect beer to drink with curry, and so Cobra was born. Even while Karan was delivering the first cases of Cobra to Indian restaurants in a battered 2CV, he had a big vision – he wanted Cobra to be the first global Indian brand! In recognition of the ongoing battle to grow in the face of competition from huge international brewers, Karan added the phrase 'to aspire and achieve against all odds' as a way of setting out his own philosophy and inspiring his staff. This remains the Cobra vision today – and it seems to be working! Not only is the business growing rapidly with sales of over £35 million and offices in four countries, but Cobra was recently voted number 35 in the '100 Best Small Companies to Work For' with more than 90 per cent of staff feeling excited by where the business is going and being inspired by Karan's leadership.

It is the power and passion of your vision that will translate paper goals and strategies into reality. It is vision which puts your dream to work, by making it something which is shared by everyone, inspirational and clear enough to help people know what kind of decisions to make in your business.

Vision creates momentum; it pulls people through the uncomfortable process of change by offering the picture of a better world. It gives people something to identify with, a meaning and purpose – just as the vision of a holiday, of marriage, or of retirement helps us to get through the daily routine.

Characteristics of Effective Visions

Drawing from these, and many other, examples, we can see that an effective vision will be

- transformational – describing a future which is significantly 'better' than today;
- inspirational – exciting people with the possibilities that the envisioned future will bring;
- passionate – based on deeply held beliefs;
- simple – easy to communicate and easy to understand;
- shared – taken up and shared by everyone;
- visible – the future state can be described using pictures and visual images;
- long lasting – describing a longer-term future that remains valid, rather than something which can be achieved in the short term;
- constantly communicated – reinforced in day-to-day work by everything you do and everything you say.

Developing a Vision

When you sit down to write a formal statement of company philosophy for instance, you will probably find that 'motherhood' statements are fairly easy. It is usually much more difficult to produce a real, relevant and inspiring vision. One of the tricks is to recognize that a vision is largely meaningless unless it is truly shared by everyone in the business. Indeed, in a business with a strong vision and culture, any employee at any time can probably tell you what the business stands for. Developing your vision, therefore, is not a job you can do sitting in splendid isolation; it is an opportunity to involve your people in its design.

There are several techniques to help you envision your future with your team. Two are described below: organization pictures and culture statements.

Organization Pictures

In diagnosing the current state of your business in Part 1, you drew a picture of how you see your business now. One way of helping you to envision the future is to draw another picture of what you would want the future to look like.

Clearly, there is no right or wrong answer to what your picture should look like. Here are some examples of future organization pictures we have seen recently:

- a circus ring – 'laydeez and gentlemen, the combined skills and synchronized talent, all under one big top';
- an orchestra;
- a phoenix rising from the ashes;
- a bus with everyone happily on board, knowing the destination;

- a racing yacht with the crew working confidently as a team and making fine adjustments to improve performance;
- a formation of Red Arrows (with ears!) flying with safety and precision.

Once you have a picture, you and your team will find it useful to put some words around it. In the 'best of all possible words', what will the future look like, and how will we know when we have got there? The following questions may be helpful in defining the characteristics of the desired 'end state':

- What is fundamentally different about the business in the future compared with how it is today?
- How big will the business be?
- What will the business be known for?
- Who will be leading the business and what distinctive skills will they have?
- How will staff behave towards customers and with one another?
- What will be the customers' image of us?
- How will staff feel about their jobs and about working in the business?
- What sort of people will we be recruiting?
- What will be our management style?

Culture Statements

In diagnosing your organization in Part 1, you also described the current culture of your business. You can also get some clues to where you are going by you and your management team brainstorming a list of words which characterize your past, present and desired future. You can see an example in Table 7.3.

You can then use this as a basis for involving each member of the management team in defining their vision of the future and agreeing an overall goal to which everyone buys in. Here is what the management team of Topnotch said some years ago:

Matthew: To build a brand that is different, delivers great results and is admired by our peers.

TABLE 7.3 Past, Present and Future

Past	Present	Future
Chaotic	Culture is diluting	Global
Inward looking	Customer service good not excellent	Total customer focus
Happy amateurs	Decisions made at top	Spin off separate businesses
Top-line driven	We tolerate failure	Professional and polished
Small motivated team	Managers want more control	Attract and keep terrific people
No politics	Disjointed	Pride and self-worth

Emma: To achieve what most cynics don't think is possible, an incredible organization which balances huge profits with breaking the rules.

Tim: To build a revolutionary retail business selling services and products, identifiable by values consumers love to consume, and staff are proud to deliver.

Steve: To maintain our values, provide fun and innovation, develop our people and products and be profitable, successful and happy!

Jonathan: To overtake immediate competitors, while continuing to develop a 'dare to be different' culture and gaining industry – City recognition and respect, and make some money!

Doing some navel-gazing in this way can also help you and the team to decide which aspects of the past you want to retain and which need to change. Sometimes, the act of articulating the words actually starts to create the desired future since everyone involved will now move towards, and make decisions in the light of, the newly described future.

Assignment 7.2: Articulating the Business Vision

Develop a statement of your company vision (or, if you prefer, your business future), through the involvement of your management team and using any combination of the methods described in this chapter.

part three
How Do We Get There?

Now that you have articulated the future you want to create for your business and yourself, all you need to do is make it happen! Arguably, this is the most important part of all in that there is little value in having a robustly thought-out strategy and plan, which meets all of your personal goals and drivers, unless it is actually implemented.

Many entrepreneurs have a natural tendency to action – in fact, we find owner-managers jumping straight into the 'how' before they have thought about the 'what'. This can be counterproductive – there is no point rowing harder if the boat is heading in the wrong direction!

Fortunately, if you have worked your way through the chapters and assignments in Parts 1 and 2, you will now have a clear idea of where you are going and so you are ready to consider how you will get there. In Part 3, we will look at how to go about the implementation of your strategy again using the four Ms (markets, money and measures, management and me) as a guide.

eight
What is Your Growth Strategy?

In the preceding chapters, we have focused on what you want the business to look like to enable you to achieve your personal goals and aspirations. Now it is time to think more about the how of making this happen.

Many of the firms we have worked with over the years have experienced, after a while, a kind of 'glass ceiling': they seem to have reached a plateau in their sales and/or profits, and cannot go beyond it. You may recognize yourself in this description! Yet, these owner-managers still have aspirations to take the business further, and so they have joined us on BGP. They have sought fresh ideas and new approaches and, from the many success stories we have heard, they seem to have found them!

In this chapter, we will review a number of options for growth strategies which have been successful in helping firms break through this 'glass ceiling'. These options are not necessarily mutually exclusive – in theory, at least, it is possible to pursue more than one at the same time. However, our experience, from having worked with hundreds of growing businesses, indicates that focus is probably the single most important characteristic of a successful growth strategy.

At the highest level, we suggest that you consider two broad options for your growth strategy:

1.   Can you improve productivity?
2.   Can you increase sales volume?

Each of these can be further broken down as shown in the framework in Figure 8.1.

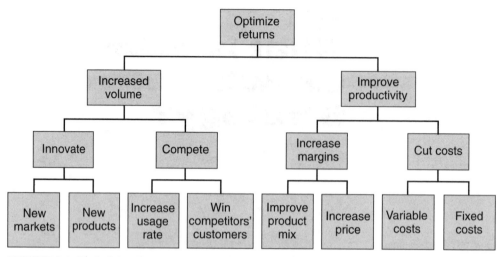

FIGURE 8.1 Optimizing Product/Service Returns.

Improving Productivity

Improving productivity should be a continuing agenda item for the growth-orientated business. Getting more value from what you have is, after all, a fundamental part of the constant search to be better than your competitors and different from them. Many, however, see this as an activity just for periods of economic recession. If this is your management philosophy, then there is a real danger that the business will swing from complacency (and inefficiency) when times are good, to frantic and unrealistic cost-cutting when times are bad – with an attendant high risk of unhappy employees and dissatisfied customers.

Cutting Costs

In any business, costs need to be controlled and balanced constantly against the needs for quality and service. The starting point for reducing costs is always to separate your variable and your fixed costs. At the start-up stage canny entrepreneurs strive to be lean and mean, to keep their fixed costs as low as possible. The implication of this strategy, of course, is that variable costs are higher. As businesses thrive and grow, so the reverse holds good: fixed costs often start to increase, as the business has the funds to invest in doing things more cheaply in-house. Information technology is a good example of this. Very few businesses start with a separate IT department, but many will create one at some stage in their growth. They will recruit an experienced professional and other staff to provide support systems across the enterprise. These people will all need office space and their own IT equipment, but the benefits of investing in coordinated, on-site business support should outweigh the costs. The same will hold for other business infrastructure functions, such as purchasing, human resources, and so forth.

Businesses, of course, move in cycles and there will come a point when you should start to question whether the emerging fixed cost structure is really necessary to run the business effectively and efficiently. Are there activities which would be better outsourced, or bought in only as and when required? Could certain operations be subcontracted to specialists? To take purchasing as an example, more and more owner-managed businesses are joining buying consortia. These aggregate their members' orders to strike better deals with suppliers, in return for increased volumes. Routine buying and low-priority purchasing (such as janitorial supplies and office stationery) are effectively outsourced at a lower cost, leaving staff to concentrate on activities that are more important to the business.

At Hotel Chocolat, Angus Thirlwell and Peter Harris keep their fixed costs under constant review: 'We are all too well aware how easy it is to let the costs run up', says Peter, a qualified accountant. 'In our case, the supply chain accounts for most of the costs. With each stage of business growth, we ask ourselves: do we need to do this or that activity, or would we be better outsourcing it to someone else?'

Here are some general guidelines on reviewing your cost structure:

1. Focus on the big items. As with most business issues, the 80/20 rule applies. Better to concentrate your energies on attacking areas where the gains will be significant, rather than those where improvements will make a marginal difference.
2. There are no sacred cows or 'no-go' areas. Just because something has always been done in a particular way does not mean it should be done like that forever.
3. Look for 'easy wins'. In many product-based businesses, for example, there is a tendency for the product portfolio to grow: the rate at which innovations are introduced exceeds the rate at which old products are discontinued. However, in any business with a wide portfolio, there is a strong chance that a handful of products are really profitable, there is a second group which is marginally profitable or trades at break even, and the rest are losing money.
4. Be ruthless!

That said, you should not throw out the baby with the bath water! Reducing fixed costs should not mean discontinuing investment in technology that brings not only economies, but also flexibility for the future. Similarly, it is not as a rule wise to outsource a 'core competence' – a set of processes, say, or technical know-how – that is part of what makes you stand out from the competition.

Increasing Margins

Increasing margins may be the result of actions to improve variable costs. It can also result from finding ways to enhance your sales product mix, or even from increased prices.

Improving Product Mix

If you have a number of different products/services, then it is almost certainly the case that you earn different gross margins on each different product/service. Clearly, if you can sell more of the higher-margin products, then you will increase overall profitability. This holds true for service-based businesses as well. As a result of BGP, Raz Khan, founder of market research company Cobalt-Sky, refocused his business on higher value-adding activities for which clients were prepared to pay. This also had the effect of determining what sort of client Cobalt-Sky was best suited to serve. Since BGP, the customer base has gradually shifted and, several years down the line, Cobalt-Sky makes better margins doing more rewarding work for satisfied customers!

Analysis of the product mix, of course, depends critically on knowing the accurate gross margins for each product/service line (net margin is often far more difficult to identify accurately, since the exact allocation of indirect costs is as much an art as a science).

Increasing Prices

In mathematical terms, increasing your prices is probably the easiest way to improve margins. But it is also nearly always difficult to convince your customers! You know instinctively what to do when cutting prices to stimulate demand: you make a lot of noise and publicity. Some people argue that increasing price should be the opposite, the increase being silently passed through to suppliers and customers alike. In some markets, this strategy seems to work: newspapers and magazines heavily publicize reductions to their cover prices, but make no reference to increases. If your business has been in existence for a number of years, you will know what the industry practice tends to be. That said, a price rise with no added value is rarely the way to generate long-term loyalty. Put another way, if the perceived added value is significantly greater, then customers will be prepared to spend considerably more.

Increasing Sales Volume

So far we have looked at strategies for growth through increasing productivity, by reducing costs or improving margins. Alternatively, you can seek growth through increased volume, in other words selling more. Increased volume consists of:

- Competing more strongly: winning market share from your competitors.
- Innovation: growing through new products or new markets.

These different strategies have different risks attached to them, popularized over many years by the US business strategist, Igor Ansoff (Figure 8.2).

The strategy of maximum risk is identified in the box called 'diversification': selling new products to new customers (or, as one of our colleagues describes it with brutal

Product /Service

	Existing	New
New	Market development	Diversification
Existing	Market penetration	Product/service development

Market

FIGURE 8.2 Product/Market Growth Matrix.

frankness, 'selling things you don't understand, to people you've never met'). Conversely, the strategy of minimum risk is to focus on the box labelled 'market penetration': selling more of what you already sell to existing customers (or ones very similar to them). Selling new products to your existing market and existing products to new markets – the other two boxes in the matrix – are strategies of intermediate risk.

There is much research to show that the most successful growth strategy for the owner-managed firm is market penetration: selling your existing products/services to your existing customers and others just like them. Our own research at Cranfield makes the case convincingly. Across our sample population of growing businesses, 50 per cent focused on a low-risk market penetration strategy, while 10 per cent pursued the high-risk strategy of diversification. However, nine out of ten of the high-performing firms, showing consistently profitable growth, focused on selling existing products and services to the market they already knew.

There are exceptions to these general rules. Businesses, for example, which are in terminally declining markets must either reinvent themselves or die. For these the strategy of greatest risk is to continue with what they are currently doing. (In chapter 1 you may recall that we profiled two businesses, Juice Technology and Pro-Activ Textiles, who have taken this path of reinvention.) However, if you are a growth-orientated entrepreneur, you are very unlikely to have set up a business in a 'sunset' industry, and the implications of the Ansoff matrix will almost certainly apply.

Competing More Strongly: Squeezing the Lemon!

In our experience, some of the hardest people to convince of the merits of this strategy can be the business's own sales force! Competing more strongly, with existing products, within existing markets, appears to be a more pedestrian, less exciting option than launching new products into new markets. For the smaller, growing business, however, improving competitiveness usually ensures better returns. Putting this into practice is normally a two-stage process. First, you sell more to existing customers, increasing their usage rate. Then, you look to capture customers from your competitors.

A simple but powerful way to think of increasing customers' usage rate and capturing new customers is to think in terms of 'squeezing the lemon'. When they cook, most people take an (understandably) relaxed attitude to squeezing a lemon for its juice. They slice the lemon, squeeze one half, discard it and may or may not retain the other half. Mostly, however, they fail to extract the maximum juice possible from the lemon. Many businesses take the same approach with their customers. There is no plan for developing the sales relationship with larger customers, no plan to encourage smaller customers to become larger ones, and no plan for leveraging existing customers to help find new ones!

Here are some tried and tested approaches to changing this situation:

- In Part 1, we introduced the idea that, in many markets, the relationship between supplier and customer often follows the same path as a marriage. To recap: in the early days, a kind of courtship takes place, when the customer and supplier get to know each other. If both like what they see, a relationship develops and, if things go well, a 'honeymoon period' takes place, in which each party values and respects the other. However, just like a marriage, if the 'partners' start to take each other too much for granted, the 'magic' disappears and, in the worst case, divorce is the end result! It is a valuable exercise to group customers by the stage of their relationship with you and to ensure that they get the right sort of care and attention. Identify those who are at risk of defecting to competitors – because they have been neglected – and those who have defected and could be won back. Then, create a plan for addressing the situation. Remember, it invariably costs far more to acquire a new customer than to retain an existing one.
- Customers who value you are your best ambassadors. Many smaller, growing businesses have customers who are many times larger than themselves. The people who buy from you may well be happy to recommend you to others in their organization – and, in particular, people you do not already know – but they have to be asked! More to the point, frequently a customer who buys one thing from you does not know, or has forgotten, that you have other things to sell. It is up to you to remind them. You can also ask your existing customers for referrals along the lines of 'Do you know anyone else who would value our product/service?'
- Big company buyers are inherently risk-averse. Becoming an approved supplier may take you years. Big companies are also, however, intensely competitive. Often, a rival to an existing customer of yours will be prepared to see you just on the off-chance that, by using your services, their rival has obtained some competitive advantage, however slight. (Also, if you supply a competitor who

operates similar policies to theirs, you must have good credentials to have made it onto their approved list!). Again, exploit this to your advantage.

■ Think carefully about the different ways in which you 'touch' different audiences. Are there untapped opportunities? Hotel Chocolat, for example, has always viewed each gift order as having two customers: the person who requests and pays for a delivery of chocolates and the person who receives them. The buyer is an actual customer; the recipient is a potential one. Hotel Chocolat makes sure, therefore, that the recipient knows exactly who supplies the chocolates, and encourages that person to become a customer in turn. For the company, a transaction is only successful if both the giver and the receiver are happy!

Innovate

Innovation, or investing in new products and new markets, is clearly a higher-risk strategy than competing more effectively. However, there are also ways in which you can manage the risks involved in innovation to a level which is acceptable.

The least risky innovation is likely to be the new product or service actively requested by existing customers. When this happens, you often have an opportunity to develop the innovation in close collaboration with one customer, or a select few. This is common practice in many technology-based industries, such as bioscience, information systems and defence procurement. The advantage with this approach, of course, is that, if successful, you have a guaranteed sale and, in many cases, help with cashflow. The disadvantage is the danger that the product or service is so customized for a limited group of customers that it cannot be sold to a wider target.

The term innovation often suggests something radically new. In fact, new products can equally mean simple line extensions to the existing core business. Measured by market value, the Coca-Cola Company has been the world's biggest food and drink business for much of its lifetime. Even today, however, more than a century after its foundation, the company derives most of its revenues from its core Coke portfolio, of Coca-Cola and a handful of variants such as Diet Coke or Vanilla Coke. In the 1980s, when the management attempted to ditch the old flavour and substitute a replacement, loyal customers revolted and forced the company to back down. Since then, Coca-Cola has focused its innovation strategy on a small number of line extensions, carefully researched and tested before they are taken to market. Outside its core cola portfolio, the company prefers to acquire or license new products, which have been successfully developed by other people. The Austrian company Red Bull has built a significant global beverages business around one product and a handful of variants!

On the same theme, what appears to an outsider to be radically new or different may in fact be a clever new combination of existing features and technologies. Many businesses have built strong positions not through innovating a particular technology, but in re-presenting existing technology in an attractive way to the customer. It has been argued that Japanese industrial strategy of the 1970s and 1980s was largely based on this idea, certainly in the field of consumer electronics, and underpinned the success of companies such as Sony, Matsushita and Hitachi. Companies at the leading edge of technological development are sometimes prone to focus on the features, as opposed to the benefits to the customer: but in the commercial world there are no guaranteed prizes for originality!

We will leave the final word on this topic to BGP past participant Jerry Sandys, who negotiated a very successful sale of his business to the industrial group Abacus in 2005. 'We built TDC through selling more of what we were already doing in new ways to existing customers, and others like them. It certainly paid off for us!'

Assignment 8.1: Assessing Growth Options

1. What opportunities are there for you to improve productivity in your business:
   - Through cutting costs?
   - Through improving product/service mix?
   - Through increasing prices?
2. How can you increase sales volume in your business:
   - By increasing existing customers' usage rate?
   - By winning customers from the competition?
   - By introducing new products/services?
   - By entering new markets?
3. What will be the focus of your growth strategy?

The Need for Clear Priorities

In theory, several of these options can be pursued at the same time. However, when considering these options, you need to recognize and manage the inherent risks of departing too far from serving your core market with your core product and service offering. Our experience, from having worked with hundreds of growing businesses, indicates that focus is vitally important and that most successful businesses concentrate on 'selling more of what you already sell to your existing customers and customers just like them', just as Jerry Sandys advocated earlier.

Cash Generation: Product Portfolio Analysis

Many businesses that have been through BGP have also found it useful to view growth in the context of cash generation. After all, the long-term value of any business is generally held to consist of its capacity to throw off more cash than it absorbs.

Most businesses which have been in existence for five years or more will have multiple revenue streams, from a mix of products and services. The common term for this is the product portfolio, although the term applies to both products and services. Some products/services in the portfolio will produce cash: others will almost certainly consume cash. The most widely used tool for analysing the product portfolio is the Boston matrix (Figure 8.3), a framework developed by the Boston Consulting Group (BCG) in the late 1970s and early 1980s, and refined thereafter.

The Boston matrix classifies products on two dimensions:

■ the rate at which their market is growing; and
■ the share of that market relative to competitors.

The resulting analysis creates a two-by-two matrix, in which the business's products/services can be located. The star box, on the top left, reflects a market which is growing strongly and where the business has a strong market position. Typically, in this situation, star products/services are either cash-neutral or consume cash. The cash cow box, in the bottom left, shows a market where the firm also has a strong market position, but the rate of growth has slowed, usually because the market is more mature. Products in this box generate the cash that powers the business. The dog box, on the bottom right, is occupied by products which have a small share in a declining market. These products tend either to be cash-neutral or to produce smaller amounts of cash. Finally, the question mark box, on the top right, is reserved for products which have a low share in a fast-growing market. These products invariably consume cash, because they require lots of financial support but are not yet producing a return. They are question marks because it is unclear whether their market share will improve, and so move them into

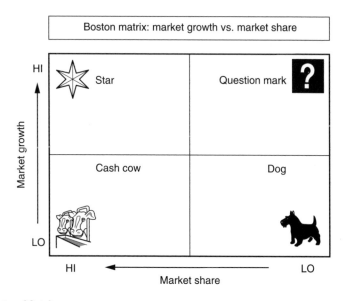

FIGURE 8.3 Boston Matrix.

the star box, or whether they will continue to underperform and, eventually, as the market matures, become dogs. (If you use this analysis when you are still a small grow- ing business, when you may have very small shares of very large markets, it is important to define share in terms of your market niche versus the direct competition.)

The Boston matrix has enjoyed widespread popularity because it is seen to be a versatile, general-purpose business tool. The analysis can be conducted at the level of an industry, within a group of companies or for the product/service portfolio of one business. The underlying idea is that businesses (above a certain size) have a portfolio of activities, developed in response to new market opportunities, and sufficiently diver- sified to spread their commercial risks (a little like the way investment portfolios are diversified to account for risk). That portfolio is dynamic, that is, it evolves over time, and should be actively managed. The key points of this active management are:

- Cash cows fund the investment needed to support stars and a selected number of question marks.
- The business must create action standards for question marks, to identify which should be encouraged.
- Dogs have no long-term future and should receive limited or no investment.
- In the longer term, as markets mature and decline, cash cows will cease to generate cash and move towards the dog box. The business needs to have other activities – ideally stars – which will become the cash cows of the future, as the market rate of growth for the current cash cows slows down. At the same time, there should be suitable question marks which are now ready to assume the role of stars.

The direction of investment is shown in Figure 8.4.

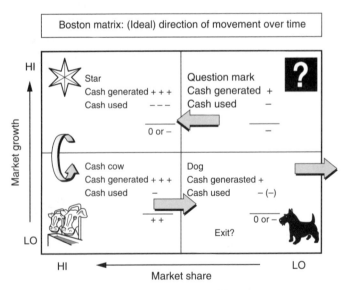

FIGURE 8.4 Boston Matrix Suggesting Direction of Investment.

It is, of course, cash flow, not profit, which is used in this model as the real determinant of a company's ability to develop its products/services. The overall business aim is to achieve market share and continuing growth while maximizing cash flow.

Arguments for Using the Boston Matrix

The Boston matrix is used by countless businesses, small and large, across the world as one of the primary tools for strategic planning. Every year, in our work with smaller growing companies, we meet business founders who rely on it heavily. It has certain undoubted advantages:

- The analysis imposes a valuable degree of rigour and clarity on your thinking about the business. Many businesses become emotionally attached to activities which can no longer be justified on commercial grounds, and thus dilute and divert their resources. A dog is a dog!
- We have already discussed the need for successful businesses to continue to respond quickly and effectively to changes in their markets. The Boston matrix forces you to think carefully about how your markets are changing, not just today but in the longer term.
- This analysis can act as an early-warning system to alert senior management to the dangers of spreading resources too thinly or underinvesting in the wrong places. In the longer term, no business can support an unlimited number of question marks, nor be reliant on too few cash cows.
- As we have emphasized before, all businesses are viable only insofar as they generate cash. The Boston matrix focuses on cash as the ultimate business driver, not profit.

See below how BGP past participant, Rod Leefe, used this approach for planning the development of his executive recruitment firm, Witan Jardine (Figure 8.5).

Proceed with Caution!

On the other hand, this approach will not work for every business. First, the analysis cannot be undertaken for young businesses or businesses which do not have a portfolio of products and services – although it may usefully prompt managers to examine whether they are too dependent on a narrow revenue stream from only one or two areas.

Second, like all managerial tools, the conclusions need to be balanced against judgement and experience. In the late 1980s, for example, the big players in the UK tea market were united in their belief that packet (loose) teas were dogs, teabags were cash cows and instant (granulated) tea was the question mark ready to become a star. In fact, things turned out rather differently:

- The technical challenge of creating an instant tea that catered for the British

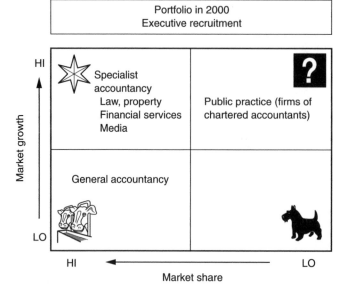

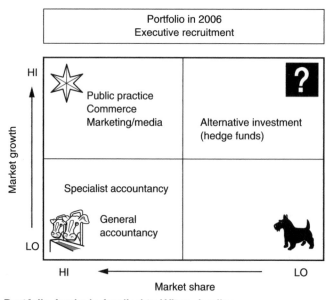

FIGURE 8.5 Portfolio Analysis Applied to Witan Jardine.

habit of drinking tea with milk proved too hard. Instant tea failed to take off as predicted.

■ The tea bag segment still had lots of potential for growth.

■ And there were still plenty of niche opportunities to make money in packet teas.

Those businesses that were very dependent on the Boston matrix for their strategic planning were paralysed in their thinking for a while, because the model had not successfully predicted the future!

The third point follows from this example. It is always dangerous to rely wholly on one way of looking at the world. We recommend using the Boston matrix only if it is appropriate for your type of business, at its stage of maturity. Then, apply your judgement and experience to interpreting the analysis and the conclusions. Discuss this across the management team and with advisers whose opinions you respect.

Revisit Your Strategy

By now, you should be well placed to answer what our colleague Professor Cliff Bowman has termed 'the five essential questions which determine whether you have a competitive strategy'. That is, do you know:

1. Where you should compete (market segment)?
2. How you can gain sustainable competitive advantage?
3. What competencies, and what kind of organization, you require to deliver the strategy?
4. What you look like now?
5. How you can move from where you are now to where you want to be? (This should crystallize in the third section of this book.)

In other words, if you know which market segment you are competing in, and can define a clear competitive advantage, you can then define your organization to deliver the strategy. Clearly, the most important of these from a strategy point of view is number 2; are the factors and the strategy still in place that enabled your company to grow?

Take the example of a business we have already referred to, Pacific Direct. When Lara Morgan completed BGP in 1999, part of her strategy to revitalize Pacific Direct Ltd was to redefine her target market. In seven years of virtually non-stop growth, Pacific had built its position selling hotel toiletries to more or less anyone who could buy. Lara had developed a large and growing portfolio of products, mostly under brands which Pacific had created itself, but some through licensing well-known skincare and cosmetics brands such as Penhaligon's of London.

Now was the time to take stock and refine the strategy. Better margins and opportunities lay in the upper end of the market, through focusing on four- and five-star hotel chains and business-class airline passengers. This was also the kind of business which Lara and her staff really enjoyed doing, and did well. Going forward therefore, Lara planned to whittle down the existing range, increase the number of licences and concentrate on penetrating the upper segments of the market. Six years later, both sales and profitability were up several hundred per cent!

Assignment 8.2: Revisit Your Business Purpose

1. In chapter 1, you reviewed your business purpose. Now that you have been through 'Where are we now?', it seems a good point to review the relevance and scope of that purpose as you defined it then. In the light of the subsequent analysis, do you think your business purpose needs modifying in some way? If so, what should that be?

2. If you have modified it, what implications does that have for:
   - How you communicate with your customers (and, perhaps, suppliers)?
   - And how you communicate with your staff?

nine
How Can You Further Develop Your Distinctiveness?

In earlier parts of this book, we considered how you win, that is, why your customers choose to spend their money with you rather than with someone else or not at all. As we have seen, this will be because, in some way, your product or service matches their needs in a distinctive way which is better than the alternatives. As you grow you will need to build on those key points of difference. In this chapter, we will concentrate on exploring how successful firms further develop their distinctiveness and customer focus.

Focusing on your customer, and delivering distinctive value for them, is the very essence of marketing and marketing planning. Surveys that we have conducted over the years have, however, consistently shown that fewer than half of businesses with turnover under £5 million employ formal marketing planning. Without some sort of formalized processes marketing is condemned to be a hit and miss operation. By the end of this chapter, you should have a clear understanding of the following key topics in developing distinctiveness and customer focus:

1 developing customer segments and product/service quality;
2 optimizing price and margins;
3 promotional activities;
4 distinctive distribution;
5 improving the effectiveness of the sales team.

Of course, not all of these components apply equally to every business. There is no single formula for achieving competitive advantage. It is the role of top management (in the small growing business, that usually means you, the entrepreneur!) to decide where are the opportunities for the business, and how these should be integrated into the marketing and sales targets set out in the marketing plan.

Developing Customer Segments and Product/ Service Quality

Through continuing analysis and segmentation of your customers, you will be best placed to identify new product/service offerings which will grow your business – but do not compromise your points of difference in the market. It is even possible to turn what look like threats to your business into opportunities.

In 1999, the Cobra Beer management team felt that they needed to take some strategic decisions about the company's portfolio, if the rate of growth was to be maintained. Although 10 years old, Cobra was still exclusively a beer business. The restaurant owners loved the brand, because it allowed their customers to both drink and eat greater quantities, and a growing number of consumers had adopted it as their first choice of beverage to drink with curry.

However, analysis of the market showed that long-term trends were against them. Beer sales in the UK were in gradual decline. Sales of wine, however, had been steadily rising over the decade. In Karan Bilimoria's experience, the basic choice that diners made was between drinking beer and drinking wine. It was clear that the balance was being tipped more and more towards wine. The strategic choice for Cobra was this: Do we fight the wine challenge, or do we turn this into a business opportunity? The answer was to create the company's own range of red and white wines. Research told them that house wines accounted for 50 per cent of wine sales in Indian restaurants. Cobra could counter this by offering a range of good premium house wines, on which the restaurant owners could make good margins, and which the restaurants could effectively present as their own house wines. The wines were branded 'General Bilimoria', and dedicated to Karan's father, Lt General FN Bilimoria, PVSM, ADC.

Launched during late 1999, the wines proved a huge success. In the words of Karan Bilimoria: 'The Cobra beer brand has not suffered at all – in fact it's stronger than ever. What we are now is a broadly based beverages business, with even better potential to grow'. In 2006, the company had sales with a retail value exceeding £100 million and offices in the UK, the USA, India and South Africa. Many entrepreneurs would feel that they had come a long way at this point: Karan reckons he has only just begun. By 2014, the company target is $1 billion retail sales worldwide!

Quality Challenges

For any business, quality is not merely a 'nice to have'. Accustomed to continual improvements in every area of consumption, today's customers have very little tolerance of poor quality. Just because you are a smaller, growing business, do not expect that your customers will see your offering any differently from that of larger competitors. Sticking with the beer market, mark the words of James Koch of the Boston Beer Company. He observed that the biggest problem for the new and growing company was in creating in customers' minds an image of quality. 'You can't sell a product you don't believe in and in cold calling the only thing standing between you and the customer's scorn is the integrity of your product'.

Nevertheless, delivering superior quality entails an endless battle or trade-off against cost and service levels. In this battle you have to seek improvements along two, or even all three, dimensions simultaneously.

Differentiation is also the fundamental rationale behind building strong brands, whether these are products or services (such as Cobra Beer), or the company itself. Brands build reputation and trust, for which customers are prepared to pay extra. The quality of your offering is not, of course, just what you do, but also how you do it. Jan Carlson of Scandinavian Airways (SAS) pioneered the concept of 'moments of truth', when a customer experiences the reality of who you are and what you do. Whether it is a sales call, a general enquiry or a telephone call querying an invoice, each business has countless daily interactions with its customers. And at each point of contact customers have expectations regarding reliability, responsiveness, competence, courtesy, and so forth. Those are the moments when the customer finds out if your organization is what it says it is, and how it measures up to his or her expectations.

At the moment of truth there is no hiding place! This is especially the case in the services sector, where typically most staff have direct and regular contact with customers. There is no substitute for spending time and resources (chiefly, but not exclusively, money) on instilling a culture of quality within a business. In the early days, this tends to be absorbed informally by employees, through observing and copying the behaviour of the boss. As the business grows, and the number of employees increases, informality has to give away to formal processes, such as employee induction and training programmes, as new recruits are told 'how we do things around here'.

Attention to Quality Pays Off

David Courteen and Steve Taylor founded Fitness Express in 1987. Both graduates in sports science and leisure management, they focused on a particular niche in the leisure industry. Their market was predominantly independent hotels who wished to offer their guests health and fitness facilities, but who did not have the expertise to manage them. David and Steve would manage and staff each fitness club under contract, rewarded through a mixture of fee and profit share.

As the business grew, so a clear formula started to evolve. First, each club was carefully tailored to appeal to a clearly defined market segment. This might be predominantly a family membership, or older people in retirement who felt intimidated by the atmosphere in a typical fitness club. Second, good systems and procedures were essential to ensuring that every member had a positive and high-quality experience every time they came. Happy members translated into renewed subscriptions, which translated into profitable business. Third, Fitness Express's continuing success depended crucially on high-quality staff: on recruiting, training and retaining the right people.

In particular, Fitness Express used the UK government-backed Investors in People (see http://www.investorsinpeople.com) method to formalize staff management. The training in all aspects of fitness club operation led their staff to obtain formal qualifications, and to improve their career prospects in sports management. As a result, Fitness Express's staff retention rate, at 67 per cent per annum, was considerably better than the industry average.

In 1997 the two founders took part in BGP, to help them accelerate the rate of growth. Four years later, they were approached with an offer to buy the business. In April 2001, David and Steve sold Fitness Express to Crown Sports plc, a large, diversified sports group, which was fast building a network of health and fitness clubs. The multi-million pound value placed on the business comfortably exceeded the value of the contracts under management. To a large degree, Crown were attracted by the quality of the systems, procedures, people and ways of managing staff which David and Steve had put in place.

Customer Retention and Adding Value

Both academic studies and our personal experience of working with literally hundreds of smaller businesses tell us the same thing: in almost every case, it costs less, much less, to retain your existing customers than it does to acquire new ones. This is especially so in business-to-business markets. Yet, we are constantly surprised by how little time, effort and money many firms devote to keeping the customers they already have. It is now over 10 years since a McKinsey study demonstrated convincingly that the biggest reason why industrial customers defect is because they feel neglected by their existing suppliers. Yet, many people still do not seem to have got the message.

Ask yourself this: would you rather spend £100 on creating a really good offer for a valued existing customer, or £1,000 to recruit a new customer to replace the valued customer you just lost? The arithmetic speaks for itself. Here are some simple but effective guidelines to help you think about keeping the customers you value, and adding value to your product/service offering:

1. Stop asking the question 'how can we make money from our customers?' – which is how most companies look at the issue most of the time – and start asking the question 'how can our customers make money from us?' (If you are selling direct to consumers, you might reframe that question as 'how can we improve the quality or lower the cost?'). To revert to the Cobra Beer example

cited above: when Karan Bilimoria decided to add wines to his portfolio, he was also creating an opportunity for several thousand restaurateurs to offer a profitable new range of beverages to their customers. Unsurprisingly, they were happy to stock the products.

2. One of the most powerful drivers of a new business opportunity at the outset can be finding an answer to the question of 'where is the pain?' That is, where are the real irritants, big or small, that you can help your customers deal with? If you are not continually readdressing that question, you should be. The only way you will find out is by being out there in the marketplace, constantly talking to your customers.

3. By focusing on identifying and creating value for the customer, you will find new reasons to talk to – and sell to – your customers. That value does not necessarily have to be a radical enhancement of what you are already offering. The UK kitchenware retailer Lakeland Ltd has built a very successful £110 million plus business through offering its customers a continuing range of innovative products, sourced from around the world. Very few involve breakthrough new technology, but incrementally they make household management easier and more pleasant. As a result, Lakeland mails customers seven or eight times a year with new catalogues, as opposed to the single catalogue of 20 years before.

Challenges for Service Businesses

One advantage which product-based businesses like Cobra enjoy over service-based businesses is that they can easily make their differences tangible and visible. Service businesses such as Fitness Express are inherently more difficult to differentiate from their rivals. Because they are intangible, services are often seen as a commodity. One insurance policy document, for example, looks fundamentally the same as the next one. Services are usually difficult to test or assess in advance and customers even play a role in determining the quality and delivery of a service: the quality of the service you receive from an advertising agency, for instance, is usually closely related to the quality of the briefing. To build differentiation in a service business, therefore, requires strong, consistent branding. The company name is frequently the brand and everything which the customer sees – the product literature, the company offices, any tangible 'evidence' of the uniqueness of that offering – has to work to strengthen the image of the brand. It is no accident that banks generally occupy big impressive offices: the subliminal message to the depositor is that this is a solid, enduring institution where your money will be safe. If you are able to make the company name synonymous with good quality, you will make the 'service' more tangible. After all, at the end of the day, your company name and reputation may be the only difference between you and your competitors.

Price and Margin Optimization

We have seen how you can further develop your distinctiveness by careful focus on the needs of different target groups of customers and through attention to quality. In the minds of most customers, quality is closely linked to price. Intuitively, we make judgements about the quality of a product or service based on the price relative to other offers in the marketplace. Charge too much for the quality, and your offer is not competitive. But charge too little, and there is an equal danger that your offer is perceived to be of low quality.

A business which has been trading for some time usually has a good idea of where to pitch its prices in the market. If that business is also trading profitably, then normally it has high enough gross margins to support its overheads and to allow for necessary reinvestment.

Beware, however, the danger of 'price leakage'. In many companies, sales force bonuses depend on sales volume, rather than profitable accounts. Discounts for order size, discounts for early payment, 'loss leaders', can all chip away at the margin. Be ruthless in examining your firm's discount policies and determining whether they can really be justified.

Margin Enhancement by Focusing on the Most Profitable Customers

It is not just across-the-board pricing and discounting that affect profitability. Even quite mature businesses are frequently unaware of other profit opportunities that they are missing. All customers are not necessarily created equal, certainly as far as margins are concerned. As we observed earlier, in most businesses the 80/20 rule applies: 80 per cent of the profit is produced by 20 per cent of the customers (and this is often true of the product range as well). But how many businesses actually know who their most profitable customers are, and which areas of business they should concentrate on?

Many businesses simply do not realize that they already have the information they need to improve their profit performance. Giles Latchford established Hidden Resource (www.hiddenresource.co.uk) in 2003. It is a consultancy that specializes in the analysis of data which client companies can use to improve their profitability. He discovered this business opportunity through a project undertaken during his MBA programme at Cranfield. This is how he describes what he found:

> The client for the MBA project designed jewellery and marketed a range of 150 plus products to the UK public via press advertising (one page, product-specific, magazine adverts) and direct mail.
>
> It had been trading since 1999 and in that time accumulated over 45,000 transactions with 5,000 separate customers, through 150 separate adverts and numerous mail shots. So there was plenty of data to work with! The primary issue was that the company wanted to improve the return on its

magazine campaigns. It also wanted to increase the number of campaigns per year that it was engaging in. This meant raising funds from a venture capital firm to increase working capital. However, there was a sense that the process was not working that well, and that, if they could improve the bottom line, they would be better placed to raise the additional money.

We were commissioned to identify, first, who their most important customers were and, second, which publications they should focus on for their future advertising.

The analysis immediately highlighted a previously unidentified regional demand for their products in the UK. Sales in this area were 23 per cent more profitable than the national average. On the other hand, the client was unaware that any customers were loss making. We were able to demonstrate that actual contribution per customer (profit before overheads) ranged from a loss of £100 to a profit of £200. Half the total profit came from the 20 per cent most profitable customers, and only accounted for 21 per cent of total acquisition costs. On the 25 per cent least profitable customers the company only broke even – but these accounted for 30 per cent of total acquisition costs.

Our analysis proved that there was no historical relationship between acquisition cost and profitability. This had a profound impact on the client's approach to advertising! We were then able to illustrate a hierarchy of profit-generating publications, and this in turn enabled our client to become far more specific with its marketing campaigns.

The analysis took less than one month to perform and the client implemented the recommendations with immediate effect. The cost of the analysis represented a small fraction of the increased profit gained from the results. The company was then in a position to decide which products should be targeted to which customers and through which publications. The bottom-line impact has resulted in a substantial increase in shareholders' return on equity. Crucially, this process enabled the company to present a much more attractive proposition to potential investors.

Promotional Activities

Word of Mouth Marketing

Many owner-managers of growing businesses rely on a small range of promotional activities. By far the most popular is 'word of mouth', that is one of your existing customers (or suppliers) recommending you to someone else. While this approach to promotion may appear to run contrary to some of the more formalized approaches advocated by marketing professionals who work with large businesses, for the owner-managed growing business it makes good sense.

First, it appears to work! Many surveys have consistently shown that the number one source of new customers for smaller business is recommendations from existing customers, suppliers and other referrers.

Second, word of mouth marketing also seems to fit more closely with the characteristics of many owner-managers who have strong preferences for personal contact and direct interchange with customers rather than impersonal mass promotions. This leads to strong conversational relationships with customers in which owner-managers can listen, and respond, to the real voice of the customer. This closeness to the customers also tends to lead to real understanding of the customers' needs. And such understanding of the customers' needs is at the very heart of successful marketing. For many owner-managed businesses, this personal contact between the owner and the customer can represent a unique selling point of the business – in other words, it is the very reason that the customers buy.

Third, word of mouth marketing tends to lead to a slow build-up of new business and, hence, a slower pace of growth. This means that the business is in a better position to manage the resources required to meet the new and increased demand.

Finally, and perhaps most importantly for the growing business, word of mouth marketing costs very little! Referrals incur few, if any, additional direct costs.

On the other hand, word of mouth marketing also has disadvantages:

- It is self-limiting. This is the flipside of the fact that word of mouth leads to a slow build-up. If a growing business is dependent on recommendations for new customers, then its growth will almost certainly be limited to those markets and segments in which the sources of recommendations operate.
- It is difficult to plan and control. You can try to influence what other people say about you and your business, but you cannot control what they say, when they say it, or to whom they say it.

Nevertheless, the ambitious owner-manager will employ a range of proactive and planned methods to encourage referrals and recommendations such as:

- Explicitly asking for referrals from existing customers, e.g. 'Do you know anyone else who might be interested in what we do?'
- 'Refer a friend' schemes where referrers are rewarded for introducing a new customer.
- Asking for citations and recommendations which you can use on sales literature.
- Merchandise carrying your brand (for example pens, mugs) which your customer uses, thus exposing the brand to others.

■ Building a favourable image of your business in the marketplace in order to encourage positive word of mouth messages about you. The most important thing you can do here is to ensure that you always deliver on your promises to customers at the quality required. In addition, there may be ways in which your business can participate in local community events, trade events, charity events and so forth, all of which contribute to the image of your business.

More Formal Marketing Approaches

As a result of this preference for word of mouth marketing and personal contact, owner-managers of growing businesses tend to spend significant amounts of their time in direct contact with customers. However, as the business grows, other, more formal, marketing approaches may also be valuable.

For historical reasons, marketing budgets are often split between advertising, referred to as 'above the line' activities, and promotional, or 'below the line' activities. As a general rule, advertising campaigns are aimed at building long-term customers, while sales promotions are typically short-term activities designed to achieve quick results. Determining the most effective ways of spending your money is equally important in each case.

Below the Line Marketing Activities

Most growing businesses will spend more on sales promotion techniques than on advertising. Some typical aims of sales promotions are to speed up stock movement, encourage repeat purchases, get bills paid on time, and induce trial purchase. The target customers for such schemes vary. For example, your target customers may be trade buyers. They could also be your own employees and you may be offering money (prizes, bonuses), goods (gifts, vouchers) or even services (such as subsidized training and development). However, for the growing business, promotional opportunities that stimulate interest and awareness among new and existing purchasers, at lowest cost, are the most important. While discounting to move discontinued or slow-moving lines may be necessary from time to time, the main positive promotional activities would include:

1. Ensuring all your company 'small items' are coordinated and convey the same image and message, from business cards to Christmas cards.
2. Participating in exhibitions, with specially designed leaflets and brochures.
3. Experimenting with direct mail and/or e-mail, using lists generated from data-bases, and telemarketing.
4. Having a website which is aligned with your overall business image and attracts enquiries.

Most smaller, growing businesses do not have thousands of customers. For this reason, in such businesses, the most appropriate use of marketing money is usually direct marketing, to a market segment you can clearly identify. Before you start, the most important thing is to be absolutely clear about the action you are hoping to encourage the customer to take. If you want the customer to make a purchase based on the direct marketing, make sure that there are minimal obstacles to their actually buying – and plenty of reasons why they should! If the purpose is to generate enquiries, make sure that there is an efficient mechanism in place to handle and follow up the calls and e-mails.

Your Website

Even if yours is not an Internet-based business, your website will be an increasingly important promotional tool. Indeed, many of the smallest of start-up businesses often now have a website right from the beginning. Although not every business has to have a website, given the all-pervasive nature of the worldwide web in many industries and sectors it has become a minimum expectation that a business will have one. It is also increasingly the case that customers, suppliers and potential new staff members will look at your website as part of their deciding whether to work with you. In effect, websites have become one of Jan Carlson's 'moments of truth'. Having a site which is attractive, welcoming and easy to use can be an advantage in the initial skirmishes of 'the battle for the customer' and 'the battle to recruit talented people'.

In addition, websites are one of the few places in which smaller, growing businesses can compete on a 'level playing field' with bigger businesses since, on the Internet, no one knows how big (or small!) you are! The flipside of this is that there is nowhere to hide. Unlike most other marketing and promotional tools, your website is open to anyone and everyone who has Internet access.

It is now relatively easy, and not very costly, to develop a basic website either yourself or by making use of the services of a web designer. However, the key decisions are not technical ones, neither are they artistic nor issues of design. The key to successful exploitation of websites and the Internet is to see them simply as one more element of your overall promotional, sales and distribution activities. The way you use your website should be integrated with other business activities and closely linked to the way in which you seek to distinguish your business. A survey by the international accountancy firm PriceWaterhouseCoopers found that businesses with an Internet plan integrated with overall business strategy grew faster than those that did not. In other words, as in nearly all other areas of your business, the key decisions are business decisions which you need to make.

The first step is to ensure that, at the very least, you meet the minimum expectation for businesses in your market. This will vary hugely by industry. In some markets, all the serious competitors will have sites and they may be very sophisticated. To be considered as a serious player in the industry, you will need a site that meets this minimum expectation. In other industries, very few competitors may have well-developed sites and there may be an advantage to you if you did. So, take a look at what the competition is doing – they cannot hide either – and see if you can do better!

After this, here are some simple rules to follow in developing a basic website to be used for promoting your business:

1. Do not confuse people.
   - Keep it simple.
   - Make sure it is easy to use.
   - Get your main messages across on the front page if possible. This should particularly include what you do and what you want visitors to the site to do.
   - Avoid effects that require the user to have special technology. Many will not have it and will be put off.
   - Ensure your web presence is consistent with your overall business, your strategy and your offline presence. Remember: the people who speak to you on the phone, and deal with you face-to-face, will also sometimes use your website. They are the same people and they want to see a consistent message in whatever way they deal with you. This applies to the 'look and feel' of the site, the content and the functionality.

On a recent Cranfield Business Growth and Development Programme, two of the participating entrepreneurs ran separate graphic design businesses. As one would expect in their industry, both had sophisticated websites. However, the two sites looked totally different to one another and had some different functionality which perfectly reflected their different offline positions and strategies.

One of the graphics businesses focused on serving customers who were themselves fairly traditional businesses. The colour scheme, layout and functionality of their site were conservative and conventional, conveying the impression of solidity and trust that their customers looked for.

The other graphics business dealt primarily with youth-orientated sports brands. The design of their website was funky, featuring more brash colours and language which reflected a younger target group. This site also included some 'off the wall' interactive games, which again suited the target marketplace.

Any customer, supplier or potential staff member accessing either of these two sites would very quickly form a view about what sort of business they were, which would be wholly consistent with what they would find in the real world.

2. Welcome all your visitors.
   - Identify all the potential types of visitors to your site (customers, suppliers,

potential new staff, people looking to buy your business, people from different countries who may not speak your language). If possible, give a clear message to them all. In some cases (for example, someone looking to buy from you in a country to which you do not deliver), this message may have to be a polite 'go away'.

■ Identify which type of visitors you really want. Make it very obvious to them which parts of the site are aimed at them.

3 Watch what happens.

■ It is relatively easy to capture information about who visits your site and what they look at. This information could be very useful in helping to improve the site and, more importantly, in helping you to understand your customers even better and to segment them more accurately.

■ Make sure that you provide a mechanism for users to make enquiries from the site. By so doing, you can ask them to provide you with their e-mail addresses and other basic data.

4. Benchmark against other sites.

■ We have already suggested that you can benchmark your site against your competition in order to meet the minimum expectations. Preferably, of course, you should have a better site than theirs!

■ For ideas to add distinctive value to your customers which none of the competition is offering, it is useful to look at other sites outside your industry. These might be customers' sites, suppliers' sites or sites that you use yourself.

5. Be good to your existing customers.

■ Continuing to satisfy your existing customers is at the core of growth and profitability for many smaller companies. At a very minimum, your website creates an additional channel through which they can communicate with you and you with them. Do you know what they think of the site? Have you asked them for feedback and comments on it?

■ Consider how you can deliver even more value to your existing customers through your site. For example, you could produce an online newsletter, you could have discussion areas for existing customers, and you could provide answers to commonly asked questions and guidance about how to use your product/service. You may even be able to allow your customers to obtain quotations, place orders, track deliveries and view their accounts online.

6. Watch out for different expectations.

■ People may behave very differently and have different expectations when dealing online. For example, most of us are quite used to the idea of queuing at the supermarket checkout. And yet, when buying online, many purchasers will abandon the sale if the processing of the payment takes more than 15 seconds! Table 9.1 illustrates a number of other differences in behaviour when people deal with you online.

Above the Line Marketing Activity (Advertising)

Good advertising is a powerful way to differentiate products and services. But advertising is expensive – and it must be carefully controlled. Advertising guru Tim Bell, chairman of Chime Communications and formerly CEO of Saatchi & Saatchi, has advised the following steps:

- Set specific campaign objectives (building sales or market share).
- Decide strategy (budget, choice of media, geographic profile).
- Target audience (market segment, demographic profile).
- Decide advertising content (highlight specific product/service benefits).
- Be sure about execution and style (humour or hard sell?). For instance, ask yourself, if your product/service was a car or a newspaper, which kind of car (a Rolls-Royce, say, or a Mini) or which kind of newspaper (the *Sun*, perhaps or *The Times*) do you want to be seen as? In these examples, both the car brands are owned by BMW and both the newspapers by News International. The individual brands, however, appeal to very different markets!

In 1997, Karan Bilimoria decided that the time was ripe for Cobra Beer's first ever advertising campaign. At this point, Cobra was available in restaurants throughout the UK, and there was an exciting opportunity to raise mass awareness and to reinforce the loyalty of existing Cobra consumers.

Working with the agency Team Saatchi, Cobra's Marketing department created the character of 'Curryholic Dave' a curry addict who would become the new spokesman for the brand. The campaign was launched in February 1998. 'Dave' offered help and advice – such as a restaurant 'hotline' for vindaloo addicts – to other curry fans. 'Dave' never actually appeared, but the advertisements were hugely successful, winning major creative awards.

Table 9.1 Differences in Behaviour when Online

Physical world	Online world
'Oh look, the new Hotel Chocolat brochure has arrived'	'Don't e-mail me without my permission'
'No, I don't mind waiting'	'If something doesn't happen in 7 seconds, I'm clicking on to another site'
'Thanks, that information was very helpful'	'Let me see what other customers have said'
'Now that I'm here, it's not worth the effort of finding an alternative'	'The competition is only a click away'
'I'll pay now'	'I won't buy unless it's easy'
'Can I pay by credit card?'	'I don't trust you with my credit card details'

'Curryholics' was discontinued in 2000, when Karan felt that the campaign had achieved its aim of raising Cobra brand awareness. New campaigns followed, retaining a humorous edge, but more subtle in tone. In 2003, the Ingenious campaign was launched, with the aim of reinforcing Cobra's brand identity. The Cobra team had been aware for some time that aspects of Indian culture, especially the Bollywood film genre, were making big inroads into mainstream British culture. The Ingenious campaign was designed to exploit this. Cobra's Indian pedigree was celebrated and linked to surreal examples of Indian ingenuity, such as a carwash operated by elephants. This campaign has also garnered awards. Cobra's calculated image of difference from the pack has been cleverly reinforced by TV sponsorship deals, which position the brand as sophisticated and at the cutting edge.

Of course, advertising embraces a very wide range of different media, such as TV, radio, newspapers, magazines, the Internet, billboards, handbills and so on. As an extra dimension, many of these media will have 'channels' which are aimed at different markets. Taking newspapers and magazines as an example, it is easy to recognize that there are national newspapers, local press, publications aimed at a particular demographic segment (such as women's magazines) and trade press aimed at people who work in a particular industry.

Typically, the criteria which drive the cost of advertising are the size of the audience, the difficulty of reaching that audience through other means, and the spending power of that audience. So, national TV advertising is usually the most expensive form of advertising. But for the vast majority of growing businesses, the most cost-effective form of advertising is usually something more focused using local and/or trade-specific channels.

It is not always necessary to take professional advice from, for example, an advertising agency. On the other hand, such professionals will be able to help you determine the most suitable advertising mix for your business. They are particularly valuable if you plan a large-scale campaign involving significant expense. One key point that Cobra learned about working with advertising agencies is to set very clear goals for each campaign. It is a great deal easier, for both parties, if the mechanism is in place to judge the results!

Distribution

Distribution is all too often the poor relation in the marketing mix, unlike advertising and promotion, which traditionally are seen as glamorous and exciting. The consequence of this is that companies who think carefully about their distribution strategy often see opportunities that others overlook. Take the issue of market share, for example. When marketing professionals are set the challenge of growing market share, they typically approach it from two ends:

- Increasing product range through launching new products.
- And taking share from competitors.

Sometimes it may be smarter to look at distribution opportunities. Figure 9.1 is an example used by leading distribution consultancy Frank Lynn & Associates.

The (simplified) model in Figure 9.1 describes an industry where a business covers 50 per cent of the market with its products. These products are present in 25 per cent of the channels through which end users are reached, and four out of ten customers in these channels buy these products rather than those of competitors. The end result is a market share of 5 per cent ($100\% \times 50\% \times 25\% \times 40\%$).

Let us assume the aim is to increase market share, from 5 per cent to 7.5 per cent, that is to raise it by half as much again. One approach is to launch new products that address the 50 per cent of the market that the business does not currently serve. Holding the other key variables – presence and customer hit rate – constant, this could be achieved by launching new products that attack half of the market not already addressed. This would increase market coverage from 50 per cent to 75 per cent. The arithmetic then looks like this: $75\% \times 25\% \times 40\% = 7.5\%$ market share.

It could be that this is an untapped opportunity, but consider the following:

- In many, if not most, markets, new product failure rates are alarmingly high, certainly well over 50 per cent of all products launched.
- The business has no expertise in this area.
- Sales of the new products might (depending on the circumstances) cannibalize existing products.

Alternatively, we can go to the other end of the process and look at raising the customer 'hit rate'. Assume the goal is still to raise market share from 5 per cent to 7.5 per cent. That implies increasing the hit rate from four to six customers ($100\% \times 50\% \times 25\% \times 60\%$).

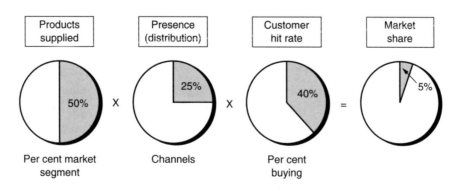

FIGURE 9.1 Distribution Model.

Four out of ten customers is already a high hit rate. How much will have to be invested in dealer discounts, special promotions, advertising campaigns and so on to gain those extra two customers?

Consider, instead, a strategy of improving channel distribution. Currently, in our example, that is only 25 per cent. To hit our market share target of 7.5 per cent, we need to achieve channel distribution of 37.5 per cent ($100\% \times 50\% \times 37.5\% \times 40\%$). That means broadening our channel distribution by 50 per cent – and we would still be covering fewer than half of the channels to the end user. In many markets this is a much more achievable target than either launching new products or increasing the customer hit rate – but it is surprising how often it is ignored by companies seeking to grow. All too often pricing is the factor identified by management as the key variable to address to improve market share, when in fact better distribution may provide the answer.

Improving the Effectiveness of the Sales Effort

Personal selling is the vital link in the communication process between company and customer, but as Professor Malcolm McDonald, the highly esteemed marketing academic and our former colleague at Cranfield, has observed, among other sins:

- Sales forces often display an alarming lack of planning and professionalism.
- They are frequently woefully unaware of which products and which groups of customers to concentrate on.
- And they lack knowledge of competitors' activity.

Studies have shown that if a salesperson's salary is, say, £50,000 p.a., the real cost to the company after travel, expenses and benefits, is frequently double that. Add sales administration support, and the real total cost is three times the salary. At the same time, less than a third of the typical salesperson's working day is spent in front of the customer. Hence, the need for responsible sales management able to:

1. set and monitor sales target achievement;
2. motivate, train and support the sales staff;
3. recruit and organize competent staff.

Setting and Monitoring Sales Targets

At the simplest level, setting sales targets may consist of ensuring enough sales to recover the salesperson's costs. To take our example of the salesperson costing £50,000: the salesperson's 'true' cost could well be £150,000. If the gross margin on the products sold is 50 per cent, then our salesperson needs to achieve a target of £300,000 just to cover the associated costs. One obvious conclusion that follows is that it pays to maximize the amount of time the sales force spend selling – yet in many businesses, as mentioned earlier, it could be as little as one-third of their salaried time, or even less. Expensive sales staff should not be spending their time in chasing unqualified leads or carrying out routine administration!

A common model adopted by many successful organizations to help their sales staff achieve their targets is to divide the selling effort into 'hunters' and 'farmers'. The hunters' role is to secure and nurture new business. The farmers' role is to take over the management of the account from the hunter, once the relationship with the customer is sufficiently established. The names indicate the different qualities required for each role: hunters are individuals who relish the challenge of being in the marketplace, are naturally competitive (and often aggressive) and can take rejection. Farmers, by contrast, are less motivated by doing deals, prefer a steady-state working routine and are happy to relieve the hunters of the routine administration that comes with selling. This kind of organization plays to people's natural preferences and helps to create effective teams who support each other. It also means that targets can be set and monitored partly on the basis of individual performance, and partly by team performance – which helps to build a sense of shared commitment and responsibility.

Sales Forecasting and Control

The best sales plans are developed from the ground up. However, your marketing analysis, and the sales and marketing plans that flow from it, tend to start at the macro level, that is to work top down. So, you will be working with:

- known industry or market segment growth rates;
- estimated market shares for yourself and your competitors;
- your own initiatives to maintain, grow or disengage from various market segments.

The task of the sales force is to turn what is a statement of intent into a detailed plan of action – and that is best built from the ground up, by looking at:

- sales by month;
- sales by individual customer account or group of customers;
- estimates of new business sales, again allocated to specific customers;
- resource needed to achieve this: people, budget, sales literature and so forth;
- and any other relevant metrics.

Sales forecasts targets that are arbitrarily imposed from the top are much less likely to be 'bought into' than sales forecasts that are built from the ground up, based on a frank exchange with the sales force. If you expect them to achieve last year's sales plus an extra 10 per cent, where exactly are the extra sales going to come from? Where are the opportunities? Where should they be focusing their efforts? And, if sales are not going to plan, is there an early-warning system in place to address the problem?

Cranfield graduate Harry Clarke has created a handy little estimating tool to predict sales at his telecommunications company, Cobalt Telephone Technologies. Keeping an eye on cashflow is always critical for a small business, but even more so when the funding is organic and the ability to borrow limited. Bitter experience had taught Harry that sales forecasting by its very nature tends to be overoptimistic. Over time, therefore, he developed the Cobalt cashflow estimator (Table 9.2) as his primary forecasting tool for new business. The spreadsheet asks three key questions when considering the new business pipeline:

1. What is the probability that this customer is going to buy anything (likelihood to buy)?
2. What is the probability that this customer will buy from Cobalt (… from Cobalt)?
3. If they do buy, when will they pay (when)?

In each step, a discount factor is applied to reflect the likelihood of the outcome. The actual timing of the payment is discounted to express the difference in value to the business of cash now, as opposed to cash in the future, even if it is only a week away. The value is free of discount factors only once it is actually in the form of cleared funds. It is a simple system, and Harry sees two major benefits from it:

1. It forces everyone to be realistic and rigorous about their assumption. (Note that the forecast actuals only produce a tenth of the apparent pipeline value.)
2. It proves uncannily accurate, not at the level of the individual project but when all the new business is taken together.

The estimating accuracy improved with time. Even today, when the business is less tight for cash, Harry continues to use this tool as a vital cash management discipline.

A company will also modify its sales forecasting in response to:

- known industry production and distribution capacity, with the effect of planned additions or deletions;
- the impact of seasonality and the effect of economic trends;
- the timing of any tactical promotional expenditure.

Assignment 9.1: Further Developing your Distinctiveness

Products/Service

1. Is your business still dependent on one product or service for over 80 per cent of profits?

TABLE 9.2 Example from the Cobalt Cashflow Estimator

Project	Value £k	Likeli-hood to buy	...from Cobalt	When Aug	Sep	Oct	Nov	?		Total discount factor	Forecast actuals
Port of Felixstowe	16	0.3	0.8			1			0.73	0.1752	£2,803.20
Cendant	40	0.2	0.1				1		0.66	0.0132	£528.00
Screwfix	80	0.6	0.2		1				0.81	0.0972	£7,776.00
NRC Phase 3	6	1	1	1					0.9	0.9	£5,400.00
British Benzol	20	0.1	0.3					1	0.5	0.015	£300.00
	162			0.90	0.81	0.73	0.66	0.50			£16,807.20

Customers

2. Do your top five customers still account for more than 50 per cent of your sales?
3. How do you measure customer satisfaction with the quality of your products and services?

Prices

4. When did you last increase your prices and by what per cent?
5. How do your prices compare with your major competitors?

Advertising and Promotion

6. What is the most cost-effective advertising/promotions medium for your business and why?
7. How much do you budget for advertising and how much for promotion activity?
8. When did you last have a press release and with what effect?

Distribution

9. Describe the distribution chain between you and the customer.
10. Do your customers and target market segments have easy access to your goods and services? How do you monitor this?

Sales Force Effectiveness

11. What targets are set for each salesperson and what incentive is there to achieve targets?
12. What was your achievement against sales forecast last year?

ten
How to Develop a Balanced Management Team

You will never have a great business without great people. Even if you have a unique strategy and the most carefully thought through plan, without great people, in the right jobs, you have very little chance of achieving your growth aims. Remember, regardless of the intentions expressed in the strategic plan, where you put your key people and money is the direction in which your organization is going to move. In addition, the quality of your people, particularly the management team, can add significant value to your business and is one of the key factors which influences potential investors and purchasers.

So, retaining and managing your people, and ensuring that they are well motivated and effective as a team, are some of the most critical aspects of any growth strategy.

Developing a balanced team will mean asking questions such as:

- How do I find the right people?
- How do I get them to deliver joined-up business results?
- How do I motivate and reward them all for today and for tomorrow's business?
- How do I assess whether the current team is working effectively together?
- How do assess whether this is the team to take the business forward?
- How do I get rid of 'traitors' and non-performers?

We will consider these factors in the following sections:

- recruitment and selection
- motivation and retention
- rewards and recognition
- performance management
- training and development
- building the team
- removing people.

Recruitment and Selection

To build a team, you are going to need some more and probably some different types of people. This will mean recruitment. In the very early stages of the business, most entrepreneurs have a very small team, primarily made up of people that they already know. As you set out on the path to growth, you will need to think more carefully about where you find the best people for your business and how to select them.

The problems of recruiting people for key roles can be a big worry for owner-managers and can place a major constraint on growth. Getting the right people takes time and money and requires considerable thought and effort, but remember, getting it wrong is even more costly for the organization. Most growing businesses have had some unsatisfactory experiences and many have made some spectacularly bad recruitment decisions. This is for all sorts of reasons. Recruitment takes time; it can take at least three to six months to find someone and at least the same time to see them integrated in the organization and performing at a fully productive level. Many owner-managers underestimate the time needed, which means that even the best of business plans may miss market opportunities because there just is not the resource internally. Another reason for failure is that although most owner-managers will think very hard about a capital investment decision such as buying a new piece of plant or equipment, they fail to see that recruitment is probably the most expensive decision to get wrong. Bear in mind that the costs of recruitment are typically at least four times salary and you will begin to see just how expensive failure can be. Think also of all the effort involved in recruiting someone only to find six months later that they are the wrong person for the job and you need to go through the same exercise all over again!

There will always be circumstances where recruitment needs to be undertaken at short notice (e.g. someone leaves unexpectedly). Nevertheless, wherever possible, the recruitment of key staff should be a planned activity, based on your growth requirements, rather than something that is left until the point at which current staff are so overloaded with work that you simply must recruit. Your business plan should enable you to identify the key staff and skills you are going to need and the time at which you are likely to need them.

Based on this staff plan, you can then provisionally plan when you need to start recruiting. You will need time to think about your requirements, to consider where to find the people, to advertise the position(s) if appropriate, to receive and review applications, to interview and select. And, of course, the person you offer the job to may well already be working for someone else, in which case they may have to work out their notice before joining you.

So the recruitment process is fraught with danger. However, you can increase the chance of success by putting in place some basic processes and disciplines which are likely to include:

- job descriptions
- person specification
- sourcing applicants
- interviewing your shortlist.

Job Descriptions

Before starting the actual recruitment for any job, it pays to develop a written job description for the role. Do not just give the job a name, such as sales manager, and expect that every potential applicant will know what you mean. Your interpretation may be very different from that of others. The job description should include the job title and overall purpose, key responsibilities, reporting lines, limits of accountability and main tasks. Do not attempt to make the job description comprehensive. You are not trying to include anything and everything the occupant is ever likely to do, merely to highlight the most significant responsibilities. Keep it short, down to a page if possible. Where you can, specify the outcomes you need rather than the inputs or tasks. Do not get too carried away in psycho-babble: keep it simple. 'To develop and roll out a conversion strategy of individual customer segments which maximize sales.' No! 'Produce a sales plan' might be better!

Person Specification

In addition to the job description, it is also good practice to have a person specification. This aims to set out the characteristics of the sort of person who you believe will be successful in the role. Once again, it is advisable to write this down rather than believe that you will know the person when you see them. The seven-point plan covers physical make-up, attainments, general intelligence, special aptitudes, interests, disposition and circumstances. It may also be beneficial to identify a minimum level and a preferred level for each of these areas. For instance, under experience, it may be a minimum requirement for the applicant to have worked in a similar role in another business, whereas the ideal would be for the person to have worked in a similar role in the same industry. The more specific you can be about your requirements, the better, since when you are advertising for the job this will help to reduce the number of inappropriate applications and aid in screening out unsuitable applicants.

It may be helpful to try out your person specification by writing down the characteristics of the sort of people who have previously been successful in your business. It is all too easy to assume you need things that you really do not. For example, you may write 'graduate needed'. Is this really the case? Have all the successful people you recruited been graduates? Why is this so necessary? So challenge your assumptions, remembering that many experienced recruiters will tell you to recruit for attitude rather than skill on the basis that you can impart skills but are unlikely to ever change people who do not fit your culture or have fundamentally the wrong attitude. Innovex is famous with its recruitment agencies for sending back many applicants who on paper look fine but who would not fit the culture: 'Just not Innovex people.' At the same time, beware of always looking for and recruiting more of the same. The last thing you want is to recruit clones of yourself!

Sourcing Applicants

The same is true in seeking potential applicants; most growing businesses rely on a very limited range of tried and tested methods. Research carried out by the MMA Group found that eight out of ten SME owner-managers prefer word of mouth recommendations for finding new employees. This may make sense but it can also mean you are not going to get anyone who will really break the mould. You may also be acquiring people with the bad habits ingrained by one of your competitors. You may need to be a little more creative and experimental to find great people. Consider your job description and person specification; how difficult is it going to be to find these types of people? Where are you likely to find them? What sort of publications will they read? Is it worth looking outside your own geographical area or approaching schools and universities? Recruiting via the web can be very powerful, although you may have your work cut out sifting through the rubbish! If you are going to use recruitment agencies, then think about the smaller boutique or one-man bands, with whom you can establish a long-term relationship, who will grow to know the kind of people you want and for whom your business is substantial enough to warrant them making an effort! They will be expensive, so make sure you get good value by really committing to an active partnership with them. Head hunters will be even more expensive – typically taking 30 per cent of the recruit's first-year salary and usually being interested only in appointments of at least £75,000 plus.

In both cases make sure you pick a recruiter who is active in your industry sector and can demonstrate their ability to attract the sort of people you are looking for.

Identify a range of different methods of sourcing applicants. You might consider:

- Speaking at local colleges, schools or chambers of commerce to let you audience know you are recruiting.
- Hosting work experience or student projects within your business.
- Using your website to advertise either specific appointments or an ongoing interest in hearing from potential recruits.

- Using local radio stations.
- Asking members of staff to recommend people they know.
- Making informal approaches to individuals you have met who impress you.
- Holding open days/evenings at your premises or in a hotel.
- Online advertising. Responses can be variable here. So before placing your ads, evaluate the various options and benchmark with other companies currently advertising on the sites. Typical sites include Monsterboard's (www.monster.co.uk), the *Guardian*'s recruitment site (www.jobsunlimited.co.uk) and www.fish4jobs.co.uk that brings together classified ads from local papers.

Interviewing Your Shortlist

Once you receive the applications, the next step is to select a shortlist. The job description and person specification will be the initial screening mechanisms. It is a good idea to get more than one person to read these, as subjective prejudices are bound to come into play and it is worthwhile to compare opinions.

You can then interview the shortlisted candidates. It is said that a typical manager takes only 45 seconds to decide whether an applicant is the right person for the job! Beware! The subjective view will always enter into the interview process, but take steps to keep it under control. This may be by using psychological or aptitude tests to provide another dimension or it may be by making sure that the person you like actually has a particularly tough interview.

There are aptitude tests for most types of role from secretary to sales manager. There are also hundreds of different types of psychometric tests that check for different things. Some are based on many years of rigorous research although others are less reliable and robust. Unfortunately, there is no policing body for psychometric testing at present. Most of the more reliable tests should be used only by a qualified or accredited person and we would recommend that you involve such a person if you intend to use one of these tests. You can find more about psychometric tests, and locate appropriate tests for your business, through the British Psychological Society (www.bps.org.uk) or the Chartered Institute of Personnel and Development (www.cipd.co.uk).

When you are interviewing, try to use behavioural questions. You will get truer answers and a better indication of what the applicant might do in the future. You might try: 'You say on your CV that you can manage teams. Can you give me an example of that?' 'What is the most difficult thing you have ever done?' 'What are you most proud of?' Often when candidates make a point of telling you that they are team orientated or strong leaders, they will turn out to be the exact opposite. The 'dynamic, high-achieving individual' will usually bear no relationship to the person sitting in front of you. By asking for examples or real evidence of that dynamism or those achievements, then you might start to get somewhere. Try to get applicants to tell you what they have achieved over and above the basic requirements of the job. Did they organize the company away-day or mentor someone? Did they develop a personal project or make a presentation to the board?

Generally, if you are doubtful about someone, then listen to those doubts, even if you cannot always articulate them properly. Contra-indicators, those little bits of behaviour which do not quite seem to fit what the CV or applicant is telling you, can be powerful signals that all is not well.

Other useful techniques to add objectivity to the interview process include:

- Inviting the applicant to undertake a short piece of work which is relevant to the job for which they are applying. For example, if you are looking for someone who can make client presentations ask them to give you a three-minute presentation on a given subject.
- Describing tricky scenarios which would typically happen in the job and asking the applicant to describe how they would deal with that scenario, preferably based on their own previous experience.
- Allowing the applicant time to meet other members of the team with whom they would be working who can often make a shrewd assessment of culture fit. Be careful though as existing managers may rule out individuals who look as though they could be a threat or are perceived as too challenging to manage!
- Involving more than one person in the interviewing for key management roles.
- Using your non-executive directors or some other impartial person who knows your business but does not actually work in it.

You will certainly want to have more than one interview with each candidate. Remember that your passion for taking pains with the recruitment process conveys a powerful message about the importance of people in your business.

One final word on interviewing: do not forget that you may have to sell the job to your preferred candidate – after all, if they are that good, they may well have other job offers! But beware creating unrealistic expectations and making promises that will come back to haunt you.

Having selected your preferred candidate, make sure that you check their references and their claims about past employment and qualifications. This sounds like such a straightforward and commonsense thing to do, and yet many growing businesses still do not do it and can get into an awful mess as a consequence. Nowadays, it is very unlikely that you will get anything in a written reference that is not a statement of bare fact about where X was employed, at what salary and for how many months. So, if you can, informally chat to previous employers or mutual acquaintances who know the individual and you may get a bit more of a feel for attitude and ability.

Assignment 10.1: Recruitment and Selection

1. What specific skills, attitudes and capabilities will the people in your business require for the future? Which of these are missing from the business currently and how will you obtain/develop these missing ones?
2. Draw up the organization chart for your business in three years' time. What are the key roles and who will fill them? Identify the roles for which you will need to recruit and when?
3. Draw up job and person specifications for each of the roles you need to fill in the next year and plan how you will recruit for them.

Motivation and Retention

Having got the right people the challenge is to keep them and keep them motivated. In most service-based businesses, in particular, all you have is your people, and demotivated people will walk. If morale and levels of job satisfaction are low, then performance will suffer, the business results will not be as good as they should be and, ultimately, people (usually the ones you really want to keep) will leave.

Let us look at some key areas under the following subheadings:

-   hygiene factors and motivators
-   attitude surveys
-   exit interviews.

Hygiene Factors and Motivators

Many owner-managers assume that money alone is the way to motivate and retain staff. But, as we have seen earlier, the motivating effect of a salary increase by itself is minor, short-lived and dependent on expectation rather than the actual amount. So, if you expected a salary increase of 5 per cent and this is what you got, then the effect is zero. If you expected 5 per cent and only received 3 per cent, then you will be demotivated. And, if you expected 5 per cent but received 8 per cent, then your job satisfaction and motivation will increase. But, unfortunately, this warm glow soon wears off.

Professor Frederick Hertzberg, an American professor of psychology, discovered that the factors which lead to job satisfaction were distinctly different to the factors which cause job dissatisfaction. His study of 200 engineers and accountants showed that five factors stood out as strong determinants of job satisfaction: achievement, recognition, responsibility, advancement and, of course, the attractiveness of the work itself. When the reasons for dissatisfaction were analysed they pointed to a different set of factors: company policy, supervision, administration, salary, working conditions and interpersonal relations. Hertzberg called these causes of dissatisfaction hygiene factors reasoning that the lack of hygiene will cause disease, but the presence of hygienic conditions will not, of itself, produce health.

So, lack of adequate job hygiene will cause dissatisfaction, but its presence will not create job satisfaction. It is the motivators, such as recognition, responsibility, achievement, etc., which do this. Both hygiene and motivator factors must be considered if you are to successfully motivate your people.

Many people would argue that you cannot actually motivate anyone, all you can do is to provide the conditions in which they can motivate themselves. But you can certainly stop demotivating your people!

Take Clive Woodward (former England rugby coach). He is modest about his motivational ability:

> I would never dream of trying to motivate people like Johnson, Dallaglio, Wilkinson. If you need to motivate people you have got the wrong people. What I can do is demotivate them, by allowing people in the changing room who are not of the same mindset. As the manager, I am just there to make sure that nothing is put in their way to stop them.

There are many non-monetary ways in which you can try to provide an environment which is motivating. First and foremost, give people motivating jobs and get out of their way!

Then think of:

- ensuring that everyone understands where the business is now and where it is going;
- consulting and involving employees in the business planning process, that so they feel much more valued;
- linking roles with company goals so that everyone can see how they can contribute;
- saying thank you for extra effort;
- creating a good working environment for all staff;
- providing new challenges;
- listening to ideas;
- having clear development plans and career paths for each member of staff;
- training and developing them;
- offering the opportunity to experience other areas of the business and other roles;
- getting everyone together for regular staff meetings, state of the nation talks, breakfast meetings;
- holding informal, social meetings (e.g. weekly visits to the pub, sporting activities);
- celebrating success!

Although good motivation and morale are often observable in the way your team works, it is good practice to have some more objective measures such as staff turnover rates, attitude surveys and exit interviews.

Attitude Surveys

If, every year or two, you carry out a simple internal survey of your team you will be able to pinpoint problem areas in the parts of your business that you cannot normally reach. In much the same way as you might survey customers to find out how happy they are with your products and services, you can survey your employees to find out just what they feel about the company, the management and their work. Attitude surveys provide an objective measure to counterbalance the more descriptive view obtained from hearsay and gossip. They also provide a useful way to benchmark morale year on year. You may also find that there are surprising differences in morale between different groups of employees, for example the top-level management team may be highly motivated, but second-tier sales or production managers much less so.

You may decide to start using attitude surveys because of a particular event or concern, such as staff turnover which is too high. Once started it makes sense to keep the practice up. At the very least, it demonstrates your concern for people and at best you will get some very useful information on how you can raise morale and remove obstacles to performance. Bear in mind that all attitude surveys tend to demonstrate an inexhaustible appetite for better communications! Nearly all employees believe that their boss knows much more than they are prepared to divulge. This phenomenon happens at all levels. The shop floor believes supervisors have secrets, supervisors believe managers withhold crucial information on plans that involve them, while those remaining managers know the directors are planning their future in secret. So, everyone becomes convinced there is a communication problem, because no one will tell them what is really going on. This may not be logical, but perception is all in business. Whether or not people's perceptions are right or wrong, they will behave accordingly. So the message is that you can never communicate too much!

You do not necessarily have to use external consultants to carry out an attitude survey, some ideas on a simple set of questions derived by Gallup, the market research and consulting organization, are given in Table 10.1 and you can find others in many places on the web, for example www.Zoomerang.com.

Exit Interviews

Of course, it is inevitable that some people will leave. Sometimes, these will be people that you would rather keep; on other occasions, you may be relieved to see them go. However, whichever way you look at it, losing people is expensive, can demotivate those remaining and can severely affect your ability to deliver the business plan. So it can be very useful to undertake an exit interview. The exit interview is a way of arranging for anyone leaving the company to be questioned by an impartial person who can establish

TABLE 10.1 Gallup Employee Attitude Survey

1.	I know what is expected of me at work
2.	I have the material and equipment to do my work right
3.	I have the opportunity to do what I do best every day
4.	In the last seven days I have received recognition or praise for doing good work
5.	My supervisor or someone at work seems to care about me as a person
6.	There is someone at work who encourages my development
7.	At work my opinions seem to count
8.	The mission or purpose of my company makes me feel my job is important
9.	My fellow employees are committed to doing quality work
10.	I have a best friend at work
11.	In the last six months someone has talked to me about my progress
12.	In the last year I have had opportunities to learn and grow at work

Rate your answers from 1, do not agree to 5, fully agree.

the real reason why. For example, is that person leaving for more money, because of a better opportunity or because they feel frustrated? Do they feel that you made promises that were not kept? Were they unable to get on with their manager or colleagues? Do they feel that your business is going nowhere?

A survey by the CIPD found that, at 44 per cent, promotion was more important than pay (39 per cent) in an employee's reasons for leaving, and at 37 per cent, lack of development and career activities was not far behind.

Most people in these circumstances are quite happy to talk freely and you can learn a great deal, which should help you improve things for other employees and ensure that your future recruitment and retention is more successful. It is always worth remembering that an ex-employee leaving in a good state of mind is much less likely to be disgruntled and much more likely to become a positive ambassador, or even a future client for your company.

Rewards and Recognition

Earlier on, we noted that what gets measured gets done. What gets rewarded gets done again. Getting your reward systems right can be crucial to moving your business in the right direction. Unfortunately, you will never find the right solution. As you go through various Greiner growth phases, the behaviours you need for success will change and therefore so should the rewards. As we have already noted, for many key staff in growing businesses, money is not the primary motivation. If it were, they would most probably be working in larger companies, which usually pay better. Provided the money is adequate, these people place great value on job satisfaction and the opportunity to make progress and build their career portfolio. It is in these two areas that the smaller, growing business may well have an advantage over bigger, more bureaucratic organizations. In other words, you have to pay enough to keep your people but, if you have done the types of things mentioned below to help them feel valued and motivated, then you should not have to pay over the odds.

So, rather than considering financial reward as the primary way to spur people on to greater performance, you should perhaps think of it as part of an overall rewards and recognition system which may include some or all of the following:

- Pay at least the going rate for the job/skill in your market and geographic area.
- Ensure that your pay system distinguishes good performers from poor performers.
- Reward little and often and use both monetary and non-monetary rewards.
- Have team-based rewards as well as individual ones.
- Make performance awards visible, for example by putting people's pictures on notice boards and internal publications or by using badges.
- Use excellence awards.
- Use rewards such as tickets for the theatre or sporting events, gift vouchers, extra holidays, etc.
- Recognize good performers in front of their peers. This could be as simple as saying 'Well done!' when other people are listening.
- Recognize that employees have a life outside work. For example, when a person works late it is not just that individual who is making a sacrifice but also the individual's family. A small gift to acknowledge this can make a big difference to how that individual and their family view the company.

Saltire Taverns

Bartenders come, and bartenders go, but Edinburgh-based Saltire Taverns makes everyone seem like family. The 60 full-time staff receive quarterly and annual sales bonuses, but the 240 part-time and temporary staff also have bonus schemes. Bar staff get involved in various sales-based incentive schemes, some run by the firm, others by suppliers. Prizes include dinners for two or bottles of wine. The firm also takes its best-performing staff across all the bars on big nights out to celebrate. There are seven pubs in the business, and the biggest one employs 90 people and has a turnover of £3 million. Three of the pubs (in Aberdeen, Glasgow and Edinburgh) are Frankenstein themed, and this also leads to staff and management merriment. Every full moon, the bar staff and management dress up in horror costumes in the bars. Everyone has a great time – and it is great for business.

As the business grows, and particularly as you start to put in place a management team, it is likely that the recognition and reward package will need to be slanted more towards encouraging:

- A sense of ownership and commitment to the business. Give people either equity or a profit share or both.
- Participation in the decision-making process. Do not be autocratic.
- Complex and challenging roles. Even with good pay, senior people get bored.
- Status. Some people might call them ego perks but they are quite important.

The first point – some sort of ownership – can be one of the easiest (or most difficult) to address. An incentive scheme is simple but make sure the individual's goals are aligned with those of the company. More attractive still is a stake in the actual business. Even though equity may be made available to all staff, it will be particularly meaningful for senior staff, who are more likely to have the money, knowledge and inclination to get a meaningful return from an exit. Options for your key players can also be attractive and can help to tie them in to your business.

Assignment 10.2: Motivation, Retention, Recognition and Rewards

1. What is your staff turnover rate and how does it compare with that of your competitors?
2. Carry out a staff attitude survey.
3. Review your approaches to rewarding, recognizing and motivating people.

What can you do to make your business an even better place to work?

Performance Management

Setting the Scene

So you have recruited great people and you are retaining, motivating and rewarding them. Is that it? Well, only if you are running an employee holiday camp! Your investment in people is an investment in delivery and that is exactly what they are there to do. Performance management is the way you align individuals with the organizational goals and track performance on a consistent basis. Gaining alignment starts with the vision and then cascades this down into objectives, action plans and outcomes. But, as Figure 10.1 shows, we must remember that is only half the story.

Although the left side of this figure provides us with the 'what' of performance management, it is the right side which gives us the 'how', and of course it will only happen if the performance you are asking for aligns with what people believe and what they are prepared to do. Whatever you say about key results, goals and measures, it is values which will drive behaviour. So it is vitally important that you translate the vision into the desired values and behaviours which will make it happen. For example, your sales

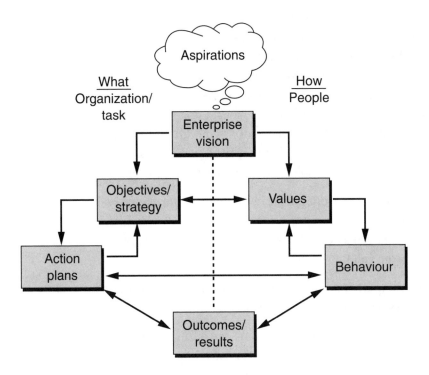

FIGURE 10.1 Aligning People and Strategy.

director, Brian, knows the strategy well, has all the qualities to perform excellently, but time and time again you get frustrated by his lack of teamwork and respect for others on the management team. Yet you know that teamwork is essential for the strategy to be a success. So either the need for teamwork is not clear to all your management team or Brian will never be an effective member of your top team and the sooner you face this the better.

The art of management is a three-stage performance feedback loop: set objectives, monitor how people are getting on and review their performance against the original objectives. It is about driving strategic goals through to performance that is measurable at individual and team level.

For this you need:

■ vision and key performance measures
■ goals and targets
■ performance reviews
■ regular appraisals.

Vision and Key Performance Measures

Performance management starts with being able to communicate your business vision and purpose and to break this down into a handful of key strategic areas. For example, the vision might be 'To be the automatic choice of first-tier investment banks who want to improve operational risk and business efficiency'. The key strategic goals for the next year might be to sell X *change* projects to the top 50 banks and to develop a further risk practice. The critical functions could be sales, delivery and the retention of key staff. Your challenge is how to translate these requirements into individual roles and goals so that everybody knows what they have to do. As we have said before, without clarity of individual roles and job specifications you cannot recruit the right people, but worse than that you cannot define what they need to do or hold them accountable for either!

This then leads to a whole host of management problems for you:

- When you confront people about poor performance and they deny it what do you do next?
- How do you assess who will or will not make the grade?
- How do you know who deserves to be paid more?

In defining what needs to be done you will have some key performance measures for the business as a whole. Obvious examples would be:

- about your customers, i.e. revenue and profit growth, market share and customer retention, high scores on client satisfaction;
- about financial growth, i.e. ROCE, gross margin and cash;
- about people, i.e. improve retention rates, upgrade skills, increase innovation, invest in training, create a younger management team;
- about internal processes, i.e. reduce the percentage of indirect costs, improve quality control, improve supplier lead times.

Goals and Targets

Taking the above example: what will be the role and specific goals of your key salespeople in achieving customer key performance measures? Do you want them to penetrate existing accounts more deeply, or to open new accounts? Will they be accountable for sales and profit growth?

Once you have decided what needs to be done and what the role is, you can go about defining the measures of performance. These should be easy to understand, open to only one interpretation, objectively determined and easy to remember.

Measures of performance for the salesperson might be the pipeline – the percentage of new customers – or it might be the number of new accounts opened. You might decide that sales coverage is the most important thing and therefore the salesperson should be tasked with carrying out x customer visits a day, an important metric if x visits translates into y new customers.

Now you are in a position to set targets! To be effective, goals should follow the SMART format. This means they should be: specific, measurable, achievable, results oriented and time sensitive. In this case, for example, an annual target for your salesperson might be to win ten new accounts in the year, each of more than £50,000 revenue at a gross margin of 35 per cent in your target market sector.

Finding the right amount of stretch for growth is crucial. If goals are too easy they do not boost performance. Goals need to challenge the individual, to be attainable, but only with considerable effort. Try not to overdo the financial goals at the cost of a balanced score card which includes all the other key constituents such as customers, employees, internal processes and perhaps also community relationships and brand and image.

Performance Reviews

Now you have the bones of a performance management system: the vision, key measures and goals. All that remains is to manage people! This entails cascading goals throughout the organization and regularly reviewing performance through both individual one-to-ones and team meetings and reviews. The frequency of the reviews will depend on how long employees have been with the business and how capable they are. For new employees, you might want a one-to-one review every month, for more experienced people every two months. These reviews should take the form of 'How are you doing and what can I do to help you perform?' sessions lasting no longer than 30 minutes or so and focusing on performance gaps and how to close them. Employees have a much larger desire for feedback on their performance than you might realize. For example, a study was carried out showing that of course people like to be praised for good work, but they also prefer being ruthlessly held accountable rather than being ignored. It is also useful to structure the discussion along the lines of 'What can you start doing?', 'What should you stop doing?' and 'What should you continue doing?'

You will probably need weekly progress checks, perhaps in the form of regular management meetings, to keep tabs on team performance as well as key individuals. In summary, beware the most likely roadblocks to effective performance management:

- lack of clear-cut responsibilities;
- lack of a tracking system;
- lack of accountability;
- lack of commitment and buy-in;
- ineffective communication;
- too many goals which are financially driven;
- goals that do not relate to the long-term vision;
- lack of time and resources;
- focusing on too many or too few goals;

Regular Appraisals

Performance appraisal is the central pillar of performance management. The CIPD performance management survey carried out in 2004 found that 65 per cent of organizations used individual annual appraisal, 27 per cent used twice-yearly appraisals and

10 per cent used rolling appraisals. The CIPD web site will help you identify the right process for you (www.cipd.co,uk).

If you have a sound performance management system and frequent performance reviews then the year-end appraisal should not come as a great surprise. It should be analogous to the balance sheet, which is an annual summary at a point in time of what the monthly management accounts have already covered.

Appraisal lies at the heart of managing performance and developing potential for the future of the business. However, to be an effective tool, appraisal needs to be approached seriously and professionally by all involved.

In its early days, Innovex had a fairly half-hearted appraisal system. It was very difficult to hold people accountable and consequently poor performance was often tolerated. The management team agreed that 'The key is to look hard at our people, look hard and develop.' The mechanism for doing this was appraisal. Innovex put all its managers and secretaries through appraisal interview training, took a good look at its appraisal system and revamped it to become a central and effective part of how the business is run.

Some of the characteristics of effective appraisal are:

- It becomes a talk between people who work together rather than a school report.
- Both appraiser and appraisee prepare in advance and then compare and discuss.
- The appraisee does most of the talking!
- The discussion is results orientated rather than personality orientated.
- The appraisal discussion is kept separate from salary review.
- The conversation starts with performance and only later moves on to career ambitions.
- The appraisal format is a narrative rather than a ratings process.
- Plenty of time is allowed for each appraisal interview (1.5 hours average).
- Appraisals are carried out at least once a year.
- Training needs are identified and acted upon by those concerned.
- Actions are agreed and they happen.

It is usually helpful to have an appraisal form to structure and record the conversation, but not essential. Below, as an alternative, is the letter one owner-manager wrote summarizing the issues and actions discussed with one of his managers:

To: Harry Summers
      Production Manager

10 March 2006

Dear Harry

Re: Performance review

Your progress over the last six months has been varied. I know that for a period of time you were not enjoying the role and this may account for this apparent inconsistency. It appears that a problem arose in dealing with poor performance. This was identified as a priority at your last appraisal; however, neither Joe nor Alan were tackled with any conviction. Concerns over Alan's performance were brought to your attention on numerous occasions and were only finally addressed once you discovered that he was apparently deceiving you. What is interesting is that this issue appears to have been somewhat of a turning point for you. Taking on the purchasing function and supplier negotiation has brought about a new lease of life and you are now very happy in your role. You have secured cost reductions, implemented supply agreements and created significant clarity about the purchasing function. You have demonstrated a high level of flexibility in responding to this change and I believe you have acted with total integrity. I also believe that you have learnt some very important lessons about dealing with poor performance.

The performance of the production team is quite mixed although significant improvements were made in the last quarter. What I am interested to see is how both you and Kevin tackle the process of beating the new targets and how any inconsistent performance is handled.

We agreed that 'excellence' did not mean 'working hard or 'trying to do the best job' – what it actually means is 'doing the best job' and 'not letting underperformers get in your way'. We also discussed that to be able to 'do the best job' meant being in the right job in the first place, i.e. one where you have both the skill and the aptitude. You have identified that procurement and supplier management is a possible career route for you and, based on your performance so far, I would agree wholeheartedly. I suggest that we scope out a potential new role for you over the coming months.

Thank you for the contribution you have made over the last six months and the flexibility you have demonstrated.

Assignment 10.3: Performance Management

1. Ensure that you have goals, performance measures and targets for all key roles in the business.
2. If you do not do them already, set up performance reviews and appraisals with your management team and ensure that they do reviews and appraisals with their reports.

Training and Development

Investing in Training

Investing in training your people is the quickest way to add value to your business. A business which has highly trained and motivated staff will always command a higher price than one in which the acquirer has to bring in his or her own management team. Of course, it takes time, money and effort, but for exactly that reason your investment in people cannot be quickly replicated by competitors and is therefore an important aspect of your differentiation and competitive edge.

Training ensures customer satisfaction, high standards and improved performance.

Ritz-Carlton has extraordinarily high customer satisfaction ratings, 92 per cent across the chain, compared with an industry average of 70 per cent. It is no coincidence that it also has industry-leading levels of training. For example once hired, new employees receive two full days' induction before starting work and are then guaranteed to receive 250–300 hours of structured training in their first year.

Training can also play an important part in retaining and motivating your staff since it demonstrates your commitment to them. Nothing is more important to most individuals than learning, acquiring experience and sharpening their skills. Your aim should be to build their worth both to your business and to themselves. Some short-sighted employers ask: 'Why train them when they will leave and it is all for someone else's benefit?' Answer: it costs 2 per cent of salary to train them, which is less than 10 per cent of the costs of their mistakes. And, once trained, who knows, they may even get enough job satisfaction to want to stay – just think how much you will save if that happens.

Jamie Paterson of Paterson Printing has built a highly successful business in a very difficult marketplace. He has done this by cascading training down through the organization. He himself went on the BGP at Cranfield. Since then, he has sent his top team on further Cranfield programmes. As this team grew, it in its turn coached and developed the next level down and sent them off on the same programmes! This way the whole organization has grown itself up the Greiner growth curve, the MD becoming the coach of the senior team and the senior team coaching the second-tier team. This has built a depth of management resource and a great team feeling. Everyone speaks the same language and shares the same goals. And they know they are important to the business!

In order to share, refine and get buy-in to the strategic plans, Jamie then took the training in-house using an external consultant to facilitate a whole series of internal workshops: longer ones for the senior staff who were shaping the strategy, shorter lunchtime sessions for all the works staff, who needed to understand what the new strategy meant for them and to feel that they had been actively involved.

In addition, training can be one of the fastest payback routes to cost reduction. Yes, you may lose some of the people you train, but you will lose them a lot quicker if you do not train them! So what if some of them eventually leave, think how favourably disposed they will be towards your business.

Smaller businesses are notoriously bad at investing in training of any type. Only 13 per cent invest five days or more in training in any one year. Amateur football teams spend more time in training than the average growing business! So, it is hardly surprising that few teams in these businesses ever realize their true potential, or come anywhere near becoming professionals.

Yet all the evidence is that training pays a handsome and quick return. In the study 'Taking people seriously: do SMEs treat HR management as a vital part of their competitive strategy?' (Cranfield Working Paper) undertaken by Colin Barrow, Lesley Mayne and Chris Brewster in 1997, smaller businesses were clustered into four categories according to the rates of sales and profit growth: businesses in decline were those where sales and profits were both dropping; unprofitable growers were those where sales were growing but profits were not; profit enhancers were those whose profits were growing on static sales figures; and the final group, called champions, were those in which sales and profits were both growing. The study compared businesses that invested significantly in people and training with those that did not. Virtually no businesses in the former category were in decline and the majority were either champions or profit enhancers. Those businesses that did not invest in people, by contrast, were most likely to be in decline or unprofitable growers. The message from the study was clear: champions and profit enhancers invest in their people.

If owner-managers are reluctant to invest in training in general, then they are even less likely to invest in training and developing themselves. And yet, investment in the development of the owner-manager is perhaps the quickest way of obtaining a return from training. In a different study, we compared businesses where the owner-manager has taken part in the BGP with a sample drawn from over 30,000 independent businesses, mostly with a turnover of between £1 million and £9 million.

The results were striking. Over the two years which were studied, the businesses which participated in BGP

- grew sales by 54 per cent (compared with the average of the sample which grew by just under 12 per cent);
- almost doubled their profitability (measured in terms of return on shareholders' funds) while the average business made only a marginal improvement.

Identifying Training Needs

It is inevitable as the business grows that, through no fault of their own, people's knowledge and skills, which were once adequate, become inappropriate for the next phase of growth. One option is to get rid of people with obsolete skills and bring new ones in. But this is both extremely expensive and time-consuming and very disruptive to your team identity and culture. Clearly, a preferable option is to keep training and developing your existing people.

Think about the knowledge levels of your staff and their attitude towards the business as shown in Figure 10.2. You can happily delegate to those who have the right knowledge and the right attitude. Those who are skilled but who currently have a negative attitude you can attempt to motivate. People with neither a positive attitude nor the necessary skills you should get rid of. The rest can benefit from training. Indeed, sometimes it is well worth being prepared to recruit people who have no knowledge but a very positive attitude as you can train them to do things your way.

Most of us are not good at defining our own training needs. It is therefore essential to spend time identifying training needs for your team, for each key individual and also for yourself. Training needs are the gap between performance now and the performance you require both now and in the future. Perhaps you have previously employed people for their immediate skills/job knowledge, but now feel that you have to develop their interpersonal and people-management skills. The appraisal interview provides one good opportunity for identifying training needs; another approach is to carry out a training needs analysis. This analysis depends on interviewing members of staff to determine key issues such as their background, role, skills needed in the job, strengths and weaknesses, and career aspirations. A good analysis will also include a discussion

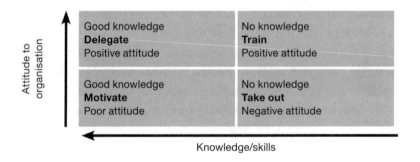

FIGURE 10.2 The Role of Training.

Table 10.2 An Example of a Training Menu

Technical/job related	Accounting or sales skills
	Negotiation skills
	Computer skills
Management skills	Leadership and motivation
(existing and potential managers)	Team building
	Appraising, counselling and disciplinary interviews
	Managing change
	Recruitment and selection
	Training and developing staff
Business	Basic finance
	Principles of marketing
	Putting together the business plan
	Understanding strategy

of changing business requirements and the gap between these demands and present capability. Table 10.2 gives an example of a training menu resulting from a training needs analysis.

Choosing the Right Training

The choices available to you in terms of training programmes are enormous. Some of these are described below.

On-the-Job Training

This is where people learn how a job should be done from someone more experienced – in effect, sitting next to Nelly. The advantages are that there are no direct training costs and no time away from work. The learning should also be immediately relevant to the individual's needs. However, the learning experience is only as good as the trainer and, if they are themselves untrained, you could end up simply replicating poor working standards.

In-house Classroom Training

This is the most traditional and familiar form of training. Some, or all, of your employees gather in a classroom either on your premises or in a local hotel. You hire in a trainer or use one of your own experienced staff. This method provides plenty of opportunity for group interaction and the instructor can motivate the class and pay some attention to individual needs. The disadvantages, particularly if it is held away from your premises, are that you can incur large hotel costs, and it can be time-consuming and difficult to release a number of employees at the same time.

Public Courses

These are less expensive than tailor-made training. Most public courses are generic and some of the other attendees are likely to come from big business or the public sector. Generally, external training of this kind is most useful if it is related to a clearly identified individual training need and if, on the individual's return, the immediate line manager takes a real interest in what has been learnt.

Interactive Distance Learning

This kind of training can be delivered by a combination of traditional training materials, teleconferencing, and Internet and email discussions. You miss out on the personal contact, but the costs are much lower than traditional training. It has been particularly effective in such areas as compliance training and health and safety training. A good starting point for what is on offer is Learndirect (www.1earndirect.co.uk).

Off-the-Shelf Training Programmes

These come in packaged kits, which may consist of a training manual, video or a CD. Once again, the cost is lower than for face-to-face training, but you miss out on a professional trainer's input. You also miss out on the buzz and culture-building aspect of bringing a group of people together for their training.

Colleges

Many universities and business schools now offer programmes tailored for the needs of growing businesses. They are usually delivered by professional instructors who understand the needs of growing businesses. They are relatively expensive but can often be very effective.

Government Initiatives

Governments have an interest in encouraging training in smaller businesses. As well as providing information on where their training schemes are being run, governments often provide training grants to help with the costs. In the UK, Business Link (www.businesslink.gov.uk) and in the US the Small Business Administration (www.sba.gov) are the relevant agencies.

Induction Training

Do also bear in mind that the most critical time to train is when someone has just joined you. At this point they offer you a clean slate, a once in a lifetime opportunity to get some powerful messages across before internal politics start to interfere! Evidence suggests that inductions can cut staff turnover by as much as 25 per cent. When you consider the full costs of replacing staff, the case for induction is compelling. There are, of course, other benefits, such as the transmission of the company's culture and vision, strengthening the brand by getting all employees singing from the same hymn sheet, improved feelings of involvement and better labour relations.

SAP UK, the software company, attributed its fast-growth success to a particular attitude. 'We pride ourselves on being bright, innovative, informal and anti-hierarchical', said the then HR manager, Anne-Marie Elliott.

The company ran a five-day induction course every six weeks for groups of between 10 and 20 new employees. All departments and all grades received exactly the same treatment. Day 1 kicked off with an informal introduction to the company, followed by a seminar with the MD, who talked about the vision, but also listened to the new employees talking about themselves. This was followed in the afternoon by an introduction to the human resources department and a talk by the sales director.

Subsequent days dealt with in-house technology such as e-mail systems, the nature of the highly specialized products they sold, plus nitty-gritty issues such as expenses, pensions, etc. The high spot of the course came on Friday afternoon when the whole company gathered for tea and cakes to welcome the newcomers and watch a video they had made about how they had felt about joining the company.

Coaching, Mentoring and Other Ways

Think also about using coaching and mentoring This can be a powerful and cost-effective way of helping key individuals to improve interpersonal skills and find ways of becoming more effective in their jobs. You can encourage your own more experienced staff to mentor new recruits. This is a great way of growing their leadership skills and looking after and encouraging joiners when it really matters, in the first few months. In the case of yourself or more senior people you may want to get an external mentor or 'wise friend' who will provide impartial support, hold up a mirror to you, give unconditional feedback, remind you of your successes as well as the failures and, not least, hold you accountable for what you said you were going to do! It can be lonely on your own.

Training does not always mean formal classroom training. There are many other small ways in which you can provide experiences to grow your people without sending them on courses. For example, you might want to think about:

- work assignments that shadow more experienced colleagues;
- asking an individual to present a paper to your board;
- sending a less experienced person to make a presentation to a client or an outside group that a more experienced person would usually do;
- job swapping, if only for a short time (BP used to insist that all senior managers spent some time manning the pumps);
- sideways moves into other departments and functions;
- training the trainers, building a raft of internal people who can train others.

Assignment 10.4: Training and Development

1. Develop a training and development plan for key individuals (including your-self!) and roles, and identify ways of delivering these needs.

Building the Team

In the early stages, the business is likely to consist of just a few people who started the business together. The entire management team would probably fit easily on the back of a donkey on Scarborough beach, or in a phone box without too much of a squash! They share the same values, like each other and probably meet informally in pubs and each others' houses. However, as the business grows, the owner-managers recognize that they cannot do all the work and make all the decisions. So new layers of management are created and new people joining do not always have the same values as the founders. Such groups can achieve much more if they perform as a team rather than as a higgledy-piggledy group. A great team will always beat a bunch of great individuals, and a highly effective team makes for a more valuable business.

Moving from a loose grouping of people who work closely together towards a more formal team structure can seem a big step. It certainly implies that decisions will be made more collectively rather than being reserved for the founding directors or part-ners. Recognizing and accepting this shift can be one of the most difficult challenges for those who started the company in its more buccaneering days.

What makes an effective team – that is a group of people united by a common pur-pose? Well, first off you cannot have an effective team without a shared vision. Team members also need to share a common language, not only in the obvious sense but also in the day-to-day business vocabulary they use. One of the advantages of train-ing your team is that you create this common vocabulary; an example might be when everyone knows about Belbin, they understand the Greiner stages of growth and they know what you mean when you talk about the business plan, ROCE and margins. You need balanced team roles and you need compatible personalities. This does not mean that everyone has to like each other. But perhaps they do need to respect each other or at least appreciate what the other person brings to the party. Mature teams do not need to consist of clones – all the same and all cosy with each other; in fact, that would be a recipe for disaster! *Vive la différence* – an effective team wants a mix of roles and a mix of personalities. Conflict can breed creativity, and sometimes the person who is a maverick can bring a lot to the team. We remember hearing one exasperated MD saying of his prima donna sales director 'I wish I had two of them, then at least I could fire one!'

Sometimes one of the most immediate and powerful ways of creating a team is to find an enemy, hopefully one outside, not within, your business! An external threat, such as a competitor, can really pull people together. Think of Pepsi taking on Coca-Cola, or Komatsu with their vision of 'Encircle, squash, kill Caterpillar'.

Finally, teams need leaders and leaders need followers. One owner-manager asked us to take away his management team and bring them back when we had trained them to be effective! Unfortunately, it does not work like this, a management team is not like having a dog that you can send away for training; hands-on leadership goes with the territory.

One thing we do know about great teams is that they do not happen by chance. This does not work for a football team and it will not work for you either. To build a team you have to work at it, getting on better with each other does not on its own improve performance.

Some of the core issues in building a management team are:

- vision and values
- size
- team roles
- leadership
- cross-functional issues
- stage of development.

Vision and Values

The more strongly you articulate your business culture, the way we do things around here, the more likely you are to hold teams together. So what are your five or six core values, which you expect everyone to buy in to? The whole management team needs to live these values, by demonstrating them every day in their actions and behaviours.

Size

There is no perfect size for a team, but as a rule of thumb around eight people is probably the optimum size for getting full involvement but still being able to make effective decisions. More than this and your decision-making may get cumbersome, less and you will miss the healthy interplay of ideas. When you start to introduce more formal methods of communication – such as team briefings, state of the nation addresses, company get-togethers and workshops – give some thought to the size of the audience. It will be well worth remembering that in any audience of more than eight or so, you will get very little participation unless you break people into smaller syndicate groups where they will feel more like contributing and less inhibited.

Team Roles

The temptation is to build a management team whose members are just like the founders. Big mistake! The last thing you need is a lot of people just like you. One of your most important deciding factors should be the commitment and motivation of those who join the management team. These factors can very often compensate for specific skills weaknesses that you can graft on later. They can be the best individuals in the world, but if they do not really buy in to what you are trying to do then you are heading for trouble.

A good way of building the team is to ensure that you have a balanced mix of people who not only like certain team roles but are good at them. These could include developing ideas, networking, chairing meetings, making things happen or ensuring that projects are completed to standard. The work of Professor Belbin has shown that teams with a mix of abilities and characteristics consistently outperform high-ability teams across a range of exercises. So if you need this mix of skills and roles, who have you got in the team at present and who should be in your team?

Belbin suggests that a successful team needs a mix of eight roles, described in Table 10.3. Completing the Belbin profiles and mapping the scores of your team members will give you powerful information on whether or not you have a balanced team and what to do about it. (The Belbin Self Perception Inventory is available from www.belbin.com.) Scores are mapped against a table of norms and can then be plotted on one sheet that gives you a clear snapshot of the team.

The table of norms identifies scores as low, average, high and very high in terms of whether or not those are the preferred roles of the individuals you are looking at. Remember there are no right answers and no one label is any better than the others – it is the balance in the team which matters. You may find that your team is full of shapers – a recipe for energy but also anarchy! Or you may find that you have lots of ideas people, plants, but no implementers to actually get the job done!

TABLE 10.3 Belbin's Team Profiles

Chairman/coordinator Stable, dominant, extrovert Concentrates on objectives Does not originate ideas Focuses people on what they do best	**Implementer/company worker** Stable, controlled Practical organizer Can be inflexible but likely to adapt to established systems
Plant Dominant, high IQ, introvert A 'scatterer of seeds', originates ideas Misses out on detail Thrustful but easily offended	**Monitor evaluator** High IQ, stable, introvert Measured analysis not innovation Unambitious and lacking enthusiasm Solid, dependable
Resource investigator Stable, dominant, extrovert Sociable Contacts with outside world Salesperson/diplomat/liaison officer Not original thinker	**Team worker** Stable, extrovert, low dominance Concerned with individuals' needs Builds on others' ideas Cools things down
Shaper Anxious, dominant, extrovert Emotional, impulsive Quick to challenge and respond to challenge Drives action Competitive Intolerant of woolliness and vagueness	**Completer finisher** Anxious, introvert Worries over what will go wrong Permanent sense of urgency Preoccupied with order Concerned with 'following through' Committed to accuracy Ensures deadlines are met

One so-called team, which shall remain nameless, asked us to work with them on a team-building exercise. They were a large media conglomerate with powerful managing directors of stand-alone geographical businesses. The new group MD was trying to bring them all together and get them to work as a team. Given the make-up of his team (see Figure 10.3) what do you reckon to his chances?

The group MD (DR) is himself a very high 'plant' or creative thinker, with an equally high score as 'completer/finisher'. His leadership score on 'shaper' is low, therefore a role best avoided, and his score on 'coordinator/chairman' is average. This means he could move into the 'coordinator/chairman' role if other members of the team allow him to. Not very likely! His five MDs are all very high 'shapers' with off the chart low scores as 'teamworkers'! They are not creative thinkers ('plant'), like DR, and neither are they particularly strong 'implementers' or 'completer finishers.' They are what they appear to be, pushy driving bosses of independent businesses with plenty of resources to get the job done who see no reason to work together.

A team destined not to succeed! So, it proved – the group MD left soon after. We hope to a role which suited him better.

Leadership

Who should lead the leadership team? The answer seems obvious: the MD or senior partner. But that person may be temperamentally unsuited to doing this. For example, in one team the owner-manager MD had such a dominant personality that it prevented the rest of the team from functioning at its best. In another case, the MD just got bogged down and was incapable of taking a tough stance in resolving team conflicts. As long as the business grows, it does not really matter who does what, as long as we match the roles to the people best suited to them. So a powerful owner-manager who is strongly technically based may conclude that he or she would be much better to become technical director and appoint someone else as MD. One of the great and welcome surprises of growing a business is that you do not have to do it all yourself and you can and should shape your role to play to your strengths and your inclination.

In an effective team, of course, leadership is also shared among the team members.

Cross-functional Issues

Building a strong team is great, but not if it means that other teams within the same organization become the enemy! Effective teams consist of people who are interdependent. Creating and managing these interdependencies can take a huge amount of time and effort. For too long, we have thought in terms of functional silos: chimneys of sales, marketing, technical, admin and accounting. It is no use each of them being a strong team if they fail to work constructively with their colleagues in other functions, or in other geographic areas. This demands clarity of roles and joined-up delivery, where everyone is focused, targeted and rewarded on delivery to the customer. Too often

Team-role profile

ABC Company Ltd

Name ....

	Roles best avoided			Roles able to be assumed				Natural roles				Roles and descriptions team-role contribution	Allowable weaknesses
	0	10	20	30	40	50	60	70	80	90	100		
	JM	RG		CH	PL		BB			DR (circled)		Plant: creative, imaginative unorthodox. Solves difficult problems.	Weak in communicating with and managing ordinary people.
		SL / JH			RI		DR (circled)	CH	BB	RG	RG	Resource investigator: extrovert, enthusiastic, communicative. Explores opportunities. Developes contacts.	Loses interest once initial enthusiasm has passed.
		CH				CO		JH / BB	SL			Coordinator: mature, confident and trusting. A good chairman. Clarifies goals, promotes decision-making	Not necessarily the most clever or creative member of a group
		DR (circled)			SH			SL	RG SL	CH BB JH		Shaper: dynamic, outgoing, highly strung. Challenges, pressurizes, finds ways round obstacles.	Prone to provocation and short-lived bursts of temper.
		RG / BB		CH		ME				JH		Monitor evaluator: sober, strategic and discerning. Sees all options. Judges accurately	Lacks drive and ability to inspire others.
		SL RG / BB / JH		CH		TW	DR (circled)	CH	SL			Teamworker: social, mild, perceptive and accommodating. Listens, builds, averts friction.	Indecisive in crunch situations.
		RG / JH			BB DR (circled) DR	IMP	CH			DR (bold)		Implementer: disciplined, reliable, conservative and efficient. Turns ideas into practical actions.	Somewhat inflexible. Slow to respond to new possibilities.
		BB RG / SL / CH			JH	CF						Completer/finisher: painstaking, conscientious, anxious. Searches out errors and omissions. Delivers on time.	Inclined to worry unduly. Reluctant to delegate.
	Low			Average				High		Very high			

FIGURE 10.3 A Team Example.

company cultures conspire to drive teams apart: through feudal power barons, targets and incentives which reward individual rather than team performance, ambiguous roles and poor cross-wise communications.

What can be done? Well think about building cross-functional project teams, intra-departmental meetings and internal road shows where one part of the business presents to another. Think of reward and recognition systems which encourage teamworking across the business and reinforce your core business values, so that you have an umbrella under which all teams will unite. Above all, get teams to meet and work together, that is within their local team and as part of the bigger business team.

Stages of Development

Just as all businesses go through predictable phases of growth, so all teams go through stages of team development before they reach the nirvana of becoming a synergistic and cohesive team. Different teams will go through them at different speeds and some stages can last longer than others. Stages of development can be usefully examined using the four-stage model of forming, storming, norming and performing.

Forming

This is what happens, as the name suggests, in the early stages of setting up a team when the first introductions are being made but the rules are not clear. People are polite and watchful. Their responses will be guarded until they see which way the wind blows. The team may apparently be making progress but the strongest desire of the group is for safety and stability and it is therefore undeveloped as a team. Its major concerns are to avoid embarrassment and making a mistake. Team members seek at all costs to reduce feelings of discomfort and vulnerability.

Storming

This is the punch-up phase of team building, when conflicts start to emerge. There will be in-fighting and pointed questioning. Some individuals' expectations will not be met and they may well opt out. The group is experimenting with different behaviours and will make only slow and painful progress. This is an uncomfortable stage in building a team, but if you have recently been forming, then storming is definitely progress!

Norming

The team is starting to develop its norms or rules, values and procedures. It is developing the skills it needs and finding routes to confront issues. This is the consolidation phase.

Performing

The team is approaching true maturity and effectiveness. It is resourceful and flexible – individuals will vary their preferred roles for the good of the team. Members are supportive of each other and will actively listen, summarize and build on others ideas. Energy is directed towards solving the goals of the team rather than meeting individual agendas.

The more you bring people together to work on becoming a team, the quicker you are likely to get them through these stages towards becoming effective. Think of team-building workshops, outward-bound events and shared social and leisure activities. Most of all, create the reasons why people want to be a member of this team in the first place. Do not fall into the trap referred to by Groucho Marx, who did not 'want to be part of any club that would have me as a member'.

If you want to know how effective your management team is or at what stage of growth, then think about having an internal workshop where you can explore team issues and enhance the bonding process. Particularly useful are some of the team questionnaires and diagnostics which you can acquire from organizations like MLR (Management Learning Resources); its website is www.mlruk.com. For example, getting team members to complete the team effectiveness profile (TEP) will graphically show you where your business is on the continuum: immature–fragmented–cohesive–effective–synergistic. A synergistic team is the holy grail – a team where $1 + 1 = 3$ – because the team results are always better than those of the best individual in the team. This questionnaire profiles your team by looking at five categories of team behaviour:

- group mission, planning and goal setting
- group roles
- group operating processes
- group interpersonal relationships
- intergroup relations.

All of the above will hugely help you in developing your first- and second-tier management teams – and in building a team culture across the whole business.

However, nothing lasts forever. Continued business growth will create new challenges which will require you to constantly reassess your top-team capability, not only for today but for tomorrow. Who are the turkeys, who are unwilling or unable to contribute to the future? Are some people getting stale and overcomfortable? Have you got the right individuals in the right roles? Do these roles need to be redefined?

Some of the questions you will want to ask yourself are:

- Is the current team working effectively as a team?
- Have I got the right people in the right jobs?
- Does the team deliver joined-up business results?

- What are its strengths and weaknesses as a team?
- Is this the right team to take the business into its next phase of growth?
- How do I reward the existing team effectively while keeping an eye on the future?
- What action do I need to take to create tomorrow's team?

Assignment 10.5: Your Management Team

1. Is your existing management team capable of taking the business through the next stage of growth and development? What specific skills do you need to develop, or recruit for, within your management team?
2. Ask each member of your management team to complete a Belbin Team Roles Inventory Questionnaire. Compile a single chart for the team showing each individual's profile. Which roles are strengths of your team? Do individuals with similar profiles ever clash? Which roles are areas of weakness in your team and what can you do to address these areas?
3. In discussion with the team, consider each individual's profile against his or her role. Is there a good fit? If not, how can you help that individual develop and/or accommodate in other ways?
4. Looking at the profiles of the team as a whole, are there any particular areas of weakness or areas where there is too much concentration (e.g. you are all trying to do the same role and getting in each other's way)? If so, how will you allow for this?
5. How effective is the performance of your management team? What needs to be done to improve the effectiveness of the team in order to implement the growth strategy?

Removing People

It is a sad fact of life that, however good your team, there will inevitably come a time when you have to get rid of people. This may be because they are no longer capable of doing the job you need them to do, perhaps because the business has changed and they are unable to change with it, or because you no longer have a need for that particular role, or because they have done something unacceptable. Whatever the reasons, you will face this uncomfortable situation at some time and it is important to grasp the nettle.

Unfortunately, growing businesses have a habit of hanging on to people long after they should have been fired. As one owner-manager says, 'Facing getting rid of someone caused me so much angst it ruined my holiday'. No one pretends firing is easy or fun – but sometimes it is essential. If people who do not perform are seen to get the same job security and rewards as those who do, you will be sending the wrong signals to everyone.

It is a most painful experience, reaching the decision that one of your team is going to have to leave, and then dismissing them. This is especially the case, if the member is, as so often happens, one of your founding team.

You may have to reach your decision to fire very suddenly – discovering, for instance, that the person has committed an act of gross misconduct, but it is much more likely to be the result of a growing realization that something is wrong. There may be a temptation to fire someone on the spot, in the heat of the moment. Conversely, the fear of the legal consequences, and of facing a claim for unfair dismissal, may make managers nervous about taking any action at all.

Your own reasons for deciding that you want to dismiss someone will probably fall into one of the following categories:

- The employee is unable to do the job properly.
- There is no longer any need for the business to continue to employ someone in that particular role.
- The person has done something unforgivable or even criminal.

Whatever the reason in your own mind, pause for thought and plan your line of action carefully. First and foremost you must get the foundations right. If you have to end up saying, 'Well, that wasn't the proper way to do it' then you will be in trouble. Do staff know, right from the first day, what they should and should not do? Can you prove it through your written documentation? Essential documentation should include job descriptions, safety rules, appraisal records, training records and many other matters, including grievance and disciplinary procedures, which should be in your staff handbook. If you cannot prove that the employee was ever shown the right procedure then your position is weak. Let us look at the various reasons for getting rid of someone and how each can be handled.

Reasons for Getting Rid of Someone

Unable to Do the Job

This can include reasons such as the person being insufficiently skilled to carry out the tasks that you need done. A key rule here is to satisfy yourself absolutely that you are right to conclude that the person is unable to do the job. Has the right training been given? Is the work environment appropriate? When dealing with long term-illness, stress-related sickness or disability remember that there are specific legal protections in place for such staff. For example, you cannot safely assume an illness will be long lasting and disabling unless you have asked the employee for permission to talk to their doctor, and the doctor confirms this. Even then, you must consider all the ways you could modify the job so that, with training, the individual can cope.

Poor Performance

If, as is most likely, your concern is with poor performance, then you need to track and record output and give the employee the opportunity to improve. Do not leave it too late. The longer you leave it the worse things will get, and just imagine what the impact might be on your business, particularly the more senior the person is or the more his or her poor performance is affecting other employees or even customers. It is also unfair to the individual concerned. Most of us know when we are not performing and to allow it to go unnoticed and un-remarked upon is to subject the individual to a lingering death. It may be a relief to all parties to bring the matter out into the open. You should be regularly checking how staff are getting on through appraisals and one-to-ones. Generally, poor performance issues do not just erupt overnight – they have been brewing for some time. It will seriously erode the company's case, for example, if it turns out that an errant salesman has never been held accountable for poor performance. If nothing has ever been done about it in the past, the individual could well argue that those standards were effectively accepted by the company.

Not Needed

If someone's job is being abolished, then technically this is called redundancy. Separate rules and regulations then apply, of course. But often things are not so clear cut. For example, a firm may grow and find that it now needs a proper finance director, and so wish to replace the current accountant's role with someone of higher calibre, doing a much bigger job. This is probably defensible as redundancy following reorganization, providing a new accountant is not then appointed in a similar role to the old one. And, provided the current person is offered any relevant suitable vacancy – such as a new post being created underneath the new finance director. And provided you have reasonable proof that your present accountant is not up to assuming the role of finance director, even if trained. You can get further advice on handling redundancy from www.dti.gov.uk.

Misconduct

Your original contract of employment with the employee should cover this area to some extent. To take an example: a violent and unprovoked physical attack on a colleague at work is a reason for dismissal unlikely to be challenged in law, provided there are good witnesses. You will want to be certain of the event's real character – that it has not been exaggerated in the telling. Likewise, if you find that someone is stealing from the till – you can and should act immediately, provided that you are absolutely certain you have proof of who the culprit is, and do not jump to conclusions without first asking for explanations.

Procedure

As we have indicated, how you go about dismissing someone is almost as important in law as your reasons for doing so. By now, most employers know that it is safest to meet formally with the person concerned, to explain fully, to give the employee the fullest possible chance to state his or her case, to keep agreed notes of the meetings, and to give at least two written warnings with full reasons. Do give the proper period of formal notice when it finally comes to terminating the employment.

Disciplinary Procedures

Poor performance is certainly one of the most tricky scenarios for you to deal with, as there is unlikely to be one single clear-cut factor – as in the case of gross misconduct. Sometimes it boils down to a feeling you have or an instinct about that person. But you need more than this – you need the facts!

The important principles are to be open and fair. You may want to take the underperformer out of the office for a no holds barred discussion. Most important of all – follow your own procedures. If you do not have a disciplinary procedure, your employee will have a field day. So get one now!

If you do, then follow it. Keep your procedures flexible so that if someone is absent the process does not grind to a halt. The ACAS web site offers guidance on what an effective procedure should include (www.acas.org.uk).

You may want to think about a termination agreement (also known as a compromise agreement). This way you offer the employee a bit more to go quietly. The beauty of it is that, once the agreement is negotiated and signed, that is the end of the matter. The downside is that, as well as paying more than you may strictly need to do, you will need to pay for the employee to have independent legal advice. Whatever you do, do not fudge the issue by creating non-jobs as a way of avoiding confrontation.

There are several critical stages to getting a dismissal right:

- Identify the areas where the employee is underperforming. You need to give the employee written notice of a meeting at which you will discuss the areas identified. The employee has the right to be accompanied at that meeting. He or she should also be warned that it may become necessary to follow a disciplinary procedure if performance does not improve.

- Hold the meeting and take notes. These will be valuable evidence should the situation escalate to an employment tribunal. You may also choose to be accompanied so that there is a third-party observer there. By the end of the meeting you need to agree a timescale within which certain objectives will be achieved. Agree a review date. You need to confirm the detail of the meeting with the employee and you may choose to give a verbal warning that any failure to achieve the agreed objectives within the agreed timescale may result in a further meeting and written warning.

- You must, repeat must, monitor the employee's performance. If he or she achieves the required objectives within the agreed time then you cannot move forward on the disciplinary procedure. If not, then you need to repeat the same procedure. You can also give another verbal warning that any failure to achieve the revised targets will result in a final written warning.
- You need to go through the process one more time. If, again, the employee has failed to achieve objectives then you can dismiss. Confirm the dismissal in writing and remember that you need to terminate the contract lawfully, dealing with matters of period of notice, monies in lieu of notice, etc. Finally, do not forget to get your own property back: keys to the office, company credit cards, papers or computer files at the employee's home.

Classic Mistakes

To keep the threat of industrial tribunals at bay, whatever you do:

- Do not dismiss anybody on the basis of information you have had as hearsay from a third party. You will always need to substantiate the facts first.
- Do not dismiss anybody just because they have got married or become pregnant, or because of race, creed, colour, sexual preference or age.
- Do not dismiss someone in the heat of the moment, however personally provoked you may be, as can sometimes happen in small teams working at close quarters.
- Do not dismiss someone for something that you have never even mentioned to them before.
- Make sure you investigate causes and possible remedies, and involve them in the process.

Handling the Termination

No matter what the circumstances, all employees are entitled to a high level of consideration and compassion, and the benefit to the company of treating dismissed employees well is that it maintains morale and your image as a caring employer. It avoids making unnecessary enemies and causing avoidable stress and pain to departing employees. Termination planned and carried out in a professional way helps to ensure this.

Plan the Interview in Advance

Decide the best time and place. Do not fire on a Friday afternoon – dismissed employees need time to adjust before facing their family. If possible, choose neutral ground for the task – a private place, quiet and free from interruptions. Rehearse the interview if necessary, and decide in advance how to direct the individual after termination.

These are the 20 responses most commonly heard from the employee being dismissed. Make sure you have your responses ready:

- Why me?
- Are the terms negotiable?
- Do I have the right to appeal?
- I intend to take the matter further!
- What about my car?
- What about my life cover and health care?
- What about my pension?
- Why was I not given prior warning?
- What help will you give me to find a new job?
- Are there any alternative jobs I could do even at a lower grade?
- Can I apply for, and will you consider me for, any future vacancies?
- Can I work my notice?
- Who is going to get my job?
- I think this is too unfair especially given my service and ability!
- Am I the only one affected?
- Can I return to my office?
- What have my colleagues been told?
- Can I tell my staff?
- Who will supply me with a reference?
- When does this come into effect?

Do Not Procrastinate

Once the decision to let someone go has been made, get on with it; otherwise, word of impending action might reach the employee's colleagues, causing them to shun him or her. Procrastination is the thief not only of time but also of the individual's self-confidence and future job prospects.

Tell Them the Truth

Explain the clear, specific and precise reason for the dismissal, without being brutal, preferably backed up by documentary evidence. Many employees cannot believe that they are being fired and will look for any sign of uncertainty as an indication that the job is still negotiable. If the reasons are held back it may cause unnecessary worry and loss of self-esteem.

Do Not be Emotional

The emotional manager will either plunge in too quickly, without sensitivity, trying to get the whole thing over and done with, or hedge about, failing to make the point and leaving the employee unsure about the situation. Defusing an emotional situation is one of the most immediate goals of a termination from the company's point of view, and one of the main reasons terminations go disastrously wrong is the emotional state of the manager as well as of the employee.

Do Not Prolong the Agony

The initial interview should last no longer than 15 minutes. There is no point in going into a great deal of detail at this stage – the person may be in a state of shock and unable to take in much of the conversation. Give them a chance to respond, though, and make a subsequent appointment to discuss details of severance pay and perhaps references.

There probably seems an awful lot to do in building your management team as we have described, but the more effectively you do it the less likely you are to have to confront unpleasant dismissals and the more likely you are to end up with a high-value business.

Assignment 10.6: Removing People

Is there anyone on your staff who you believe should be removed for whatever reason? If so, plan carefully and then do it!

eleven

How Do You Manage The Changes?

Threats and opportunities come from so many different directions, and at such speed, that it is no longer sufficient to glance up occasionally to scan the horizon. You have to be on constant watch for new technology, for legislation, for competitors from overseas with better ways of doing things, and for changing consumer tastes, any one of which could wipe out your business or create golden opportunities almost overnight. The lesson for entrepreneurs is a harsh one: if you are interested in staying in business there is no alternative but to change. Readiness to change is essential. Change has become an everyday management preoccupation.

So it is by getting people on board to translate your business plan into reality that you will achieve success. When examining your organizational capability earlier in this book, you will have already identified things you need to change. For example, you may be thinking of introducing new systems, structural reorganization, strategic repositioning, relocation, bringing in new people, building a new culture or moving into new products. The question which this chapter addresses is how best to manage people through these inevitable but painful transitions.

But there is a central dilemma here, and it is about the speed of change. Your job is to drive change, and very frequently there will be only a small window of market opportunity, so you must move fast, yet at the same time people do not like change and take time to get used to new ways of doing things. So the challenge is to get your team to make the changes you want as quickly and as painlessly as possible.

Change Hurts

We have only to observe people in a meeting or the staff canteen or relaxing in the pub to know that the human being is a creature of habit, who likes familiar patterns: the same bar stool, the same group of friends to talk to over lunch. Most of us do not like change, we like things to stay the same. It is easier to lead a defence of the status quo than it is to lead people into something new with all the attendant uncertainties and the innate fear of the unknown which change implies. As the owner-manager it is quite likely that you love change, you probably thrive on the adrenalin kick, the challenge, the excitement and the buzz. That is great as it is your job to create change, but do not expect everyone else to feel the same way!

Many employees see change as a temporary and unnecessary disruption of the status quo; they tend to believe that once management have got it right, change will go away. The people who have to make changes happen can find it a very disruptive process. They will tend to respond negatively even to changes which seem to you entirely reasonable. This is because change is an emotional process and the typical reactions will be those of fear, loss, anxiety, distrust, confusion, anger and shock. In other words your employees will naturally tend to resist change, unless you can encourage them to see the positives, what they stand to gain as well as what they will lose.

Here are some comments from people within ICL when it was going through a huge programme of change:

- *Fear*: 'Do not think the company realize how frightened people are.'
- *Loss*: 'Teams broken, relationships broken, lack of commitment to keeping our unit.'
- *Discomfort*: 'We feel very battered.'
- *Stress* (causing personal overloads): 'In the past we worked hard and played hard, and people laughed – they do not any more.'

So individual resistance to change should not be a surprise – it is the normal reaction stemming from things such as:

- fear of the unknown
- lack of information
- threats to status
- threats to established skills and competencies
- fear of failure
- lack of perceived benefits
- threats to the power base
- low-trust organizational climate
- fear of looking stupid
- feeling vulnerable and exposed

- loss of control of one's own destiny
- loss of team relationships.

Change Means You Too!

There is a famous quotation which goes, 'Change is something that the top asks the middle to do to the bottom' (Rosabeth Moss Kanter). But change imposed top down rarely works. Particularly when the boss has no intention of changing! Remember the words of Gorbachev in the years of *perestroika* 'I thought I was the driver of the engine of change but instead I was a passenger on a runaway train'. Perhaps there are only runaway trains and you as the owner-manager really do not know how things will work out; you cannot because the future has not arrived yet. So why should anyone else be prepared to change if you are not? You are the most important role model in the business, so it is up to you to model the new behaviours you are looking for and lead from the front. Try as hard as you will, you cannot actually make anyone else change, you can only encourage them to do so. At the end of the day you are the only person who you can actually change and, as years of experience will have taught you, even that is pretty difficult. However, if your employees see that you are at least trying to change and do not consider yourself immune from the process, it will help them do the same.

The Predictable Process of Change

Almost any major change will make things worse before it makes them better. The concept of the productivity curve means that the immediate impact of change is a decrease in productivity as people struggle with new ways of doing things, cope with their own learning curve and desperately try to 'keep the shop open'. It may be months or even years before productivity recovers let alone exceeds original levels (Figure 11.1).

The management challenge is to reduce the drop in productivity to a minimum and achieve the benefits of change as fast as possible. The more you consult and involve your people in the early stages, the quicker this is likely to happen. Unfortunately, the inevitable fall-off in production increases the likelihood that managers who have an unrealistic expectation of how long change will take to achieve will panic and pull the plug on the change, just when they are about to start to see the pay-off. This phenomenon is well described by John Philipp and Sandy Dunlop as 'the long dark night of the innovator' (Figure 11.2).

Everything looks like a failure halfway through. It takes courage to stay with the vision during this period, to persevere, to maintain enthusiasm and commitment. For Richard Williams' father and grandfather, change was something they might have considered occasionally; but for Richard it was a case of change or die.

Richard Williams has automobiles in his blood. His family have been selling new cars

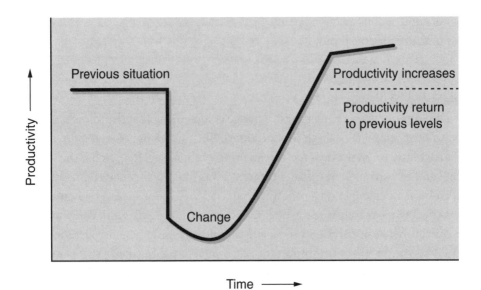

FIGURE 11.1 The Productivity Curve.

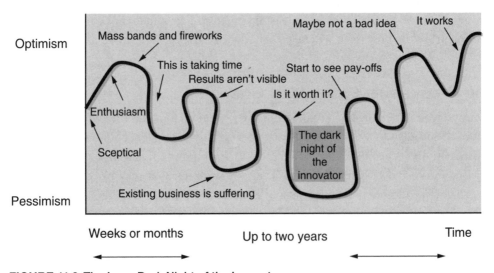

FIGURE 11.2 The Long Dark Night of the Innovator.

for three generations, ever since his grandfather first signed a dealership contract with Austin Morris in 1911. For the first 78 years, the business ticked over, but when Austin was taken over by Rover in the eighties, the Williams business sank into a gentle but dangerous decline. Crisis point was reached in 1988, when British Aerospace acquired Rover and announced a 30 per cent staff discount on all cars. After the acquisition, the 60 Rover dealerships around Bristol declined to one. So in 1989, Williams bravely decided to dissolve his arrangement with Rover and move out of the cut-throat, low-margin, high-volume sector. He struck deals with Saab, Suzuki and Lotus and went into speciality cars. He was just in time for the violent economic contraction that was the recession of the early 1990s!

Williams weathered the storm but found it was a whole new ball game. When he moved the dealership into the speciality sector, Williams had 36 staff, all deeply entrenched in the ways of the volume market. 'We ran retraining programmes and indoctrination sessions to get them to accept new ways of doing things', he says. Nonetheless, half of them walked. No sooner had the dealership settled on a nice steady growth path than the Internet exploded, providing a great opportunity for marketing cars but necessitating not only new skills but a complete new culture. Although it was possible to buy in some of the technical skills, it was hard work getting staff to understand the impact of the Internet on the business. The Internet changed what was basically a sales-led operation into a marketing-led enterprise. So after almost 80 years of comparative stability, the family business had to radically reinvent itself not once, but twice, within a six-year period. At the same time it had to re-equip itself on both occasions with new skills, staff and ways of working for its new markets.

Change always takes longer than you think. Even in a small, responsive business, the temptation is to assume that change can be made to happen overnight. For example, one chief executive we know asked his directors to devise a totally new culture and to have it in place by the next board meeting!

The risk of not allowing sufficient time for the change to bed down is that the embryo change plant will be pulled up and thrown on the rubbish heap, to be succeeded by yet another change and another after that – all equally likely to meet the same fate. The change process predictably takes time, costs money and effort, and causes an immediate fall-off in productivity. In responding to a significant change, people also go through a predictable pattern of personal response. This has been described as a transition curve, showing an individual's response to change over time (Figure 11.3).

Figure 11.4 describes a four-stage process through which people typically pass as they learn to adjust to a personal change, such as bereavement or an organizational change such as a relocation, redundancy or restructuring. This means that change usually only happens after people have passed through the stages of denial, resistance, exploration and commitment.

How you manage the change process will determine just how quickly and painlessly change will happen. Managerial support is crucial, just as support for a grieving spouse is crucial. It is an interesting but sad fact that most people who are trying to cope with bereavement get the support from friends and family when they least need it, in the early stages of shock. When they most need encouragement, months later, most of the relatives have gone home.

You can use specific management strategies depending on where people are in the process. For example, people in denial are at their most intractable so the best approach is to keep confronting them with the reality of the situation, that change is needed and

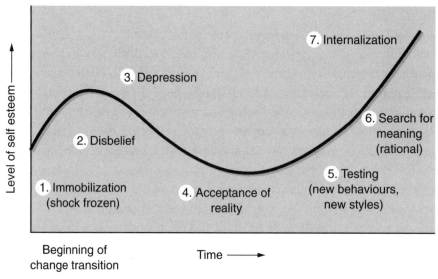

FIGURE 11.3 Personal Reactions to Change; based on Adams, Hayes and Hopson (1976) *Transition – Understanding and Managing Personal Change*, Martin Robertson & Company, London.

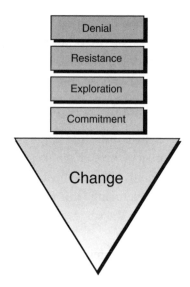

FIGURE 11.4 Change is a Predictable Process.

will not go away and that they must change too. When you find resistance, then actually you should be pleased, for resistance at least means that denial is over! The way to handle resistance is by listening to people's concerns and letting them talk themselves into believers. During the exploration phase, people will be really starting to engage and there will be a renewed buzz of energy. Your role is to harness this energy but make sure that people do not revert to old behaviours. By the time the commitment phase is reached, you are well on the way to success and can start to think about recognizing and rewarding success, and of course celebrating!

Increasing the Odds in Your Favour

If change is a predictable process then the good news is that there are things you can do to increase your chances of success. The change process has its own dynamic. This balance can even be expressed as an equation, which states that unless C (the cost of changing) is exceeded by A (the weight of dissatisfaction with what you have got), plus B (the desirability of the proposed change), plus D (its practicability), the change will not happen.

$$C = (ABD) > X$$

For example, you may see a house that you and your spouse find very desirable. But unless you are pretty dissatisfied with the one you have already got (too few bedrooms) and unless the move is practicable (does not disrupt school arrangements) then the cost of changing will outweigh the benefits and you will not do it. The same applies to organizational change. Consider this example.

An oil company in the United States decided to reorganize into independent oil and gas companies. The change involved relocation, causing geographic and personal dislocation for hundreds of people. Senior managers were surprised by 'significant resistance' from employees. Given the following comment from their consultants should they have been surprised by strong resistance? 'The rationale for change was obscure since the existing organization was very profitable and displayed no obvious evidence of the need for transformation.'

Let us look at the three parts of the change equation:

- dissatisfaction with the status quo;
- desirability of the proposed change;
- practicality of change.

Dissatisfaction with the Status Quo

The more you can encourage your staff to find things wrong with your business, then the more you create a positive dynamic for change. Of course this is precisely what management consultants do when they come into an organization, telling everyone what is wrong with it, which they nearly always knew perfectly well anyway, and thereby justify the programmes of change which were already in the mind of the CEO! So fermenting dissent and encouraging revolution, in a controlled way of course, are good ways of creating momentum for change.

Desirability of the Proposed Change

Change always involves risk, because it is moving from the known to the unknown and unknowable. Why would anyone in their right mind do such a thing unless the destination is very tempting! So the clarity and passion of your vision or dream is a very important component in persuading your team to pull away from the past and take the risk of changing.

Practicability of the Change

Even the best change plan is doomed if is just too ambitious, too expensive and too difficult to do. So break the change down into little bits and give yourself twice as long as you think you need to achieve it

So, some clues are beginning to emerge in this business of managing change. First and foremost, it is people who make change happen so:

- Communicate why change is needed.
- Encourage people to challenge the status quo.
- Involve people as early as possible in the change.
- Make it their change not yours.
- Do not underestimate likely resistance.
- Identify the key influencers.
- Use coalitions and alliances to build critical mass for change.

Of course it is always easier to say how not to do change! Here is Rosabeth Moss Kanter's spoof Ten Commandments for making sure that change will never happen in your business:

1. Regard any new idea from below with suspicion because it is new, and it is from below.
2. Insist that people who need your approval to act first go through several other levels of management to get their signatures.
3. Ask departments or individuals to challenge and criticize each other's proposals. (That saves you the job of deciding; you just pick the survivor.)
4. Express your criticisms freely, and withhold your praise (that keeps people on their toes). Let them know they can be fired at any time.
5. Treat identification of problems as signs of failure, to discourage people from letting you know when something in their area is not working.
6. Control everything carefully. Make sure people count anything that can be counted, frequently.
7. Make decisions to reorganize or change policies in secret, and spring them on people unexpectedly. (This also keeps people on their toes.)
8. Make sure that requests for information are fully justified, and make sure that it

is not given out to managers freely. (You do not want data to fall into the wrong hands.)

9. Assign to lower-level managers, in the name of delegation and participation, responsibility for figuring out how to cut back, lay off, move people around, or otherwise implement threatening decisions you have made, and get them to do it quickly.

10. Above all, never forget that you, the higher-ups, already know everything important about the business.

Your Change Toolkit

We will introduce you here to three useful pieces of toolkit which will help you anticipate in advance whether a change you are thinking of is likely to succeed and will help you plan how to implement it:

- force field analysis
- commitment charting
- the change star.

Force Field Analysis

Kurt Lewin's force field analysis is a powerful technique for assessing whether a change you are thinking of making is likely to be a goer or not. There will always be forces working both for and against any change you are proposing. The forces for the change are the drivers, the forces against, the restraining forces. It is fairly obvious that if the drivers equal the resisters then the status quo will prevail, inertia will rule and the change is probably doomed. By identifying each of the drivers and each of the potential resistors, or restraining forces, you will get a good idea of what you are up against and, more importantly, what action you may need to take to change the balance by reducing the restraining forces or increasing the drivers. You can even put a rough weighting on each factor, so that you can then have the satisfaction of adding up the driving forces and seeing if they exceed the resistors.

The process of force field analysis takes us through six phases:

1. What is the problem?
2. Where are we now?
3. Where do we want to get to?
4. What are the driving forces?
5. What are the resisting forces?
6. Action.

The heart of the process are stages 4 and 5; you can see this in more detail in Figure 11.5.

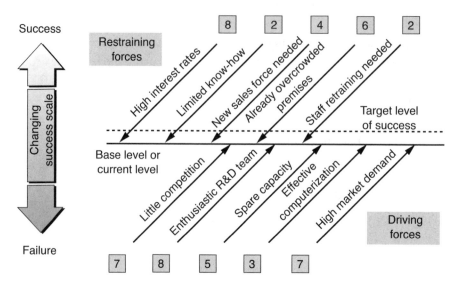

FIGURE 11.5 Kurt Lewin's Force Field Analysis.

When you have carried out the force field analysis and listed your driving and restraining forces, you may find that they are too equally balanced for your liking. Perhaps the most obvious action to take would be to accentuate the positive by piling on more benefits. Research shows that by far the more productive course of action would be to eliminate the negatives by seeking to reduce or remove some of the restraining forces. It is a bit like meeting a sales objection; although it is tempting for the salesperson to put renewed efforts into selling the benefits, they would be much better off trying to understand and reduce the objections.

Commitment Charting

Readiness for change is more likely to exist when there is considerable external pressure for change (i.e. from new market or technology trends) combined with internal pressures (i.e. from disgruntled shareholders or eroding margins). There is also greater readiness for change if there are new people at the top with new questions to ask, the proverbial new broom sweeping clean.

Readiness for change is greatest where there are neither very high security levels nor very low security levels. If people are too insecure then they tend to dig in, retrench and resist change; when they are too secure then they become apathetic. So how are we to secure the critical mass for change to happen?

The likely commitment levels or readiness for change of key individuals can be plotted using the technique of commitment charting (Beckhard and Harris Organization Transitions).

The steps in developing a commitment plan are:

- identify target individuals or groups whose commitment is needed;
- define the critical mass needed to make change happen;
- develop a plan for gaining commitment of the critical mass;
- monitor progress.

Commitment charting will help you to form a diagnosis and an action strategy for getting on board the key players you need to push the change through. The technique works on the assumption that for each key player it is necessary to gain some degree of personal commitment but that it is neither likely nor essential that everyone is in the 'make it happen' box. To make a commitment chart, list all the key players in the change, whether they are individuals or groups, on the vertical axis of the chart. Then consider the degree of commitment you really need from each (Figure 11.6). The range of possibilities is:

- active resistance;
- no commitment;
- let it happen;
- help it happen;
- make it happen.

The 0 indicates the minimum commitment you need; the X indicates where you think that person's commitment is at the moment. When the 0 and the X are in the same box, breathe a deep sigh of relief; when they are not, draw an arrow connecting the two, this will give you a map of the work to be done. So, for example, we do not need to worry about key players 5 and 8, their level of commitment is exactly where it needs to

Key players	Active resistance	No commitment	Let it happen	Help it happen	Make it happen
1			X ———→		0
2			X —→ 0		
3	X ——————————————→				0
4			0 ←— X		
5				(X0)	
6	X ———→ 0				
7			X ———→		0
8			(X0)		
9		X ———→ 0			
10				0 ←— X	

FIGURE 11.6 A Sample Commitment Chart.

be. Player 3 is worrying: he or she is actively resisting but needs to be prepared to make the change happen. Players 8 and 4 are also interesting: they are keen to make change happen, but perhaps by being too gung-ho they will hold back others from owning the change, so perhaps we need to pull them back a little to create space for change.

The Change Star

The change star model (Figure 11.7) has proved a useful framework to help get people through the change process as quickly and painlessly as possible.

The star provides a useful summary of the ground we have covered. It starts from the belief that if you want to get to the centre-point where our business is change then you have to consider four main strategies:

- Why change?
- Make it manageable.
- Involve early.
- Create a climate for change.

There is no right place to start on the star; it is an iterative model. 'Why change?' may seem the obvious start, point but unless you have made it manageable it may be that the resistance you will meet will make the change too hot to handle. Similarly, you cannot

FIGURE 11.7 The Change Star.

afford to wait until the later stages of the change to involve early, this must come right at the beginning. The fourth pointer of the star talks about the need to create a climate for change in order that people feel safe enough to take the risks of change. This climate of positive thinking and a 'people matter' style cannot be built overnight. If you have a punitive culture where people keep their heads below the parapets and come out of every meeting with their boss feeling uncomfortable, then it will be a long time before your employees will feel they can risk making mistakes without being cut off at the knees.

When you are testing out your change plan check it against the change star to make sure you have answered questions such as:

- How well have we put across the rationale for change?
- How much dissatisfaction is there with the current situation?
- What specific benefits does change offer to those who must carry it out?
- How many people/customers will be affected by the change?
- How can we break the change down into manageable chunks?
- Will existing teams be broken up?
- Is a change of boss involved?
- Will retraining be needed?
- How many people will perceive themselves as losers?
- What levels of resistance do we anticipate?
- How will career opportunities be affected?
- How long will the change take to achieve?
- What are the effects on travel time to work, social and domestic arrangements?

A change plan is really no different from any other project plan – it should stipulate what actions need to be taken when and by whom. You will find that even the most rudimentary change planning on the back of an envelope will vastly increase your chances of success.

Assignment 11.1: Managing the Changes

1. Identify the key change projects that you will need to implement within the next year in order to achieve your business and personal objectives. There are unlikely to be more than about five or six such projects.
2. For each change project, complete the 'change toolkit' templates consisting of:
   - force field analysis.
   - commitment chart.
   - change star.
3. For each change project, identify the resources you will need to allocate in order to complete the project and estimate the time and costs required.

twelve
How Do You Fund Growth?

Whatever strategic direction you propose to pursue in order to grow your business, it is almost certain to require money. By now, you will have discovered that a healthy business has an equally healthy appetite for cash! For the first years of a business's life, its strategic choices are invariably limited by the availability of funds. Once it gathers momentum and begins to plan its strategic direction, the 'corset elastic' is usually the limited availability of good opportunities and the management to exploit them successfully.

The constant search for funds is not in itself necessarily a cause for concern. Businesses, after all, exist in part at least to turn money into goods and services, which can be sold on for a profit. It usually takes a while for the business cycle to move from strategic ideas to profit and so, as long as you are growing, more money will be needed.

What should concern you, however, is where that money comes from. There are two main sources of money – internal and external – with a number of subdivisions of each sector. Getting the right balance of funds from these different sources is one of the keys to profitable growth – and perhaps even to survival itself.

By the end of the chapter you should have a clear understanding of the following key topics.

- identifying how much cash you will need to grow your business;
- internal sources of funds including squeezing working capital and ways of making more profit;

external sources of funds, in particular debt (or borrowing) and equity, and the different expectations of the providers of these types of funding;

other ways to fund growth including franchising and corporate venturing.

How Much Cash Will I Need to Grow My Business?

Essentially you will need to find cash to do two things:

1. fund working capital – debtors, stock, suppliers etc;
2. fund any capital investment – new plant, equipment, factory, etc.

That is it!

It the first of these two that is the most challenging because you have to understand the way cash comes in and goes out of your business. So let us start with the most difficult area – calculating working capital.

Calculating the Working Capital Requirement

This is not rocket science and it is in fact quite common sense – but it is amazing how many business people struggle with this. There are some totally cash businesses with no physical product – a window cleaner springs to mind – which will have no real working capital requirement. However, most businesses do buy in some materials, convert these and sell them on either as a product or together with a service. In all probability if they are selling to another business they will have to give credit and with a bit of luck they are getting some credit from their suppliers. Let us look at an example to see how the requirement for working capital can become quite sizeable.

Ashcroft Engineering buys in raw materials, which it marks up and sells on to its customers. The brief extract below shows sales, cost of sales, annual gross profit (all figures are shown excluding VAT and come from the profit and loss account).

Sales	100%	£2,500,000
Cost of sales	60%	£1,500,000
Gross profit	40%	£1,000,000

In addition, we know that the company has to hold a lot of stock to make sure it can satisfy its customers' needs. When the managers looked at the balance sheet they found that the company had stock at the year-end that was worth £430,000. When they calculated their stock days (we covered this ratio earlier) they got quite a shock – they were holding on average 105 days' worth of stock, which was far more than they thought! The figures used to calculate this are shown below.

Stock	£430,000
Cost of sales	£1,500,000
Stock days	105

But there were further surprises in store when they looked at who owed them money (debtors). When they looked at the balance sheet they saw that they were owed £482,877 (including VAT). Knowing that their sales were £2,500,000 excluding VAT they were able to work out how long their customers were taking to pay. They added the VAT to this to get back to the VAT-inclusive sales figure of £2,937,500 – this enabled them to compare like with like as the debtors figure already included VAT and to calculate the correct working capital requirement. They then calculated their debtor days (we covered this ratio earlier) and found they were giving their customers on average 60 days' credit. The figures used to calculate this follow.

Debtors (incl. VAT)	£482,877
Sales (incl. VAT)	£2,937,500
Debtors days	60

Having taken a little time to recover from the shock of how much stock they were holding and the credit they were giving their customers, the managers remembered that all their suppliers gave them credit for the materials they purchased. Again they converted their cost of sales figure to a VAT-inclusive figure, which was £1,762,500, and, by comparing this with the outstanding trade creditors figure in the balance sheet, which was £265,582 (including VAT), they were able to work out their creditor days (we covered this ratio earlier). They were taking on average 55 days to pay their suppliers. The figures used to calculate this follow.

Trade creditors (incl. VAT)	£265,582
Cost of sales (incl. VAT)	£1,762,500
Creditor days	55

This again came as slight shock as their standard suppliers terms were 30 days, and they realized that they were always paying late. No wonder some suppliers were always chasing them and sometimes refusing to supply them.

When all this was put together it gave a very good picture of the business's working capital requirement, which is shown below. In addition to showing each figure in days, which had already been calculated, the figures were shown as a percentage of sales (excluding VAT). The reason for this is that, since most profit forecasts show sales excluding VAT, it makes sense to have a working capital requirement model that reflects this. It did come as a bit of a shock to find that for each pound of sales about 2.5 per cent (or £0.25) would be needed to finance working capital. The figures that follow show how this is made up (Table 12.1).

So now we have a very good measure of how much working capital the business needs. Assuming that there are no changes to the way the business is run, i.e. customers pay in 60 days, suppliers are paid in 55 days and 105 days' worth of stock is held, we can predict the working capital requirement for the business if we were to, say, grow sales by

35 per cent to £3,375,000. As mentioned above, it is not rocket science, but it does come as a bit of a shock to find that if the business does this it will need to find an additional £226,553 cash (£873,848 – £647,295) (Table 12.2)! Just as well to know that now before you start off on a rapid growth plan!

So now we have a dynamic model of the working capital requirement for this business if it grows but does not change, i.e. it continues to pay, be paid and stock up in the way it has done before. What if you want to grow and improve the business at the same time? What effect would this have on the working capital requirement?

The business we have been looking at, Ashcroft Engineering, has decided that it is going to improve its business before growing. The proposal is that it will put up prices by 15 per cent, chase customers faster and harder to get debtor days down to 40 days (its terms are 30 days) and reduce stock to 70 days. It is anticipated that as result of this it will lose customers and in fact sales will probably fall by 5 per cent as a result. At the same time, they plan to pay their suppliers quicker and have set 40 days as the target. How will the new Ashcroft Engineering look alongside the old? The figures show the before and after picture (Table 12.3).

You would hardly recognize it as the same business – the financial transformation is almost too good to be true! Despite reducing sales, each sale made has much better

TABLE 12.1 Working Capital Requirement

	Days	Per cent of sales
Current assets		
Debtors	60	19
Stock	105	17
		36
Less creditors		
Trade	55	11
Net current assets (working capital)		25

TABLE 12.2 Effect on Working Capital of Growing and Improving Business

Working capital requirement	Days	Per cent of sales	Current	Proposed
Sales			£2,500,000	£3,375,000
Current assets				
Debtors	60	19	£482,877	£651,884
Stock	105	17	£430,000	£580,500
		36	£912,877	£1,232,384
Less creditors				
Trade	55	11	£265,582	£358,536
Net current assets (working capital)		25	£647,295	£873,848

TABLE 12.3 Working Capital – Before and After

		Current position		Proposed position	Benefit from
Sales		£2,500,000		£2,375,000	−£125,000
Margin		40%		55%	15%
Gross profit		£1,000,000		£1,306,250	£306,250
Working capital					
Debtors	60 days	19%	40 days	13%	
Stock	105 days	17%	70 days	11%	
Less creditors	55 days	−11%	40 days	−8%	
Working capital/sales ratio		25%		16%	−9%
Working capital		£647,295		£380,000	£267,295
Other benefits					
Interest costs					Reduced
Asset Investment					Reduced
Fixed costs					Held/reduced
Gearing					Reduced

margin and hence gross profit contribution – up £306,250. And, assuming fixed costs (overheads) remain the same, net profit will also be improved by the same amount. The reduced volume of business (sales down) and improved working capital requirement (just 16 per cent of sales as opposed to 25 per cent) means that some £267,295 less working capital is required. That will ease the overdraft position, which will cut interest costs and reduce gearing. Reduced sales will ease the pressure on the need for new capital investment and help keep the lid on fixed costs.

Identifying the Funding Requirement

Let us just show how we calculate the complete funding picture by showing the steps we need to take.

1. Calculate the working capital requirement (NCA).
2. Calculate the net fixed asset required (NFA).
3. Add NCA and NFA to get the total funding requirement.
4. Deduct what the shareholders can provide.
5. What is left is the actual borrowing requirement.

Let us show how this works with our previous example, Ashcroft Engineering, which has decided to grow sales from the current £2,500,000 to £3,375,000 but without making any of the improvements we have just shown. We know that to achieve this it will need £226,553 extra cash (we calculated this earlier) to meet its working capital (NCA) requirement. Let us also assume that it has decided to invest another £200,000 in fixed assets (NFA) to help make sure it can meet the extra business. In total, we can see that the company will need £426,553 to meet its total funding requirement. This should be met from a combination of shareholders' funds and borrowings (bank etc.).

Now, we know that if sales do grow from £2,500,000 to £3,375,000 this is an increase in sales of £875,000, which, if it achieves the gross profit of 40 per cent, will produce an additional £350,000 of net profit (£875,000×40 per cent) assuming no extra overheads. Assuming that the shareholders leave all this in business (i.e. they reinvest), this still leaves an additional £76,553 to be found (£426,553 – £350,000). Now, assuming that things are reasonable with the company's bankers, then this should be a bankable deal. (Table 12.4).

Now let us look at a more extreme situation. Let us assume that Ashcroft Engineering is contemplating aggressive growth plans to double sales to £5,000,000 but for various reasons it will make a loss of £750,000 initially.

In the base year, when sales are £2,500,000, the shareholders are funding the business to the tune of £323,648, which we assume is being matched by the bank. However, as the ambitious sales growth plan escalates we can see that, as a result of the proposed loss and fixed asset investment, both the shareholders and the bank would have to more than triple their support of the business. Since the business is not making any profit for the shareholders to reinvest, this would represent a real investment of extra cash. On the face of things, this plan is not fundable (Table 12.5).

TABLE 12.4 Calculating the Funding Requirement

1. NCA requirement	£226,553
2. NFA requirement	£200,000
3. Total funding requirement	£426,553
4. Less shareholders (improved profit)	£350,000
5. Additional borrowing (balance)	£76,553

TABLE 12.5 Funding Growth when Loss Making 1

		Current	Proposed
Sales		£2,500,000	£5,000,000
1. Ratio of NCA to sales	25%	£647,295	£1,250,000
2. Additional fixed asset investment		£0	£200,000
3. Proposed loss		£0	£750,000
4. Total funding requirement		£647,295	£2,200,000
Shareholders' funding	50%	£323,648	£1,100,000
Borrowing requirement	50%	£323,648	£1,100,000
Total funding		£647,295	£2,200,000

TABLE 12.6 Funding Growth when Loss Making 2

		Current		Proposed
Sales		£2,500,000		£5,000,000
1. Ratio of NCA to sales	25%	£647,295		£1,250,000
2. Additional fixed asset investment		£0		£200,000
3. Proposed loss		£0		£750,000
4. Total funding requirement		£647,295		£2,200,000
Shareholders' funding	50%	£323,648	15%	£323,648
Borrowing requirement	50%	£323,648	85%	£1,876,352
Total funding		£647,295		£2,200,000

Assuming that the shareholders could not make the further investment to support the business the picture would be as shown in Table 12.6.

The gearing of 50 per cent at sales of £2,500,000 would have to move to 85 per cent at £5,000,000. This is just not going to happen. The bank, although usually happy to match shareholder funding (50 per cent gearing), is most unlikely to go to 85 per cent gearing. What these figures demonstrate quite clearly is that growth and losses are by and large unfundable.

Internal Sources of Funds

Surprisingly enough, many businesses have much of the money they need to finance growth already tied up in the firm. It may require a little imagination and some analysis to uncover it, but a financial position audit (as described in chapter 3) should give some pointers to how this might be done.

Squeeze Working Capital

Working capital is an area rich in possibilities to release cash for expansion. Debtors and stock control are perhaps the most fertile areas to start with.

Debtors

According to research at Cranfield School of Management (Business Finance in Today's Challenging Environment, an Independent Business Finance study, 2003), collecting money from customers is still a major problem for most owner-managed businesses, despite copious legislation across Europe to outlaw late payment of bills. It is salutary to note that the total cost of providing customers with the extra 48 days of credit, the difference between the best and worst collection periods in different countries in Europe, is equivalent to 5.7 per cent of the average business's turnover, and, assuming a net profit margin of 10 per cent, more than half its net profit. Instead of businesses being able to borrow to grow the business, they often need to borrow just to fund their sales ledger.

Listed below are some things you can do to manage your debtors more closely and so make better use of your working capital.

1. Carefully consider your terms of trade. Can you ask for part payments up front, or for staged payment? Do you need to allow credit? If so, how much?
2. If you are going to give credit, always take trade references and look at the customers' own accounts to see how sound they are.
3. Make sure that your invoices are accurate. Do not give your customers an excuse to query them.
4. Send out invoices promptly, if possible on delivery.
5. If you sell on credit, set out your terms of trade very clearly on your invoices. Unless customers know when you expect to be paid, they will pay when it suits them.
6. Find out when your biggest customers have their monthly cheque run and make sure your bills reach them in time.
7. Send out statements promptly to chase up late payers, and always follow up with a phone call.
8. Bank cheques and cash promptly. It is not only safer, but the sooner you get money into the banking system, the sooner you are either saving interest cost or earning interest income.

Stock Control

Stock of all types (raw materials, work-in-progress and finished goods) ties up capital. You benefit from this investment only once the finished goods are sold and you receive the payment in return. Stock also occupies space and needs people to manage it. Therefore, minimizing the amount of stock and maximizing the speed with which stock flows through the business are key levers of releasing working capital.

On the other hand, you need enough stock to meet demand. So, it is important to have detailed and accurate forecasts of demand and then to match your stock requirements to these forecasts. In larger businesses, this is often done through sophisticated software known as material requirements planning (MRP) and enterprise resource planning (ERP). Growing businesses can achieve considerable improvements in stock management by relatively simple changes in the way they purchase and monitor their stocks including

- Having accurate stock records for each individual stock item. Regularly reviewing for any slow-moving items.
- Regularly forecasting sales for each individual stock item. Review forecasts against actual sales so that you can improve the accuracy of your forecasts. Match stock and work-in-progress to these forecasts.
- Where possible, buying from suppliers with short delivery times.

- Buying more frequently but in smaller quantities (e.g. monthly instead of quarterly). You may need to consider the effect of price discounts for bulk orders but generally speaking the working capital advantages outweigh these discounts.
- Much of the cost of many products is incurred in the final stages of manufacture. So, potentially big stock savings can be made by holding stocks of semi-finished items. Only put the finishing touches to an item when the customer wants it.
- Re-examine any automatic stock reorder points to see if lower levels can be set.

For businesses which have failed to monitor stock levels closely, the introduction of tight controls can prove daunting. A 'quick and dirty' way of making improvements can be achieved by grading stock as A, B or C according to the value of individual items or of the total number held. Attention is then focused on items in the A category which can provide the greatest savings. These items can then be subjected to regular stock-takes; patterns of demand can be studied to see how frequently orders are placed, if there are peaks or troughs, or whether demand is seasonal. Managers can then decide the quantities they require and when to place their next order, or start their next production run if they are making the item in-house. B and C items can be brought into this programme once it is well established.

Other Ways to Squeeze Working Capital

You can also improve your working capital management by managing your own credit and cash better.

- Take the maximum credit from your suppliers. Once you have a good track record, try to negotiate extended terms with major suppliers. Many will say no, but some may not. A good time to start these negotiations is when a price rise comes along!
- Make any cash you have work harder. Overnight money markets, now more easily accessible through Internet banks, could allow you to get interest on cash, rather than having it sitting in the banking system doing nothing.
- Work out if it makes sense to pay bills quickly to take advantage of early settlement discounts. Sometimes, usually by accident, suppliers offer what amounts to high rates of interest for settling promptly. If you are offered 2.5 per cent to pay now rather than in two months' time, that is equivalent to an annual rate of interest of 15 per cent $((12/2) \times 2.5$ per cent$)$. If your bank is charging you 8 per cent then you would make a good extra profit by taking up this offer.

Make More Profit and Plough It Back

Another internal source of finance is to make your present business more profitable and plough that profit back to grow your business. Five steps you can take to unlock the extra profit potential in your business are described below.

Recognize the Iceberg

Just as the small tip of the iceberg showing above water conceals an enormous mass below, the small(ish) percentage of profits the average business makes (typically under 10 per cent of sales) conceals a great volume of money being used to arrive at that profit. It requires only a few percentage points reduction in costs to dramatically improve profits, as Table 12.7 illustrates.

In the example given in Table 12.7, the last profit margin was 5 per cent. Costs, the 'below the water line' mass, are 95 per cent of sales. By reducing those costs by a mere 2 per cent, bottom-line profits have been increased by a massive 40 per cent (this is a simplified example from a real-life case).

This extra profitability can then be used to finance extra investments, saved as a reserve for bad times, or be used to compensate for lower sales. In Table 12.7, when costs are reduced by 2 per cent, turnover from sales can drop by over 25 per cent to £714,000 before profits will dip below £50,000. That should take care of even the worst recession seen since the 1920s and 1930s.

Now much of this will come as no surprise to you – after all most of this is your money, so, naturally, you are well informed as to where it goes. But the people who work for you have probably never considered, or been given the chance to consider, the phenomenal impact that relatively small savings in costs can have on the bottom line. So, why not tell them? You could start by giving your key employees a copy of Table 12.7 and inviting their comments.

Use the 80/20 rule

Obviously, you cannot leave the whole responsibility of reducing costs exclusively to the people who, after all, created the costs in the first place. Just as with any other business task, objectives have to be agreed and strategies adopted.

Fortunately, here you have the 80/20 rule working in your favour. This rule states that 80 per cent of effort goes into producing 20 per cent of the results. Look at Table 12.8, which is a real case of a company on a recent BGP at Cranfield. This more or less confirms the rule, as 18 per cent of customers account for 78 per cent of sales.

A quick glance at figures in your own business will, in all probability, confirm that 20

TABLE 12.7 The Effects of Cost Savings on Profits

	Before		After 2 per cent cost saving		Extra profit		But if sales drop ...	
	£000	%	£000	%	£000	%	£000	%
Sales	1,000	100	1,000	100	–	–	714	100
Costs	950	95	930	93	–	–	664	93
Profit	50	5	70	7	20	40	50	7

per cent of your customers account for 80 per cent of your sales, and yet your costs are probably spread evenly across all your customers.

As an example of the way in which this affects your business, consider the way that sales staff spend their time. Sales staff tend to make their calls in a cycle that suits their administrative convenience, rather than concentrating on customers with the most potential.

Interestingly enough, when the salesman in the company used in the previous example was asked where he thought his sales in two years' time would be coming from (see column 3, Table 12.8), he felt that his top 18 per cent of customers would account for 88 per cent of sales (up from 78 per cent of actual sales this year). And, yet, an analysis of his call reports showed that he spent over 60 per cent of his time calling on his bottom 68 accounts, and planned to continue doing so. This activity-based – rather than results-based – outlook was being used to make out a case for an additional salesperson. What was actually needed was a call-grading system to lower the call rate on accounts with the least sales potential. So, for example, accounts with the least potential were visited twice a year and phoned twice, whereas top-grade accounts were visited up to eight times a year.

This grading process saves costs, as phone calls are cheaper than visits; it eliminates the need for an additional salesperson, which at first glance the projected growth would have justified; and it even frees up time so the salesman can prospect for new, high potential accounts.

The 80/20 rule can be used across the business to uncover other areas where costs are being incurred that are unwarranted by the benefits. In some areas, you just need to open your eyes to see waste. Did you know that the average executive spends 36 minutes a day looking for things on or around the desk? This can waste up to £6,000 a year for a fairly senior person – you, for example. The same survey, conducted for the British Institute of Management, revealed that a quarter of the 500 executives they questioned spent 11 hours a week in meetings – equivalent to 13 weeks a year. Few were satisfied with their investment.

The chances are, if you are anything like many other chief executives, you feel that you and your management team waste too much time on the wrong priorities. It is not that managers are not working hard enough – on average they work 20 per cent more

TABLE 12.8 The 80/20 Rule in Action

Number of customers		Value of sales		Value of potential sales	
	%	£000	%	£000	%
4	3	710	69	1,200	71
21	18	800	78	1,500	88
47	41	918	90	1,600	94
116	100	1,025	100	1,700	100

hours than a decade ago. It is just that organizing time and daily priorities in a world in which there has been a 600 per cent increase in business information, and the average manager is interrupted every eight minutes, is difficult to say the least. But the 'cost' of wasting time is very real in two senses. First, you end up buying more management than you need – and that cost has to be spread across your products. Second, people are too busy doing the wrong things to have time to do the right things.

Zero-based Budgeting

The 80/20 rule is helpful in getting costs back into line – but what if the line was completely wrong in the first place?

When you sit down with your team and discuss budgets, the arguments always revolve around how much more each cost centre will need next year. The starting point is usually this year's costs, which are taken as the only 'facts' upon which to build. So, for example, if you spent £25,000 on advertising last year and achieved sales of £1 million, the expense would have been 2.5 per cent of sales. If the sales budget for next year is £1.5 million, then it seems logical to spend £37,500 next year. That, however, presupposes that last year's sum was wisely and effectively spent in the first place, which it almost certainly was not.

Popularized by Robert McNamara, zero-based budgeting turns the cost argument on its head. It assumes that each year every cost centre starts from zero spending and, based on the goals of the business and the resources available, arguments are presented for every penny spent, not just for the increase proposed.

Cut Out Mistakes Through Training

According to the former CEO of a major bank, basic mistakes by employees account for between 25 per cent and 40 per cent of the total costs of any service business – and not just in banking. It is certainly true that people learn from experience, and the more often they do a job, the faster and better they get at it (up to the stage where indifference sets in of course)! What a pity, however, that so many growing businesses let their employees practise on their customers, losing money and goodwill in the process.

As we have already seen in an earlier chapter, training your people, on a regular basis, in all aspects of their jobs, is a sure-fire way to reduce mistakes, and get costs down and customer satisfaction up. Training can be one of the fastest payback routes to cost reduction.

Incentivize Everyone Around Profit

Lots of businesses have incentive schemes, but most end up rewarding the wrong achievement. Some firms actually reward people by how much they spend! So, for example, buyers with the biggest budget get the highest pay and perks. Production staff are paid for greater output and salespeople for more sales, whether or not either activity is particularly desirable at the time it is achieved. In one company (name withheld to protect the embarrassed) one of the largest creditor items on liquidation was salespeople's commission.

There are always hundreds of reasons for giving people intermediate incentives, such as sales commission. But, unless you build profit targets into your goals and incentives, nine times out of ten you will end up with the wrong result. You get nothing if the company does not make a satisfactory profit, so rewarding others if they do not make money is only encouraging an illusion of reality.

Building incentives for everyone around the profit you make focuses the whole business around customers and costs, and that has to be good. It will make everyone look for

- cheaper ways to do things;
- ways to eliminate waste;
- more effective ways to spend their time (and your money);
- ways to get more money out of more satisfied customers.

In short, all the ways to unlock the profit potential in your business.

Increasing Margins

Increasing margins has the double effect of increasing the flow of cash into a business by increasing profits, while at the same time reducing the amount of money tied up in producing low- or even no-profit items.

To achieve increased margins, you need first to review the mix of your sales. This requires accurate costs and gross margins for each of your products or services. Armed with that information, you can select particular product groups or market segments that are less price-sensitive and potentially more profitable.

For example, Robert Segesser, MD of Dairyborn Foods, a cheese component business, spent his first five years in business building sales – £3 million a year's worth – without making much profit.

Then he defined the company's principal objectives as being to move its profit margin from 16 per cent to 25 per cent. This moved the business into what he likes to refer to as 'margin-protected' business: in other words, things that only Dairyborn can do, that certain groups of customers want badly and will pay for. Segesser believed that, if his customers get to the future before he does, they would leave him behind. He had to create solutions for customers' problems before they even realize they had one.

Refocusing on solving problems rather than selling cheese, and aiming for profit margin growth rather than turnover growth alone, has transformed the business so that it now has annual sales of £15 million and annual profits of £2 million. From being worth little, within two years the company had turned away a potential suitor with £20 million on the table.

Pricing

Pricing is one of the biggest decisions your business has to make, and one that it needs to keep constantly under review. It is certainly the decision that has the biggest impact on company profitability. Try the consultant's favourite exercise of computing and comparing the impact on profits of:

- a 5 per cent cut in your overheads;
- a 5 per cent increase in volume sales;
- a 5 per cent cut in materials purchased;
- a 5 per cent price increase.

All these actions are usually considered to be within an owner-manager's normal reach. Almost invariably, the 5 per cent price increase scores the highest, as it passes straight to the net profit bottom line. Even if volume falls, because of the effect price has on gross margin, it is usually more profitable to sell fewer items at a higher price. For example, at a constant gross margin of 30 per cent with a 5 per cent price increase, profits would be unchanged even if sales declined 14 per cent. Yet, if prices were cut 5 per cent, an extra 21 per cent increase in sales would be needed to stand still.

Frequently, resistance to increasing prices, even in the face of inflationary cost rises, can come from your own team members, eager to apportion blame for performance lapses. In these instances, it is important to make detailed price comparisons with competitors. Mark Saunders, for example, when designing and launching his innovative folding bicycle, the 'Strida', into the mature 100-year-old bicycle market, recognized that (a) his manufacturer's capacity was strictly limited and (b) his target market was 'well-to-do, city commuters' or 'lifestyle weekenders'. An initial price of nearly £300 per bike was well above established competitive models, but gave good margins to dealers in taking up the product and left room for manoeuvre later in the product life cycle when competition would react to the Strida's unusual features. By selecting a less price-sensitive market segment, Strida's margins were maintained at a much higher level than they might otherwise have been had they gone for a blanket approach to the market.

Working Smarter

Making more of your own money, rather than having to raise money outside, does not always have to mean working longer hours. You could just work smarter and, who knows, you may even end up working fewer hours than you do now and still make more money.

One way to get everyone's grey matter working overtime is to create smart circles (and smart rewards). You could formalize the process of encouraging employees to rethink the way they work, and reward them in such a way as to make their working environment better still, as the owner-manager has demonstrated in the following case example.

Smart Circles, Smart Rewards

Dairyborn Foods products are used in the chilled ready-meal market, frozen ready-meal market and the convenience food market. The mar...... is one of the most dynamic sectors of the total food market in Europe. The market is relatively new but is developing quickly in response to consumer expectations.

For the past decade the total market for all chilled food has grown at a compound rate of 7.7 per cent and is forecast to continue this rate of growth over the foreseeable future. The market for chilled ready meals has grown at a compound rate of 10 per cent and is expected to continue this growth rate.

Operating in such a dynamic market has forced Dairyborn to find innovative ways to get even more output from its small production facility. To motivate and involve employees, 'Smart Circles' have been introduced to develop a culture of working 'smarter not harder'. Any employee can arrange a meeting with other staff members, to discuss a new idea or operational change that will be of benefit to the customer or company. This meeting has a set time of half an hour, to ensure they are productive, but if the idea is worth pursuing there is the opportunity to have as many meetings as required. However, after six weeks, the idea must be 'taken on' or dropped.

This gives the staff a sense of belonging and responsibility for the way the company develops, and a Smart Team award acknowledges any 'outstanding' ideas for each quarter. This award is presented by the managing director and published in the company's newsletter each quarter.

The Smart Team Award consists of a sum of money, relative to the value of the innovation. The money has to be spent on things of value to the team. It could be an evening out, or any other social event. It could also be used to buy a business asset that is nice to have but could not really be justified on business grounds. One winning team decided to buy their own photocopier to save them going up and downstairs to use the one in the general office.

Consider Outsourcing

One final thought on internal sources of finance: does your business really need to do everything it currently does itself? If not, you could release all the working capital and fixed capital tied up in that process and use it for better things.

Despite all your efforts to generate more funds internally, there may well be times when you need to access additional funds from outside.

There are two fundamentally different types of external money which a growing company can tap into: debt and equity. Debt is money borrowed, usually from a bank, and which one day you will have to repay. While you are making use of borrowed money you will also have to pay interest on the loan. Equity is the money put in by shareholders, including the proprietor, and money left in the business by way of retained profit. You do not have to give the shareholders their money back, but they do expect the directors to increase the value of their shares, and if you go public they will probably expect a stream of dividends too. If you do not meet the shareholders' expectations, they will not be there when you need more money – or if they are powerful enough they will take steps to change the board.

Debt (or Borrowing)

Borrowing someone else's money to help you grow your business has many attractions. High gearing is the name given when a business has a high proportion of outside money to inside money. High gearing has considerable attractions to a business which wants to make high returns on shareholders' capital, as the example in Table 12.9 shows.

In this example, the business is assumed to need £60,000 capital to generate £10,000 operating profits. Four different capital structures are considered. They range from all share capital (no gearing) at one end, to nearly all loan capital at the other. The loan capital has to be 'serviced', that is interest of 12 per cent has to be paid. The loan itself can be relatively indefinite, simply being replaced by another one at market interest rates when the first loan expires.

Following the columns through, you can see that ROSC grows from 16.6 per cent to 30.7 per cent by virtue of the changed gearing. If the interest on the loan were lower,

TABLE 12.9 The Effect of Gearing on ROSC

	No gearing	Average gearing 1:1	Average gearing 2:1	Average gearing 3:1
Capital structure				
Share capital (£)	60,000	30,000	20,000	15,000
Loan capital (at 12%) (£)	–	30,000	40,000	45,000
Total capital (£)	60,000	60,000	60,000	60,000
Profits				
Operating profit (£)	10,000	10,000	10,000	10,000
Less interest on loan (£)	None	3,600	4,800	5,400
Net profit (£)	10,000	6,400	5,200	4,600
Return on share capital	16.6%	21.3%	26%	30.7%
Interest cover	N/A	2.8×	2.1×	1.9×

the ROSC would be even more improved by high gearing, and the higher the interest the lower the relative improvement in ROSC. So, in times of low interest, businesses tend to go for increased borrowings rather than raising more equity, that is money from shareholders.

At first sight, this looks like a perpetual profit growth machine. Naturally, if they could increase the return on their investment, owners would rather have someone else lend them the money for their business than put it in themselves. The problem comes if the business does not produce £10,000 operating profits. Very often, in a growing business, a drop in sales of 20 per cent means that profits are halved or even eliminated. If profits were halved in this example, the company could not meet the interest payments on its loan at the highest level of gearing shown. That would make the business insolvent.

Bankers tend to favour 1:1 gearing as the maximum for a small growing business, although they have been known to go much higher. Gearing can be more usefully expressed as the percentage of shareholders' funds (share capital plus reserves) to all the long-term capital in the business. So 1:1 is the same as saying 50 per cent gearing.

All loans from banks take time to set up and attract an arrangement fee, and it is generally frowned upon if you go back a few weeks later and ask for more money. The days when you could expect to cultivate a lifetime relationship with either a bank or a bank manager are long gone. Banks are into market segmentation and profit generation, so you need to be prepared to (a) shop around and (b) manage your relationship with the bank carefully.

As a rough guide, if you are with the same bank for over five years, you have not pushed them hard enough. The Cranfield study mentioned earlier in this chapter indicated that around half of all owner-managed businesses had either changed, or seriously considered changing, their bankers in the preceding two years. There are a myriad number of things to negotiate with your banker, and there is even a new breed of consultants who advise on banking relationships.

Once your business is up and running you will have a wider range of financing options, including those described below.

Working Capital Finance

Customers often take time to pay up. In the meantime, you have to pay those who work for you and your less patient suppliers. So, the more you grow, the more funds you need. It is often possible to 'factor' your creditworthy customers' bills to a financial institution, receiving some of the funds as your goods leave the door, hence speeding up cash flow.

Factoring is generally available only to a business that invoices other business customers, either in their home market or internationally, for its services. Factoring can be made available to new businesses, although its services are usually of most value during the early stages of growth. It is an arrangement which allows you to receive up to 80 per cent of the cash due from your customers more quickly than they would normally pay. The factoring company, in effect, buys your trade debts and can provide a debtor accounting and administration service. In other words, it takes over the day-to-day work of invoicing and sending out reminders and statements. This can be a particularly helpful service to an expanding business. It allows the management to concentrate on expanding the business, with the factoring company providing expert guidance on credit control, 100 per cent protection against bad debts and improved cash flow.

You will, of course, have to pay for factoring services. Having the cash before your customers pay will cost you a little more than normal overdraft rates. The factoring service will cost between 0.5 and 3.5 per cent of the turnover, depending on volume of work, the number of debtors, average invoice amount and other related factors. You can get up to 80 per cent of the value of your invoice in advance, with the remainder paid when your customer settles up, less the various charges just mentioned.

If you are expanding more rapidly than other sources of finance will allow, this may be a useful service that is worth exploring. If you sell direct to the public, sell complex and expensive capital equipment or expect progress payments on long-term projects, then factoring is not for you.

Invoice discounting is a variation on the same theme. Factors collect in money owed by a firm's customers, whereas invoice discounters leave it to the firms themselves. However, the majority of growing businesses continue to prefer factoring to invoice discounting because it enables them to outsource their financial management controls. Invoice discounting is, in any case, typically available only to businesses with a turnover in excess of £1 million.

Invoice factoring and invoice discounting now account for £8 billion of business financing, up from £2 billion in 1990.

In the first few years, Cobra Beer sales turnover grew rapidly as more and more Indian restaurants chose to stock the beer that was designed specifically to eat with Indian food. As is customary in the industry, the restaurants were allowed credit. In the meantime, Cobra had to commit to increases in production, to meet the increasing demand, and to pay the brewing, bottling and importation, before receiving payment from the restaurant owners. Founder Karan Bilimoria, a qualified accountant, realized that the business would run out of cash if this situation continued. He decided to bridge this gap by means of an invoice-factoring arrangement whereby Cobra would receive 75 per cent of the value of the goods as they were delivered to the restaurants, with the factoring company then responsible for collecting the payments.

Asset-backed Finance

Physical assets such as cars, vans, computers, office equipment and the like can usually be financed by leasing them, rather as a house or flat may be rented. Or they can be bought on hire purchase. This leaves other funds free to cover the less tangible elements in your cashflow.

Leasing is a way of getting the use of vehicles, plant and equipment without paying the full cost at once. Operating leases are taken out where you will use the equipment for less than its full economic life, for example a car, photocopier, vending machine or kitchen equipment. The lessor takes the risk of the equipment becoming obsolete, and assumes responsibility for repairs, maintenance and insurance. As you, the lessee, are paying for this service, it is more expensive than a finance lease, where you lease the equipment for most of its economic life and maintain and insure it yourself. Leases can normally be extended, often for fairly nominal sums, in the later years.

The obvious attraction of leasing is that no deposit is needed, leaving your working capital free for more profitable use elsewhere. Also, the cost is known from the start, making forward planning simpler. There may even be some tax advantages over other forms of finance. However, there are some possible pitfalls, which only a close examination of the small print will reveal. So, do take professional advice before taking out a lease.

Hire purchase differs from leasing in that you have the option to eventually become the owner of the asset, after a series of payments.

Government Assistance

Unlike debt, which has to be repaid, or equity, which has to earn a return for the investors, grants and awards from governments or the European Union are often not refundable. So, although they are frequently hard to get, they can be particularly valuable.

Almost every country has incentives to encourage entrepreneurs to invest in particular locations or industries. The US, for example, has an allowance of Green Cards (work and residence permits) for up to several hundred immigrants each year prepared to put up sufficient funds to start a substantial business in the country.

In the UK, if you are involved in the development of a new technology, then you may be eligible for a Research and Development award (previously called a SMART award). This is open to individuals or businesses employing fewer than 50 people. The grant is in two stages and can be for amounts as high as £100,000 in total. You may also get help with the costs of training staff, gaining quality recognition, or carrying out market research to identify export opportunities.

Support for business comes in a very wide variety of forms. The most obvious is the direct (cash) grant, but other forms of assistance are also numerous. The main types of grant also include soft loans, which are lent on terms more advantageous than would usually be available from a bank, equity injections, free or subsidized consultancy or access to valuable resources such as research facilities.

Many grants are location specific. There are several schemes that operate across the whole of the European Union, and are available to all businesses that satisfy the outline criteria. In addition to these, there are a myriad of schemes that are administered locally. Thus, the location of your business will be absolutely crucial, and funding that might be available to you will be strongly dependent on the area into which you intend to grow or develop. Additionally, there may well be additional grants available to a business investing into an area of social deprivation, particularly if it involves sustainable job creation.

For further information on grants and support available in the UK, try Business Link (http://www.businesslink.org/), the Department of Business, Enterprise and Regulatory Reform (http://www.berr.gov.uk/), Funders Online (www.fundersonline.org) and Grants Online (www.co-financing.co.uk/).

Money for 'Free'

If you enjoy publicity and like a challenge, then you could look out for a business competition to enter. Like government grants, business competitions are ubiquitous and, like national lotteries, they are something of a hit or miss affair. But one thing is certain: if you do not enter, you cannot win.

There are more than 300 annual awards across Europe, aimed at new, small and growing businesses. For the most part, these are sponsored by banks, the major accountancy bodies, chambers of commerce and local or national newspapers, business magazines and the trade press. Government departments may also have their own competitions as a means of promoting their initiatives, for exporting, innovation, job creation and so forth. The nature and the amount of the awards change from year to year, as do the sponsors. But looking out in the national and local press, or contacting one of the organizations mentioned above, should put you in touch with a competition organizer quickly, as will an Internet search.

Money awards constitute about 40 per cent of the main competition prizes. For the most part, these cash sums are less than £5,000. However, a few do exceed £10,000, and one UK award is for £50,000. Other awards are for equally valuable goods and services, such as consultancy or accountancy advice, training, and computer hardware and software.

Equity (or Venture Capital)

Venture capital is a medium- to long-term investment, of not just money, but time and effort.

Venture capital is rarely a means of financing start-up ventures, but for development, expansion or for pursuing a strategy of acquisition this means of financing comes into its own.

The venture capitalist acquires an agreed proportion of the share capital (equity) of the company in return for providing the requisite funding. Venture capital firms often work in conjunction with other providers of finance in putting together a total funding package for a business.

Venture capital providers are investing other people's money, often from pension funds, and seek to achieve large returns by investing in businesses with the potential to grow and develop into major businesses of tomorrow. Worldwide there are several hundred venture capital firms.

Venture capitalists will go through a process known as 'due diligence' before investing. This process involves a thorough examination of both the business and its owners' past financial performance. Accountants and lawyers subject all the directors' track records, and the business plan, to detailed scrutiny. Directors are then required to 'warrant' that they have provided *all* relevant information, under pain of financial penalties. The cost of this process will have to be borne by the business raising the money, but will be paid out of the money raised, if that is any consolation.

In general, venture capitalists would expect their investment to have paid off within 3–5 years. But they are hardened realists. Two in every ten investments they make are total write-offs, and six perform averagely well at best. So, the two stars in every ten investments they make have to cover a lot of duds. Venture capitalists have a target rate of return of more than 30 per cent to cover this poor hit rate.

Raising venture capital is not a cheap option. The arrangement costs will almost always run to six figures. They are not quick to arrange either. Six months is not unusual and over a year has been known. Every venture capitalist has a deal that they did in six weeks in their portfolio, but that truly is the exception.

Venture capital providers will want to exit from their investment at some stage. Their preferred route is via floatation on a stock market, but a trade sale is more usual.

Although venture capital is big business, the value of funds invested in early-stage companies has remained modest, at just a few per cent of all the funds invested. While this is mainly attributable to the risk–reward relationship, the due diligence and transaction costs involved in investing in smaller businesses are similar to those associated with investments in large companies, and so they are far higher per unit of funds invested. But do not despair. New venture capital funds are coming on stream all the time and they too are looking for a gap in the market.

Mezzanine Money

Mezzanine finance (also known as subordinated debt) is a type of debt that, from a security perspective, typically ranks behind senior debt finance such as invoice discounting and factoring, leasing, traditional bank loans and overdrafts, but ranks in front of equity investment. This means that the mezzanine finance provider has the second claim on a company's assets should the loan need to be recovered.

This increased risk, and the fact that there is often little security available, means that an increased charge is required to justify the risk. Charges vary but can be up to 8 per cent more than the cost of ordinary debt and can also include share options or warrants that can be converted into a company's equity. Options or warrants may be necessary if the available cash flow is insufficient to support a level of interest that will compensate for the risks associated with a given transaction.

The benefit of mezzanine finance is that it often bridges the gap between the funds that a clearing bank will provide and the funds provided by the company's management and a venture capital or private equity backer. Between 15 per cent and 30 per cent of management buy-out finance is provided by mezzanine finance, making it a crucial element in successfully structuring a transaction. Mezzanine finance can now also be considered a stand-alone funding solution, often as an alternative to more expensive equity finance. Mezzanine is now commonly used to provide acquisition finance, development capital and replacement capital as well as finance for the more traditional management buy-out or buy-in scenarios.

Sources of mezzanine finance include many of the clearing banks and insurance companies as well as specialist finance boutiques. With larger transactions, it is possible to access the capital markets using an investment bank to achieve public offerings of high-yield or 'junk' bonds. These are typically sold to institutional investors such as insurance companies and pension funds.

The amount and cost of funds under a mezzanine arrangement will depend on many factors including industry sector, historic performance, credit ratings, seasonality and predictability of revenues, forecasts for future cash flow and profitability, as well as the strength of management, nature of a company's financial backers and structure of the overall financing package.

It is usual for mezzanine finance to be provided on an interest only basis until some or all of general bank debt has been repaid, typically after four to five years, with typical loan terms ranging up to 10 years. Loans are usually secured with a second charge on a company's assets such as property, plant and equipment.

Other Ways to Fund Growth

Franchising

Have you ever wondered why Tie Rack is surviving in this turbulent economy and Sophie Mirman's Sock Shop has gone to the wall? Both are (or in Mirman's case were) niche retailers; both need small high street locations; both founders came from Marks and Spencer's and knew all about their product; neither product is essential for survival – indeed, if anything socks seem more essential than ties!

One of the key differences lies in the way these businesses were funded and managed. All the Sock Shop outlets were funded by the company itself and, in the last year of its life, this was largely provided by the banks. In Tie Rack's case, the situation is rather different. Most of their outlets are effectively owned by the people who manage them. These franchisees, as Tie Rack's 'managers' are called, have stumped up at least £60,000 each for the privilege of following the Tie Rack formulae for business success. That was a fairly staggering £6 million of new money for every 100 franchisees, which is completely risk and cost free to Tie Rack. For Mirman, a similar sum would have cost her £1.25

million a year in interest charges alone – and it probably did as £2 in every £3 in Sock Shop was put up by the banks.

Miles O'Donovan's franchise, Material World (named after the Madonna hit record, Material Girl), is a good example of how to turn a successful conventional business into a franchise. O'Donovan is an upmarket version of a market stall trader, buying up manufacturers' ends-of-lines and seconds and selling them to an apparently appreciative public. 'It is a very simple business', he says. And he never doubted that it would succeed because, the way he looks at it, it is providing a service at both ends of the equation. Not only is he helping out those people who would love to make their home 'very Sanderson' but currently find themselves strapped for cash, but he is also helping out the manufacturers who have to rid themselves of their surplus stock somehow.

This mutually beneficial system is already well established in the clothing business, where disposing of chain store cast-offs is the basis of several retail chains. O'Donovan, however, operates with goods from rather further up the market. Much of what he stocks would normally sell at £15 to £20 per metre but he has a blanket price of £7.95 per yard. The fact that he sticks to yards is not just hankering for days gone by; it gives him a 10 per cent price advantage.

O'Donovan woke up one morning and decided that, with nine of his own shops, he was about as exposed as he would like to be. Watching others in his sector sink without trace, he decided the time had come to share the risk with others. After a brief flirtation with the idea of venture capital, he plumped for franchising and has never looked back. His new franchisees have helped lift turnover significantly and his business is now expanding fast both in the UK and Europe. Best of all, he can sleep easy at night with the comfort of knowing his franchisees are as exposed as he is to the consequences of failure.

Corporate Venturing

Corporate venturing is a term widely in use for an activity that has been around for at least 50 years. However, there is quite a lot of confusion about what exactly it is, since the same term is frequently used to describe different things.

Internal corporate venturing essentially describes large companies' attempts to generate new business activity from inside the organization, but outside their existing core activity. Usually, in internal venturing, the new activity is set up as an entirely separate unit, and sometimes as a stand-alone business, so as to maximize the sense of entrepreneurism in the new venture. IBM attempted this in the 1980s, with mixed results, when it created the PC division, to compete head-on with Apple. Until that time IBM had focused solely on large, centralized computing systems. More recently, several big UK financial institutions, notably Halifax, Abbey and Prudential, have successfully incubated and launched Internet-based banks, which not only have very different business models from the parent business, but are also entirely separate businesses.

External corporate venturing, on the other hand, refers to investments made by big businesses in new or early-stage ventures that are outside their organizations. Sometimes, these investments are made directly, sometimes indirectly through an investment fund controlled by the company but typically managed by investment professionals. In both direct and indirect investing, the usual model is that the investing company injects cash, and possibly other resources (e.g. industry know-how, customer introductions), in return for a minority shareholding. This is the dimension of corporate venturing that is of interest to us here, since it is a potential source of funding for growth-hungry, early-stage businesses. As a general rule, external corporate venturers will invest in early-stage businesses, but not start-ups.

What is in it for the larger partner?

In 1999, the UK's employer organization, the Confederation of British Industry (CBI); surveyed its members to find out the benefits of corporate venturing from their point of view (the report is called 'Connecting Companies'). CBI members are overwhelmingly medium and large-sized companies, and those who took part in the survey replied that the main advantages are:

- access to new ideas, people and skills;
- developing a more entrepreneurial culture;
- exploiting managerial talent and intellectual property to their full potential;
- pre-empting competitors.

Those views have been echoed in other surveys (e.g. the 'Captains of Industry' report compiled by MORI and featured in *Corporate Venturing* Issue 1 in April 2003), although profit has also figured strongly as a motive!

What is in it for the Growing Business?

For the growing business partner, the principal reasons given for entering joint ventures with larger firms were:

- access to sales and distribution;
- collaboration on research and development;
- access to products and processes.

In every case, however, there is one common purpose shared by the partners: achieving growth.

Corporate venturing can be a great option where the parties bring complementary skills and assets to the table. However, the growing business needs to think carefully about this method of building the business.

- The corporate venturer will behave in a very similar way to a venture capital firm. It will require the current owner of the business to surrender some shares in return for the investment and, as a corollary of this, it will usually be in the picture for the long term. Therefore, you will need to give careful thought – and take some (expensive) legal advice – on what to do if the relationship goes sour, and how to provide for that in a shareholders' agreement.

■ Corporate venturing has something of a reputation as a management fashion, and tracks the economic cycle closely. Thus, Venture Economics, a leading consultancy in this area, estimated that European corporate venture investing peaked at US$5.1 billion in the last quarter of 2000, and dropped to $2.8 billion in the first quarter of 2001. Since then, it has been in steady decline, as the technology bubble burst and the European economy has hovered uneasily between recession and low growth. The implications for the investee company are clear:

1. Be clear that the interests of both partners are aligned for the long term.
2. Make provision so that, if the corporate investor is not prepared to invest more money if needed at a later stage, there are no obstacles to other investors putting money into the business.

If this does seem like a suitable route forward for your business, where should you start? A good place to begin is with your existing network of business contacts. If this leads nowhere, then look to see who is making trade investments in your industry – usually not too difficult to discover via the trade press or the Internet. Professional advisers often have good networks and, increasingly, government agencies are seeking to act as brokers between large businesses and growing businesses seeking finance (see, for example, www.corporateventuringuk.org). To see how one large multinational corporation presents its corporate venturing activities look at www.unileverventures.com.

Do not forget, however, that this is one aspect of business where it definitely pays to get expert advice!

Assignment 12.1: Funding Your Growth

1. How much money can you squeeze out of your business by greater working capital efficiencies, i.e. getting paid faster, reducing stockholding, reducing the amount of fixed assets tied up?
2. How much extra capital is required to fund each £100,000 of growth in sales?
3. So, how much new funding is required to meet your growth objectives?
4. Which sources of funds would be most appropriate for you?

thirteen
What is Your Future Leadership Role?

The characteristics needed to be a successful entrepreneur are very different from those required as the CEO of a mature business. It is unusual to find an individual who has both sets of skills. Entrepreneurs from Bill Gates to Stelios Haji-Iannou have, at a particular stage of business growth, stepped aside to allow a more fitting CEO to take over.

In chapter 5, we took stock of your current leadership capability. You probably found that you have many of the strengths and weaknesses of the typical entrepreneur; that means that, on the plus side, you are innovative, energetic, visionary, hands-on, great with customers and totally committed. On the minus side you are likely to be a control freak, you probably do not communicate well enough or frequently enough, you have not built a management team and you tend to criticize and be exasperated by your staff. Sound familiar? By and large, the most frustrating problem for growing businesses is the personality of the owner! Many owner-managers are not natural leaders; they cannot delegate, are poor at recruiting and retaining staff and dislike confrontation on performance issues. For most founders, there is therefore a substantial transition to be made from owner to manager and leader. Many cannot, or will not, make this transition, thus becoming the major restraint on business growth.

Managing and Leading your Business

If you started work for a large organization you will be familiar with the principles of good solid management: planning, controlling and organizing resources. These principles work well in environments where there is little change and much predictability, but in the twenty-first century this is not the world in which we live. Managers maintain order and do what they do efficiently but they cannot cope with change. To respond to and exploit change effectively you need to be a leader as well as a manager. Leadership and management are not the same thing. A leader challenges the status quo, a manager accepts it. A leader creates change, a manager behaves as if everything will always stay the same. A leader thinks long term and inspires trust whereas managers rely on short-term fixes and control mechanisms.

What is Leadership?

Leadership is a commodity most growing businesses lack. The first task of the leader is to articulate the vision or direction and communicate this to all staff. The second task is to get everyone on board with this vision. That's it! Leadership implies, first, that you know where you are going and, second, that when you turn round people are following you rather than hiding or running in the opposite direction as fast as they can! Leadership is all about people; management is about things. Good management will give you a well-run business but it will not grow the business.

Leaders set the values and maintain the culture needed for success. They also ask the un-askable questions, always challenging people to find better and different solutions. For manager, think of your bank manager, great for ensuring the safety of your assets but not about to set the world on fire. For leader, think of yourself as a magnet drawing people irresistibly after you, like iron filings, further and faster than they ever thought they could travel. Your job is not just to respond to change but to create it. You will want to become the change master of your business.

Leadership, as we have seen earlier, demands certain behaviours and attributes. It will also make huge demands on you in terms of:

■ *energy*: the capacity to engender excitement, stay passionate and enthusiastic even when you are flagging, work all hours and meet inevitable setbacks;
■ *drive*: knowing where you are going and being determined to get there;
■ *honesty*: staying true to yourself and behaving with integrity;
■ *mental and emotional health*: the robustness to survive isolation and disappointments and sustain good relationships and the capacity to withstand the inevitable stress that goes with high rates of change.

How do you feel about stretching your own capacity for leadership in the interest of growing a bigger and more successful business? Here are some comments from owner-managers who are coping with the transition towards leadership:

> I have a leadership problem. I have always found it difficult to put my name at the top of the tree. I have strong managers underneath me and it is difficult

to stamp my authority. I want to be liked, yet I have to do tough things and do not have too many friends.

It is hard to face up to the fact of being the solo leader, it is very uncomfortable, and I'm not sure it ever will be comfortable.

Entrepreneurial theory assumes that everyone has the same goals as you, it's not true.

It is taking me out of my comfort zone.

I have made the transition from unconscious incompetence to conscious incompetence.

As a leader I was in the past hesitant about taking control, feeling I was not quite ready. I still feel this but times have changed, I am coming out of my shell.

Becoming a Leader of Leaders

Your business will need different amounts of leadership and management at different stages of life and according to the turbulence of your business environment. As a start-up business, life is fairly simple but you have an enormous challenge in creating something out of nothing. You need little management but an enormous amount of leadership to take your original idea, inspire a small team and direct them towards customers. Internally things may be chaotic, but so what. However, as the business grows, there will be a stage at which you are consolidating progress within a relatively stable environment. This calls for lots of management to put in systems and infrastructure but little leadership drive. But later on, if you want rapid growth plus the capacity to do different things, you are likely to need both leadership and management in depth. The myth of the solitary hero leader has been exploded. A recent headline in the *Daily Telegraph* read, 'British brigadier attacks America's John Wayne generals'. Brigadier Alan Sharpe was commenting critically on the strong streak of Hollywood and heroics he had observed working alongside Americans in Baghdad. He suggested, 'Loud voices, full body-armour, wrap-around sunglasses, air strikes and daily broadcasts from shoulder-holster wearing brigadier-generals proudly announcing how many Iraqis have been killed by US forces today is no hearts and minds winning tool'.

Clever companies can develop leadership at all levels and your job will be to become a leader of leaders. Of course, you need management potential too, and sometimes in a small business leadership and management potential have to reside in the same person.

So look out for leadership attributes at all levels in your business, build them into your recruitment process and develop those who have these characteristics. You can do this not only through formal training but also by giving potential leaders challenging assignments, moving them across the business into different roles or sending them abroad or to other parts of the business. This way you will grow them out of their functional specializations by exposing them to all areas of the business and to all sorts of relationships.

Assignment 13.1: Leadership and Management

1. How much management and how much leadership does your business need? Do you have the right amount (not too little and not too much) of each for the position you are currently in?
2. How much management and leadership will your business need in the future in order to achieve your growth strategy and plans? Where will these capabilities come from?

Letting Go to Grow

Growing into leadership requires a fundamental shift in attitude. Lack of skills is only part of the problem. The single biggest obstacle to the development of your business will be your inability to let go.

Why do you have to let go to grow? The reason is that, if you alone are the source of all power, decisions and leadership in your business, then the business cannot grow beyond the limit of your, inevitably finite, resources. It does not matter who you are or how charismatic you are, you need a team in place to provide the launch pad for long-term growth.

Brian Wiseman, manager director of electrical switch gear manufacturer Terasaki, let go. He realized that as he started to withdraw from the day-to-day business his managers and staff grew in status and ability. 'I started to refuse to be drawn into problems, which was fine as long as I thought others could handle them' he said. It did not come easily. Wiseman had to work hard at giving himself less to do. He instituted some control and bean-counting measures but now leaves all other major projects to his staff. He now spends his time thinking about how the company can work better, developing a vision for the future and travelling the world seeking out new ideas and setting up new alliances.

So how do you know if letting go is a problem for you? Well, you might consider some fundamental business and personal questions. First, let us look at you. Successful people have a lot invested in the past. They did not get where they are today by giving things up! How easy do you find it to let go of familiar habits, familiar roles, familiar relationships? Do you always sit in the same seat in the pub? When did you last throw out possessions and cross people off your Christmas card list?

Then you can ask yourself some business questions around how indispensable you are to your business:

- Who runs the business on a day-to-day basis?
- Is there an established management team?
- Who manages client contact?
- How many family members are involved in my business?
- Am I working all hours and regularly taking work home?

If your answers are 'me', 'no', 'I do', 'lots', 'yes', then you have made yourself so indispensable that you can never retire, leave, exit or grow. You need to step back from the day-to-day running of the business unless, that is, your intention is to go on running a static business forever.

The benefits of letting go and delegating are huge: it is a win–win proposition for you, the employees and the business. Letting go:

- liberates the management team, motivates and involves employees;
- develops new competencies, thereby adding value to the business;
- produces faster and more effective decisions;
- assists in mentoring, developing and empowering individuals;
- releases your time to focus on the vision of the business;
- builds trust and confidence throughout the organization.

Building Trust

Trust is an important part of the delegation process. You will never delegate to people you do not trust. Without trust nothing happens.

Ken Lewis, Chief Executive of Dutton Engineering, said, 'I realized I was the problem, the starting point for lack of trust in the company. Because I wasn't trusting, I had recruited and promoted for technical ability alone. So I hadn't built a team, I had built a series of clones.' His first move was to shut down the quality control function, organize the workforce into multifunctional teams and give them more and more power. There is no time clock or set working day. People set their own budgets and even their own salaries: 'My role is simply to set the vision, agree goals and to be a resource', says Ken. The results in terms of turnover and customer satisfaction have been startlingly good. Ken concludes, 'It was me controlling everything that limited the business. I had to change. I admit I found it very difficult to let go. But once I had learned to trust – something that you have to do gradually – it worked very well. Anybody else who leads in the old-fashioned way will be limiting their business'.

So the starting point for delegating responsibility and letting go of power is to trust the people in the business. After all, if they are not worthy of your trust why did you recruit them and why are they still there? Trust means getting to know your people better. When an admiral was asked by a new naval commander what was the secret of commanding a large vessel, his answer was that as commander he should not only know the names of all 200 men aboard, he should also know for every single one of them:

- what ages are their children;
- what makes them laugh;
- what motivates them;
- when is their birthday.

Mutual confidence and trust will also be encouraged if you go first! This may mean making yourself vulnerable and sharing with your employees something of yourself. You do not have to make a strict separation between work and private life. Tell them something about your leisure activities, your holidays and your children. Talk about your hopes and fears, admit the areas where you are trying to change and develop your own skills. Nobody expects you to be perfect! By trusting them not to use such information against you, you encourage them to return the compliment.

Empowering others means literally that you pass to them some of your powers. Some people think that if you give power, then you have less power. The opposite is true. If you give power to others you will end up with more power; yours plus theirs.

So why on earth do people find excuses not to delegate? It is because of fear, often expressed as:

- It is my business and my baby! I built it up from nothing.
- I cannot trust them – they will make mistakes.
- This looks risky!
- Nobody can do the job well enough.
- But what if they can do it better than me and show me up?
- The routine is preferable to the difficult.
- What do I do with myself if I do not meddle?
- I do not have the time to delegate.
- I am afraid of losing control.
- I am afraid that if they know as much as me they will start challenging me more.
- There is no one to delegate to.
- It is faster if I do it myself.

We will all recognize some of these fears in ourselves. Delegation is about having the confidence first to let go emotionally and then to transfer your powers to others. You may have to physically force yourself to let go by moving your office, coming in only three days a week or giving yourself a fundamentally different role which takes you out of the business!

Ask yourself:

- What are the powers that I can transfer to others?
- What value will this give my business?
- What powers am I not prepared to transfer?

How to Delegate

It may be, for example, possible for you to delegate all the day-to-day running of the business in order to build your management team and free yourself up to become the strategist, not the meddler. However, you may decide that there are certain things you are not prepared to let go of: monitoring key financial ratios and cash, recruiting senior people, reinforcing the culture, management by walkabout. You will find delegation much easier if you feel you have personal control of whatever you feel to be the vital parameters. Get yourself a one-pager of the key performance indicators you intend to monitor – leave the rest to your management team. Decide what role you want to play in the recruitment of your key people and stay away from the rest. Do your MBWA (management by walkabout), but do not make snap decisions, just listen and then pass on anything that needs fixing to the appropriate manager.

Some people think that delegation is abdication. Nothing could be further from the truth. Delegation is a very demanding management style, but you have to do it. Here is your five-point delegation plan:

Define the Boundaries

Be clear about the scope within which you are empowering people. Decide what you are delegating and what not to delegate. Make it quite clear to people what is off-limits and where they are not empowered to take decisions. For example, you may empower them to make any day-to-day decision to enable a customer order to be met but not to change product pricing or offer discounts.

Decide Who to Delegate To

You will need to consider an individual's skills, motivation and workload. It is annoyingly true that some individuals whom you feel have great potential will choose not to use it. You can lead a horse to water ...

Communicate Your Decision Clearly

The task you are delegating should be SMART: specific, measurable, achievable, relevant and time-bound. Give the person enough information, perhaps using a written brief. Make yourself available for further clarification as the employee works through the assignment. Make sure that individuals know the limits of their accountability and that they are perceived as having the authority to do as you have asked. This may mean that you have to brief others that so and so is acting on your instructions and has full authority. Otherwise other managers may block progress by refusing to take the individual seriously.

Provide the Tools to Help Staff Succeed

They may need specific training or access to information; they will certainly need your ongoing support. Think of teaching a child to swim. You need to set the boundaries, i.e. there has to be a swimming pool, a defined and safe environment within which the child is empowered to move. But you do not then just throw the child in to sink or swim.

First, there will be a rubber ring, then armbands, then floating supports, and only when the child has gone through this process and gained confidence do you remove the props. You may graduate to putting the child on your shoulders, but at no point do you decide to dive under water just for the hell of it! It is exactly the same when you are empowering your employees. You are trying to create the conditions for success. You are not opening the window on the twenty-fourth floor and saying 'You are empowered to fly! Ouch, they crashed. Knew they couldn't do it!'

Review, Feedback and Reward

The secret of delegation is follow-up. Results that are rewarded will be repeated. Organize a debriefing meeting. Ask questions that encourage thinking about improvement. Ask the individual to reflect, with the benefit of hindsight, on what they could have done differently or better. Review what has been learnt and give praise and credit for success.

Empowerment can be seen as the result of good leadership. Your people will feel a sense of ownership, they will feel important, they will feel work is exciting, they will feel that they are strong and capable and they will feel that they are in control of their own destiny and are part of a team. Heady stuff – and real motivation! Oh, and by the way, you will have the enormous satisfaction of getting some nice surprises when you see just what some people are capable of doing. Growing your own heroes is what differentiates leaders from managers and creates additional value in the business.

Assignment 13.2: Delegation

1. Does your management role in the business need to change in order to achieve your personal and business objectives? If so:
   - What specifically do you need to do more of and how will you achieve this?
   - What specifically do you need to do less of and to whom will you delegate?
2. How much of what you currently do could you and should you delegate and to whom?

3. Is each person to whom you will delegate tasks capable of undertaking those tasks? If not, how will you help them develop?

What will Your Role be in Future?

As your business grows and changes you may find yourself standing at the crossroads, deciding whether to stay and learn new skills or pack it in and move on. At the very least, your role is likely to change over time, both because the business demands on you will change and also because you, yourself, and what you want, will change. As we have seen, few people make the leap from founding entrepreneur to visionary leader and professional manager, so now is the time to take stock.

In other chapters you have looked at the core skills of the business – what it does best. Now take a look at the implications of your own strengths and weaknesses. To back out of what you cannot do well is not a failure. Many founders return to their roots; reading financials and managing people may leave you cold, but perhaps becoming the chief engineer or sales director would revitalize you. There are no rules that say because you are the owner-manager you have to be the managing director.

Your existing role in the business will consist of three components:

- employee
- director
- shareholder.

As an employee of your business you will want to ensure that, just like everyone else, you are giving as much value as possible. Is it possible that you are the most glaring example of a square peg in a round hole? Does your existing role really play to your strengths and are you enjoying it?

As a director, you are responsible to the board for maximizing the performance of the company. You, yourself, are a key resource and you need to deploy yourself in the most effective way.

As a shareholder you want to make as much money as possible from your investment. Who does what is largely irrelevant. If you decide to take a back seat or take a lower level role, why should you care if it is going to help to make you rich?

So swallow your pride and your assumptions about status and title. Your answers to the following questions should determine your future role:

- Where can I add most value to the business?
- What is my unique contribution?
- What does the business need right now?
- What are my major strengths and weaknesses?
- What would I like to stop doing?
- What would I enjoy doing?

Perhaps you would be best employed as the MD, but equally you may be the best person to solve technical problems and, if this skill is critical to the future of the business, why not make yourself technical director? Similarly, if manufacturing is core to your business and you do not have a production director, this may be a role that reluctantly you decide to assume as a stop-gap measure until you can recruit the right person.

After taking stock, other owner-managers have concluded:

I am a journalist rather than an entrepreneur.

I am a natural networker and my skills are best applied in establishing alliances, reinforcing customer and supplier relationships.

I am the best ideas man in the business, so I will spend more time outside the business sourcing new technology and product development.

I am a lousy manager but I'm great at building new businesses.

At the end of the day, if you are not in business for fun and for profit, why are you wasting your time?

If, however, you excel in creating vision and getting your followers excited about it, then the best decision for you and the company is likely to be that you stay as chief executive. After all, you presumably had the drive and energy to dream your dream and make it happen so perhaps you still do this better than anyone else!

One of the founders of Innocent Drinks, Richard Reed, says: 'We gave birth to this thing and we are in it for the entire ride'. Innocent has doubled its turnover from £17 million to £35 million and operates in five countries. Richard goes on to explain: 'We are very clear about what needs to be done and we bring in people who are smarter and more experienced than us.'

Even in this case, however, you may feel that you are short of serious business skills such as finance, marketing, negotiating, team building and strategic thinking. You can graft these on through formal business training.

You may also want to make some changes about how you allocate time so that you spend more time:

- on the business, not in it;
- on strategic thinking rather than day-to-day operations;
- leading leaders, not meddling;
- empowering others rather than directing;
- recharging your personal batteries;
- bringing in new ideas, technology, resources and relationships.

When you have decided on your role, then write yourself a role or job specification. This will help you remind yourself what you should (and more important what you should not) be doing and will enable you to map whether you are allocating your time as you had intended. We will look at how you best go about managing your time later in this chapter.

Managing Succession

Eighty per cent of companies that reach maturity change leadership. Yet it has been estimated that eight out of ten entrepreneurs put the future of their business at risk by staying on too long. The Chartered Institute of Personnel Development (CIPD) urges owner-managers to start planning for their succession at least two to three years before they hand over. A 2004 survey by the government's Small Business Service estimated that 100,000 companies fail each year through lack of succession planning.

It is difficult to find founders who mature at the same rate as their businesses. People like Richard Branson tend to be the exceptions. So look long, hard and coolly at yourself and whether the time has come to replace yourself as CEO. Certainly this means letting go of your company, yourself, your baby; but if that is the best way of bringing up baby then do it! The pressures to do so can come from many different directions – pressures from investors and board members, pressures from a flotation, pressures of health and age, pressures from your partner and family, pressures from a hungry young management team.

Here are some of the signs that you need to replace yourself:

- You are tired and bored by the big picture.
- Shareholders ask you more questions about your golf handicap than business results.
- Conversation goes quiet when you approach.
- People who used to ring you now ask for your finance director or operations manager.
- Your get up and go has gone.
- You read the sports sections before the financial pages.
- Your idea of hell is making major changes.
- You spend five days, 9 to 5, in the business.
- When you step back temporarily, the business does better without you.
- You doodle and daydream during your board meetings.

Working out when to let go is a delicate balancing act. Letting go is never easy but do you really want to run a bigger company? Sadly, many entrepreneurs become the victims of their own success, ending up running companies very like the ones they set up on their own to escape! In the end, if your business is going to succeed and have lasting value it has to be without you. What is most important is the success of the company, not your own position.

You have many options: replace yourself and meddle with and alienate the new CEO; replace yourself and exit leaving employees feeling cheated; or cling to the helm at all costs. It is not all that common for people to step aside – perhaps they ought to do it more often? Most owners have to be forced to the edge of the precipice before they will conquer their own ego and let someone else have a go.

In 1999, James Carling replaced himself as CEO and co-founder of Prime Response. He had founded the company in May 1990 and built from scratch an international business that in 1998 sold $18 million worth of software. During the last nine years, he has frequently worked 80-hour weeks as chief executive. Now he has all afternoon to talk! 'It is a shareholder issue really', said Carling. 'I felt this was really getting into the big league and I wanted my investment and the previous 10 years to be protected'. It was while negotiating the exchange of 33 per cent of his company for £24 million, in the first round of venture capital funding, that Carling decided that his lack of experience would hurt the company's global ambitions. He also felt that he would feel uncomfortable managing top-level talent. Carling became chief technology officer. He concludes: 'It would have been great to ride over the horizon as CEO of an important technology company, but it is just too high risk. I would rather be the technology officer of a very successful big business – with a large number of shares'.

So take an honest look at what you want from the business and look quite ruthlessly at your succession options. This is particularly important in a family business, in which case, once you have put emotion to one side, you may decide that the best people to replace you may not be family members. Any succession plan to transfer power should be looked at as a process, not an event. This will be one of the biggest transitions the business has ever seen and it needs to be sensitively managed as a change project in its own right (see chapter 11).

You need to consider, for example, how you will handle the process of letting go and what your role will become. The risk of bringing in other people is that they will have their own ideas and take the business off in directions you do not agree with. We all know painful examples of ex-CEOs languishing at home feeling neglected by their former management team and finding that their visits to the office are unwelcome and their ideas ignored. The founders of Friends Reunited have been more successful in achieving a smooth transition.

Friends Reunited founders Steve and Julie Pankhurst and Jason Porter launched the website from their back bedroom in 2000 and orchestrated a successful management buy-in before selling the business for £120 million to ITV in December 2005. Porter comments that: 'It had come to a point where Friends Reunited had taken over our lives …it had been an incredibly exciting time but we were tired and lacked the skills necessary to take it forward.' Steve Pankhurst goes on to say; 'handing over something that we'd toiled over day and night was difficult, but we knew that making the break was the right thing for the business. We had a huge emotional attachment to the company, and the option to retain majority ownership while bringing in a professional management team was very attractive to us.' The chemistry between the founders and Michael Murphy, who they brought in as CEO, was strong and they gave him complete autonomy and basically withdrew from the business.

Handing over control of the company can be hard on employees too. They may be fiercely loyal to you as the founder of the company. They may feel that you have deserted them and sold them out. Often there will be fears that the culture will change because your replacement will bring in different values and practices. Some may feel that they should have been appointed CEO. The exit of a dynamic leader can really dampen the spirit of the company: an important role model has left and employees will have their own letting go and grieving processes to go through. As with any significant change, you need to clear the air quickly and then give people time to get used to the new situation. Your succession planning should include:

- identification of the new or potential leader(s);
- how the new leader is to be trained for the role;
- a definition of the roles of other key members during the transition, particularly yours;
- mechanics of the handover and the purchase of shares;
- a timetable for the process;
- a procedure for monitoring the process and dealing with disputes and problems.

Assignment 13.3 Succession

1. Does your management role in the business need to change in order to achieve your personal and business objectives? How do you see your future management and leadership role?
2. Who would take over your current role if you were incapacitated for an extended period of time?
3. For how much longer do you see yourself fulfilling your current role in the business? Who would take over your role? What do you need to do to identify and develop this person?
4. What role do you see yourself fulfilling in future? Write yourself a job description for this role.

Managing Yourself

You cannot be effective unless you manage yourself. There are at least three aspects you need to keep under review: how you spend your time, how you manage meetings and how you communicate.

How You Spend Your Time

Time is your most scarce resource, yet most owner-managers have only the haziest idea of where their days go. In chapter 5 you were asked to complete a breakdown of how you currently spend your time in order to decide what you should do more of and less of. Let us take an example, by looking in Table 13.1 at how Bob uses his time and what changes he might anticipate making:

Bob was horrified to find that 22 per cent of his time went into lots of bits and pieces of administration, such as treasury, health and safety and IT. None of these are high value-added activities. Of course, freeing himself up from these activities partly depends on recruiting other people to whom they can be allocated. But it will be worth it. Bob concluded that he should allocate more than 2 per cent of his time to the all-important recruitment of senior people and that 8 per cent of his time is too much to spend on his outside interests in other start-ups.

Bob thinks that about 15 per cent of his time goes on strategy planning and forward thinking; time drawing up business plans, assessing acquisitions and monitoring development in the States. It is interesting that he defines values/culture as a strategic issue, reflecting his passionate concern with 'the way we do things around here'. However, if management development is of strategic importance, 1 per cent seems like inadequate time to allocate to it.

Sixteen per cent of Bob's time goes on meetings off-site with customers and suppliers. This included a figure of 9 per cent on customer contact, which seems a bit low, especially as some customers are an important source of new ideas and potential new income streams. It is good that Bob includes a 5 per cent figure for his own personal development. Adding on the 6 per cent of time he spends on business travel, such things as trade shows and foreign business development takes his time off-site to 24 per cent.

Another 16 per cent of Bob's time goes on reviewing business performance, communication activities and management by walkabout. Bob does not see any reason to change this, particularly as his walkabouts are so successful and help him reinforce his unique company culture. However, as he lets go a bit more to the management team, his performance management should become by exception.

In summary, Bob anticipates he would like to spend roughly 40 per cent of his time on external focus, another 40 per cent on internal management focus and he believes he is probably wasting about 20 per cent of his time. Bob concluded that he should aim to spend no more than two days a week in the office, so that ties in well with the 40 per cent focus on internal management. At the moment, if he is not careful, he could get drawn back into the business and can find that he is there five days a week and, of course, if he is there, he will always find problems and things that need doing! Less time in the

TABLE 13.1 How Bob Spends his Time

Major activity and breakdown		Total percentage on this activity	
Strategy planning and forward thinking		15	
Business plans	5%		
Acquisition/disposal	1%		
Management development	1%		
Other	8%		
Board meetings		6	
Planning	1%		
Actual	4%		25
Follow-up	1%		
Meetings with management		19	
In groups	3%		
One to ones	11%		
Visits/travel together	5%		
Review of business performance		8	
Sales/income/Costs/Cash data	2%		
Monthly accounts	1%		
Key performance indicators	5%		
Other in house activities		8	
Walk the floor	5%		
Sales and marketing/business development	2%		
Staff meetings	1%		
Meetings off site		16	
Suppliers	1%		
Customers	9%		24
Trade organizations	1%		
Personal development	5%		
Trade/travel (not holidays)		6	
Conferences/trade shows/exhibitions	2%		
Market research tours	2%		
Foreign business development	2%		
Other (please specify)		22	
Outside investments	8%		
Recruitment	2%		
Legal/H&S	2%		
Facilities	4%		
IT	2%		
Payments and cash management	3%		
Social events	1%		
Total		100	

office may help him to stop him meddling – reacting to crises that the management team should be solving. It will also reduce his frustration levels and send him home at weekends in a better mood. He thinks that 40 per cent of time spent on the business would be about right, as this translates into two days out of the office. If he can stop doing some of the things in the rather unproductive other category he feels he can find himself a day a week to spend on himself, his development, his fishing and his family. Of course, it will not work out like that, but at least having done this exercise Bob has an ideal use of time against which to measure his actual time allocation.

On the subject of family, Bob also felt that it would be a good thing to maintain only one diary that would combine business and family engagements. This way he might avoid arriving in the middle of forgotten dinner parties or finding that they have all gone off on a planned excursion without him!

There are some important principles here that should inform how you choose to spend your time in future.

- You have to decide the priorities in your business. There will always be more tasks around than resources to meet them. There will be constant pressure on you to do a little bit of everything. That way you might make everyone happy but you can guarantee that there are no results. One of your most critical and difficult jobs is to say 'No' and to stop doing things.
- Remember, as Drucker said, that inside the business there are only costs. Results are on the outside. If you are spending five days a week in the business you can be sure you are making no progress on the business. A sure way of stopping yourself meddling and growing your team is to spend less time in the office.
- Nothing requires as much time and effort as people decisions. There will be critical people decisions that only you can make. Do not let your time be wasted on low-level, routine administrative matters.

Making Your Meetings More Effective

As Bob's diary showed, meetings can typically consume a great deal of time in a working week. Of course, meetings are a vital ways of exchanging face-to-face information, but anything you can do to make meetings more effective must be a good idea. Here are some pointers to help you manage meetings effectively.

Define the Purpose Clearly

Meetings without set objectives demotivate people. Do you need a meeting at all?

Decide Who Should Attend

Invite the people who can make things happen or who really need to know.

An Agenda is Vital

Your meeting will be much more successful if you send out an agenda beforehand and everyone prepares in advance. If there is information such as budgets, sales reports, proposals that need to be absorbed, send them out beforehand as well. The agenda provides your control device, establishing order and sequence, assigning tasks and providing guidelines for the timing of each item.

Order of the Items

Really think about what goes on the agenda and the ordering of the items. Most management meetings become a routine, predictable and unproductive sleepwalking through the usual headings of financials, sales forecasts and departmental reports. Are these really the most important issues for your business? The first item on your agenda will indicate what is really important to you! Why not make it recruitment, motivation or culture for a change? Getting a boring individual report from each of your departmental heads is a recipe for defensiveness and sending everyone to sleep. Make your meetings issue led.

Be a Good Listener

As chairman of the meeting you need to listen more carefully than anyone else in the group, since it is the chairman's job to make sure that the real point of someone's conversation is not lost, to pick the right point to move on and to clarify when people get in a muddle.

Involve All Participants

People are much more likely to feel committed to the decisions you reach if they have had their say. Indeed, you should expect and insist that everyone at the meeting makes a valuable contribution, or else why are they there? It is always better to use open-ended questions. The what, why, how, when and where questions work much better than closed 'do you' and 'can you' questions.

Keep to the Point

Keep the meeting on course and stop people going too far off the point. Red herrings and ramblings abound so do not be too tolerant of people who take the meeting off at a tangent.

Control Aggression

Stop signs of aggression before the situation becomes too ugly and confrontational and people are forced into extreme positions and lose credibility. Conflict can be healthy in encouraging new ideas, but you do not want personal arguments and, of course, never lose your own temper, come what may.

Check Progress

Check understanding by regularly summarizing using the words 'so, what you are saying is …'.

Decide on Action

How are actions to be taken, by whom and when? Ensure that there is a record of what has been agreed. It is very difficult for the chairperson to take minutes as well, so get someone else to do this.

Follow-up

Make sure agreed decisions are implemented. If the meeting was worth having the decisions are worth implementing.

Communicating

Leadership is all about people and therefore all about communication. Very little of the job of the leader can be done in splendid isolation because the essence of leadership lies in communicating a vision and then getting people excited enough to follow it willingly. The data from many years of owner-managers completing the visionary leader questionnaire (see chapter 5) clearly demonstrate that of the ten leadership facets entrepreneurs score consistently low on communicative leadership, defined as the ability to get one's message across, interpersonal skills, listening skills and rapport.

This is a serious weakness, perhaps the other side of the coin of the entrepreneur's energy and drive, but one which means that the typical owner-manager tends to want to put across his or her own ideas rather than listen to others and tends to have a short fuse in the face of people not understanding the message. The reality of business is that you have to communicate regularly, repeatedly and effectively if people are ever to understand and act on your messages. Apparently TV advertisers know this fact well: they appreciate that an advert needs to be shown eight times before the message sticks!

You need to do the same. So part of managing yourself will be to manage your own frustration levels when people, deliberately it sometimes seems, fail to see what you are on about. You need to overdose on communication – some have suggested that as much as 80 per cent of the CEO's time should be spent in face-to-face communication. This means having many and regular channels of communication such as staff meetings, state of the nation talks, one-to-ones, staff newsletters, management by walkabout-social meetings. If you communicate the same thing, passionately, clearly and repeatedly, the message will eventually get through. Remember that in any communication the onus is on you to get the message across convincingly.

Good verbal communication is a two-way process, which means giving the listener a chance to ask questions, clarify misunderstandings and make comments. Many small businesses forget this and specialize in one-way communication from the boss downwards. Build into your communications question and answer sessions, divide people into smaller groups where they are less inhibited and allow time for them to participate in the discussion. There are a number of barriers that get in the way of and distort communications, such as noise, interruptions, personal prejudice, assumptions and values. Some words can stop us listening altogether. So a good start point for communicating is to talk to people in an environment free from interruption and to avoid phrases and tones that will rub the other person up the wrong way. Stay calm and neutral; if you sense emotional barriers keep your conversation brief. Sometimes you will need repeated small bites at the cherry, giving an individual time to think and reassess before reinforcing your point.

Research has shown that in any piece of communication only an astoundingly low 7 per cent of the message is conveyed by the actual words. The tone of the voice accounts for 35 per cent and non-verbal or body language for a massive 58 per cent. It is not just what you say but the way that you say it that counts. As most owner-managers have impatient and assertive personalities, it is easy to see how tone and body language might become a barrier to effectively getting the message across! Furthermore, at the beginning of any conversation note that 87 per cent of the information is via the eyes and only 9 per cent via the ears (the rest is through other senses such as touch). So establishing rapport early is vital to a successful conversation. You can do this through smiling, eye-to-eye contact, listening, summarizing and avoiding defensive body language.

Your checklist for communicating is:

- communicate at least twice as much as you think you should;
- listen well – this is the best compliment you can pay another person;
- establish rapport so that the other person is willing to listen;
- be prepared to repeat and repeat again important messages;
- make sure the conversation is truly two-way – you have two ears but only one mouth!
- keep it simple stupid;
- be passionate about communicating your vision;
- count to ten next time you want to explode;
- use language that will be meaningful to the person to whom you are communicating;
- use your eyes.

Assignment 13.4: Managing Yourself

1. Keep a log of how you spend your time over the next week and analyse it as suggested above. Do you need to improve the way you manage your own time? If so, how?
2. Review the last three meetings you have run and identify ways in which you could improve the way you manage meetings in future.

3. Get some feedback on the way you communicate verbally. What could you do to improve the your verbal communication?

Investing in Your On-going Development

While investing in training and developing everyone else do not forget about YOU! You are the most important role model in the business, the source of vision and energy for the future, so it is vital that you look after your own well-being and develop any skills you need as your role changes. Sometimes, it is not so much that you need to graft on new skills as that you need re-energizing and refreshing because you have become stale. Sometimes the issue is to deal with the fact that leading a company is a lonely business and you need someone you can offload your worries to, someone who will listen to you. Developmental experiences can take many forms.

Appropriate Role Models

It is perhaps surprising how often a father is a powerful role model, along with people like a former boss or a commander in the services. Role models are hugely influential, although sometimes it must be said that the role model of a successful parent can actually hold you back:

> I am the son of a very successful father who created something fantastic and is still chairman. At 20 I wanted to impress my father but I will never be him. They all look to him for expert knowledge and quick decisions, he does not nurture people and his approach is based on fear. My concept of leadership was entirely based on him, leaving me no room to develop. I now see there are many successful leaders who do not rule by fear.

Broader Experiences

As one owner-manager comments: 'When it has been the same business all your life and you have never experienced anything else, it is easy to fall back into what you are comfortable with.' Travelling abroad, working for different companies, meeting different people or carrying out charity work will all help widen your horizons.

Making Mistakes

You learn by doing and failing, then doing and succeeding. You will make an awful lot of mistakes before you grow into the leader you can be.

Formal Management Training

Formal training can be invaluable, not only in equipping you with business skills but in bringing you in contact with other people who have similar problems. This provides you with a consolation, a source of encouragement and a source of new ideas. The views of your trainers and fellow participants will stimulate your thinking, broaden your horizons and challenge your assumptions. You are guaranteed some light bulb flashes of inspiration!

Books

Well, for some!

Get a Mentor

Find yourself an executive coach you trust and with whom the chemistry works. You will find this relationship an invaluable support, a constant challenge, a way of being held accountable, a mirror on what you have achieved and a reminder of your own strengths and weaknesses.

Work With Other Owner-Managers

No one understands the issues and challenges you face quite in the same way as another owner-manager! Try to find other owner-managers or 'kindred spirits' with whom you can network, share issues and challenges, and with whom you can exchange input, advice, support, encouragement and challenge.

Such groups can range from very informal self-managed networking groups to highly organized, structured processes offered by commercial organizations.

There is no doubt at all that owner-managers who invest in themselves grow bigger and more profitable businesses, and have more fun!

Assignment 13.5: Your On-going Development

1. In what ways does your leadership need to develop in order to achieve your business and personal objectives? How will you achieve this development?
2. Are there any other skills and capabilities that you need to develop in order to fulfil your role now and in the future? How will you develop these skills and capabilities?
3. What do you need to do in order to achieve your personal goals outside the business? How will you continue developing in this area?

fourteen
Acquisitions, Mergers, Divestments and Joint Ventures

Up to this point, this book has focused on organic approaches to growth, that is developing your business through using your own resources and asset base.

In this chapter we review alternative approaches to growth. These may or may not apply to your business, subject to your market position, the opportunities that present themselves and your personal appetite for risk! First, a word on definitions.

Acquisition describes the takeover of one organization by another. (In this chapter we are assuming that you are doing the acquiring: the next chapter covers the topic of being acquired, as a means of realizing value from your business.) Where privately held businesses are concerned, this typically means the acquisition of a controlling interest, if not the entire shareholding.

A merger takes place when two businesses of a similar size agree to merge their interests into a larger entity, which usually requires the formation of a new legal vehicle. The allocation of shares reflects the assets – in the broadest sense – which each party brings to the table. The standard outcome is 50:50, but sometimes the balance varies a little depending on the deal.

A divestment takes place when you dispose of a part of your business's trading activity, or sell a significant asset (or assets), which is valued on the balance sheet (such as surplus plant and equipment). As divestment by a growing business is normally a tactical activity, and not part of the mainstream strategy for building the business, it is not discussed at length.

A joint venture, as the name suggests, is a business activity initiated by one or more organizations in which each participant has a stake. It can take a variety of forms. It might be little more than an informal arrangement, governed by a loose understanding. At the other end of the spectrum, it might consist of the creation of a new business entity with its own balance sheet and profit statement, in which the parent organizations hold shares.

Acquisitions

It is hard to know just how many businesses change hands annually in the UK. Most businesses are sole traders and their fates are not comprehensively tracked. When it comes to limited companies and limited liability partnerships, industry estimates would put the number of acquisitions at over 2,000 in a typical year. The pattern tends to track the fortunes of the economy. In boom times there is more activity: acquirers are feeling expansionist and sellers are more optimistic about getting a good price. The converse occurs when the economy turns down.

Most of the businesses bought and sold in Britain will have a turnover of under £20 million – unsurprisingly, since fewer than 2 per cent of UK businesses actually have a turnover above £20 million!

Why Would You Want to Make an Acquisition?

Acquiring a business is rarely something that happens by accident, although events can sometimes force people's hand. In its early days Pacific Direct was critically dependent on a supplier in the Czech Republic. When the owner disclosed that the company was facing a cash crisis, Pacific Direct founder Lara Morgan concluded that she had little choice but to mount a rescue. Pacific Direct became the majority shareholder, a move that, as things turned out, has proved extremely beneficial for both parties.

Strategic Reasons for Making an Acquisition

Of course, you would not consider buying just any supplier, but only ones that are of strategic importance to your business. Pacific Direct's Czech supplier formed a key component of the company's international supply chain. Ensuring continuity of supply can in itself be a strong enough reason for acquiring another business. There are a number of other equally valid reasons.

Complementary Portfolios of Products, Services or Customers

It often happens that there are other players in the market who have businesses that could dovetail nicely with your own. It could be product or service ranges that will enhance what you are currently doing, or providing access to a customer segment that you do not currently address. Two main factors should influence the decision to go ahead: first, the conclusion that this approach will deliver bigger benefits more rapidly than growing organically (such as reduced unit administrative costs, as a result of improved overhead allocation); second, that the act of acquisition will not jeopardize the anticipated benefit (customers will not defect, for example).

Increased Production or Warehousing Capacity

If you are a manufacturing or logistics business, it may make better sense for you to acquire extra capacity outright rather than lease it. In an owner-managed business this decision is frequently influenced by considerations of pension fund arrangements.

As a Means of Diversification

Rather than 'grow your own' business in a market segment that is not your core, you choose to acquire a business with a proven track record.

As a Means of Entry or Expansion into Foreign Markets

The process of scaling up activity in overseas markets often culminates in buying an established business in the market(s) concerned. In certain markets – notoriously France – it is difficult to be taken seriously unless you have a local presence on the ground. Buying a business can both accelerate that presence and mitigate the trading risks.

Taking out Excess Capacity

Many markets, especially in advanced economies, are simply oversupplied. Motor industry analysts put excess global automotive manufacturing capacity at over 20 per cent. It is no surprise that, since the year 2000, car plants have been closing around the world (although some new ones have also opened, generally in low-cost economies). It can, on occasion, make commercial sense to buy a competitor with a view to transferring production to your own facilities.

As a Means of Acquiring Scarce Resources

When you buy a business, you acquire not only the assets but also the skills and people that come with it. In business services such as advertising, law or investment management firms, access to scarce and valuable 'talent' can often be a prime reason behind the acquisition.

This list is not exhaustive, but is representative of the drivers behind the acquisitions made by the many owner-managed businesses that we have worked with over the years. If your primary reason for making a potential acquisition does not feature in this list then you need to think carefully about why you are doing so.

Process of Acquisition

The process of acquisition is complex and there exist innumerable specialist publications that can provide detailed guidance. In a general book of this kind, our role has to be confined to presenting an overview of what takes place. There are a number of well-trodden paths to getting started. The search process most frequently starts with targets that are already known to the prospective acquirer, especially if the target is an industry competitor or supplier. If you are broadening your search, or are looking in a sector with which you are not familiar, you have three main choices.

- Appoint an agent, normally a broker who specializes in this area, who will act on your behalf.
- Consult the financial press or the financial pages of national newspapers and trade journals, which advertise businesses for sale (perhaps augmented by a trawl of the Internet).
- Place your own advertisements in the relevant media.

Many people who are doing this for the first time will seek the help of their professional advisers before they start. This could be either your auditor or your legal adviser. However, it is important to have confidence in their ability to act on your behalf, and to check carefully that the partners are experienced in this type of activity. If they are not, you need to find advisers who know what they are doing. In our experience the most reliable method is to ask around your network of friends and colleagues and take the recommendations of people whose opinion you respect. Armed with some names, you would do best to compile a shortlist and then to interview, say, the top three for the privilege of handling your business! One recent BGP participant we know went through this process and discovered that law firms that looked pretty much the same on the outside were really quite different once they got beneath the surface.

Making contact with your target can be done directly by you, or via an intermediary you appoint. The advantages of the intermediary approach are obvious: your identity can remain concealed until a time of your choosing and an experienced professional is doing the legwork. On the other hand, it will cost you professional fees and you do not directly control the process. Whether you do this yourself or through a third party, the initial objective will be the same: to establish whether there is a possible deal that can be done.

Assuming that both parties conclude there is a deal to be done, the valuation process now begins. This works at two levels. Informally, you will have conversations with managers within the target business as well as with your adviser and other people whose opinion you will want to canvass. Formally, your advisers will begin on the process of commercial and legal due diligence. Due diligence is a technical term, but is in fact no more and no less than part of the duty of care which the directors of a business are required under law to exercise on behalf of the shareholders. The act of acquiring another business exposes the shareholders to a new set of risks, and it is the duty of the directors to mitigate the business's exposure.

In practical terms this means confirming all the claims about the business made by the owners, and identifying all the risks that come with the acquisition. Accountants and lawyers have standard checklists that run to many pages and which the directors of the target business are obliged to reply to. The major risks are typically associated with ownership of physical assets and intellectual property, contracts of supply, employment contracts, historical risks (such as risks associated with land and buildings), outstanding or contingent litigation, and so forth. The due diligence process is also the reverse side of the valuation process. The target business will be attempting to talk up the valuation through emphasizing aspects of the business that are more difficult to value, such as future cashflows, while the acquirer will frequently use the due diligence process to talk the value down through identifying risks that need to be mitigated or provided for. Eventually, if a deal is to be struck, a compromise position will have to be reached.

In an acquisition process that runs smoothly, a price is sometimes agreed early on subject to satisfactory completion of the due diligence process. There is no one, universally agreed, method of valuing a business, especially when its shares are not listed on a stock exchange. There are rules of thumb that exist in different industries (generally multiples related to either turnover or net profit), and you will be familiar with those that exist in yours. Similarly, professional valuers have their own methods based on both their experience and their knowledge of current market conditions. At the end of the day, the business will be worth what you, the acquirer, are prepared to pay for it. Caveat emptor!

Mergers

A merger in many ways looks similar to an acquisition – and all of the issues in the previous section apply. A process of due diligence takes place, two entities become one, a single set of assets is created and, often, a new legal entity is created. The critical difference, of course, is that the term merger is used of a marriage of equals, or near-equals. The unspoken presumption is that each party brings something roughly similar to the party, and emerges as an equal partner in the relationship.

That may well be the outcome, but often the reality is a little different. Where the corporate cultures are very different, sooner or later after the merger has taken place one will prevail as dominant – and the situation will look very much like a takeover. This is even the case where the shareholding is evenly split between the shareholders of the old businesses. What tends then to happen is that the staff from the 'losing' partner either adapt to the new environment or leave. In instances when people leave, it is common for the shareholders of the 'loser' to follow until virtually all traces of their old business have been effaced.

If that sounds a little brutal, it is better to be aware of it in advance, rather than go through the process naively and live to regret it! Indeed, if you can see in advance that there is a high possibility that this will happen, it may be better to assume that the deal will be an acquisition – and then work out which side of the acquisition you will be on!

The People Factors in Acquisitions and Mergers

When you are contemplating merging with, or acquiring, another business you should be aware that around 50–70 per cent of mergers and acquisitions fail, that is they fail to meet their objectives. The deal goes through but then it falls apart. The expected synergies which justified the whole thing do not materialize, the economies of scales prove illusory, corporate cultures do not mesh and frightened employees underperform.

That represents a very high failure rate for an expensive habit and the failure lies as much in the people factors as the strategic and financial ones.

Is the Logic Compelling?

In the throes of early romance and courtship, it is all too easy for owner-managers to fool themselves about their prospective partner. Pre-merger targeting will go much better if you have some sort of template of what you are looking for. If a merger decision is a stool with three legs – strategic fit, financial fit and culture fit – all three legs need to be in place if the stool is not to wobble and fall over.

Do the two businesses share the same values? Fights over anything from management style to company picnics can foul up business marriages. So weigh up a prospective partner's culture as well as its finances before doing the deal. All too many CEOs just want to throw everything into the blender and push the mix button – but it does not work like that.

The urge to merge can be powerful but just because you are part-way down the track and there are some potential synergies does not mean there is an overpowering logic for spending the rest of your life together.

Stages of an Acquisition or Merger: the Cultural Perspective

Typically, there will be at least three stages to manage your way through:

1. romance (due diligence);
2. courtship (culture fit);
3. managing the marriage.

Romance

During the early stage of romance everything looks wonderful! The dating agency has come up with the goods and due diligence is, you believe, a simple matter. Not a bit of it, however! Your proposed partner will be running a fine-toothed comb over every aspect of your business, and you of course will want to do the same. Again, the people issues are surprisingly important in making a well-informed decision. Not just the most obvious things such as conditions of employment and contracts but the lock-in of key players. In a small business, it is particularly vital to retain key personnel.

In one IT company, a significant part of the value rested in the know-how of the staff. When it transpired that employees did not have formal contracts of employment and could leave at any time, the purchaser was able to negotiate a greatly reduced price.

One can indeed argue that, in a service business, all you have is the people; so of course value ultimately depends on them. Therefore, making some sort of assessment of the quality and personality of the management team, their skills and future capability, will be crucial to success. You will find a checklist of some of these factors at the end of this section.

Courtship

As in the case of an enforced marriage, a merger between two partners who have incompatible values, philosophies and working practices is unlikely to work. How does your management team get on with theirs? Test out the culture just as you might test out whether your new partner picks their teeth, likes bad pop music or wears awful clothes. Investigating the softer issues will help avoid derailment later on. If you are informal, sales-led, passionately fun people and you are contemplating marriage to a quarterly driven, investor-conscious, financially managed business, you are not going to make sweet music together!

It is also perhaps a surprising fact, but a company that is up for sale will not automatically gravitate towards the highest bidder. In a significant number of cases, the selling company will go for the bid that is the most accommodating to the preservation of jobs and spares them the imposition of a new and draconian style.

So it is interesting to see how and why a merger succeeds. That is what seems to have happened when Mobile Media and Freight Media merged.

Karen Olsen started Mobile Media in 1987, the same year Nick Lees founded Freight Media. Both companies did the same thing: they ran poster campaigns on big trucks for major advertisers. It was a new medium and both expanded quickly, having overcome competition from lots of small operators, which had scared them both. Now that they had the market to themselves, Olsen and Lees competed on some occasions and collaborated on others. Finally, Olsen suggested that her company buy half of Freight Media, the half that focused purely on mobile advertising.

It helped that they had known and respected each other for years. 'We got on well while also being deadly rivals', laughs Lees. They shared similar values about how business is done. And they knew that they would lose business opportunities if they did not get bigger. Strategically and culturally it seemed a good fit. Most mergers do.

But then they tackled the issues so many companies fudge. From the outset, it was explicit that Mobile Media was the acquirer and that Olsen would be the new boss. 'We considered the two of us running the combined entity and we just knew it wouldn't work', says Olsen. There was no nonsense about joint leadership or everything staying the same.

Turning two workforces into one is never easy. 'I hadn't realized how much loyalty there was to the Freight Media brand', admits Olsen. 'That brand was wiped away overnight. So I've seen every person and explained the philosophy and the benefits and that they're now part of a bigger, better team.' It was crucial there were no redundancies. 'We've brought in lots of policies to make everyone feel part of the team. There's a newsletter for drivers and everyone's on the same mobile network, which isn't simple given our geographical spread. We've lost two drivers but, otherwise, there haven't been any casualties.'

Nick Lees says mergers are like marriages and he is right. Everyone talks about the wedding but it is the marriage that matters. Everyone talks about mergers and deals – but what counts is having the time, energy and commitment to ensure that everybody can live happily ever after.

Managing the Marriage

So, it is a done deal and everyone lives happily ever after? Well, not quite. As one wag said: 'The end of one man's deal is the start of another's ordeal.' There is the small issue of managing the combined business. Who will run what? What pressures will that put on a management team that perhaps is already stretched running the current business? Most acquirers tend to run away from the challenge of integrating two businesses then get surprised when the synergy of $1 + 1 = 3$ turns out to be elusive. There will be a lot to think about: you need to create changes which have a clear people shape to them so that it is soon clear what jobs and responsibilities people will have. A transfer of technology will take place and you will face the challenge of combining different systems and procedures.

Integrating two businesses is a real challenge, which involves

- leadership
- anticipating employee reactions
- communication
- team building.

Leadership   Be in no doubt that the costs to you as the owner-manager will be huge. Managing the intended merger or acquisition will take your eye off the ball and business may suffer. You may be up all night as the deal closes, things go wrong, the price may be renegotiated, your stress levels will be sky high and the deal will consume at least 60 per cent of your working time for months and most of your emotional energy for 100 per cent of the time! The end result had therefore better be worth it. Apart from you, the people who will have to manage the merger, the management teams on both sides, will themselves be in the invidious position of managing themselves through denial while trying to do the same for others! Everyone will be working through their own doubts and what the implications might be for them personally; everyone's workload will be much greater, as well as their anxiety levels. Yet at this time strong and visible leadership is essential, which makes still more demands on the top management.

You will also need a process, a project plan. Projects do not come much bigger than this and you will forget things if you do not plan in advance. You will need to assess well before completion just how and by whom is the company going to be run. As one owner-manager said, 'We were basically trying to run two businesses which were 100 miles apart, and we should have put the right person in from day 1'.

Employee Reactions   A merger or acquisition is an exceptional event, which will inevitably cause distraction and tensions in both companies. There will be strong feelings of loss, betrayal and fear. People will ask, 'What about me – is my job safe?' They will feel vulnerable, almost as though they are being asked to apply for their own jobs, which they well might be. They may fear loss of status, a change of team or a new boss, new roles and responsibilities. The questions will come thick and fast and you may not yet know the answers to all of them. You will find that your employees fall into one of three camps: the ready, who are raring to go; the resistors, who did not get what they wanted and are adjusting to new realities; and the wrung-out, who are listless, cynical and demotivated. All need your attention if they are to successfully climb on board the new enterprise. Listening to their concerns and actively communicating with your people are the key here.

Communication   Communicate like crazy, as much as you can and as early as you can, from the due diligence process onwards. Be as open and honest as you possibly can. Acknowledge that people will be preoccupied with their own interests. Put together a communication plan to ensure you reach all employees and, just as importantly, that you talk to key customers and suppliers. Go out and about the two businesses, trying to put over an exciting story and vision and explaining the benefits and future opportunities for the combined new business. Try to get face to face with teams and individuals as much as you can. A direct and personal approach will win more supporters. If you can, tell people what will not be changed for a few months: you will be providing a welcome reassurance.

Do plenty of management by walkabout, hold regional road-shows, produce a special merger edition of your newsletter, hold voluntary lunchtime sessions where employees can express doubts and talk through their concerns, have one-to-one conversations wherever possible and think about taking the combined new team off for an away-day.

Team   In any merger or acquisition, if you are not careful there will be the perception of a winning team (us) and a losing team (them). This is dangerous and potentially divisive as it may stop you ever successfully integrating the businesses and realizing your planned synergies.

The way to integrate the businesses is not by one team lording it over the other but by creating a totally new team with a new, shared vision. Get them all together at an off-site meeting, get them talking to each other and leave only when you have bashed out a new vision and a set of agreed values which everyone will buy in to.

Acquisition or Merger People Factors Checklist

Although the odds are stacked against acquisitions and mergers fully meeting the original objectives, paying attention to the people factors both before and after the transaction can shorten the odds in your favour.

Use this checklist to help you make your pre-merger people due diligence more effective and to enable you to put in place appropriate post-merger management.

Terms and Conditions of Employment

- Employment contracts for all staff including directors.
- Details of benefits, i.e. share option schemes/pensions/cars/mobile phones.
- Lists of key managers and staff.
- Accident records.
- Salary ranges and banding/pay structures/promotion guidelines.
- Details of employment disputes, appeals or pending legal cases.
- Employee handbook.
- Accustomed practices (which may be undocumented) like holidays/travel allowances.
- Training schemes and management development.
- Trade union matters.
- Policies for health and safety/redundancy/maternity leave, etc.
- Employee turnover.

Conditions for Key Managers and Staff

- 'Lock-in' arrangements: who, for how long, on what terms?
- Share ownership, minority shareholder issues.
- Non-compete clauses.
- Key man insurance.

Strength of Management Team

- What is the management structure?
- What are lengths of service/educational backgrounds?
- What is the typical management style?
- What previous experience do managers have?
- How much potential is there for future growth?
- To what extent do people enthuse about company values?
- Do senior managers operate as a team?
- Who will run the new business?

Organization Structure

- What are the existing organization charts?
- What are the areas of critical core skills?
- What synergies are likely when the two businesses are put together?
- How would possible synergies influence the culture?

Culture Fit

- What image is portrayed by reception staff, accounts, internal memos, advertisements and so forth?
- What do people say they believe in (value statements)?
- Does the evidence back this up?
- Is there a healthy organizational climate?
- What are the communications practices?

Post-merger Management

- How will both parties want to handle communications issues?
- Who will be the key contacts between both parties to ensure effective transition management?
- Clear post-merger management processes and management structures.
- Post-merger communications plans including employees, customers and suppliers.

Joint Ventures

As we said earlier, joint venture is a term that covers a spectrum of activities, from a loose declaration of intent to a jointly held incorporated company. In the middle are a variety of agreements which have some sort of legal force and impose a binding commitment on the parties involved.

At Cranfield, during 2003 and 2004, we undertook research into venture collaboration between firms, typically between larger and smaller firms, since that is the form which most joint ventures seem to assume (David Molian and Quentin Solt, as part of Mastering Innovation, *The Financial Times*, October 2004). As a result, we compiled a set of guidelines designed to enable prospective partners to think clearly about what they were embarking on. They are reproduced below.

Articulate Clearly the Strategic Aims of the Deal

What is the rationale for the deal, and what are the anticipated benefits to each party? Too often the strategic rationale is little more than 'it seemed like a good idea at the time'. If the ultimate destination is unclear, how will either party know whether or when they are getting there?

Align the Interests of the Parties

Two parties to a deal, especially firms which are very dissimilar in many respects, may have common ground. But they will also have interests which diverge. Potential – as well as actual – conflicts of interest, however, have to be identified and pre-empted right at the outset. A skilled advisor will identify latent conflicts, seek agreement as to the principles for resolving these, and provide the mechanisms for resolution. To be effective, the advisor needs to build the trust of both parties.

Identify Rights and Responsibilities

It is important to be explicit over who brings what to the table: not merely intellectual property, but physical assets and access to certain resources. With rights go responsibilities. What is expected of each party in return for their enjoyment of the asset base? Again, vagueness is the enemy of a good joint venture. If things go well, then a certain lack of clarity probably does not matter too much. When things do not go according to plan, ambiguity in the agreement will be the source of endless disagreement and finger pointing.

Set Out a 'Prenuptial' Agreement that Provides for the Dissolution of the Deal

Most of us shy away from contemplating divorce at the time of getting wed. Unfortunately, this is not a luxury a joint venture can afford. Change of ownership, insolvency and a major change of strategic direction are just some of the more obvious triggers for dissolving the deal which need to be explicitly provided for.

All of these may be classed as execution issues. They are not 'just' legal issues, best left to the lawyers. Leaving things to the lawyers usually guarantees only that the costs will rack up!

BGP past participant Ian Turner of Juice Technology has based his electrical power distribution business on the joint venture model. Juice provides the research and development to create new technology. Partners which are hundreds of times larger than Juice provide the route to market through their sales and marketing expertise. Every time an installation takes place, Juice takes a royalty payment. It is an arrangement that plays to the strengths of both parties.

Founder of Currencies Direct, Mayank Patel, who, like Ian, took part in BGP 2001, has a strategic alliance with banking giant HSBC. Currencies Direct provides remittance facilities for HSBC customers wanting to send small sums overseas. As Mayank explains, 'We are set up to do this cost-effectively, whereas it is more difficult for HSBC. So we can provide their customers with the exact service they require, and HSBC knows that we will keep their promises!'

A Final Word

It should by now be clear that the role of advisers in these types of transactions is paramount. It has been justly said that, if you think good legal advice is expensive, how much do you think bad legal advice will cost you? Since the earliest days of Cobra Beer, Karan Bilimoria has sought to hire the very best auditors and legal advisers that the business can afford – and he is qualified both as a lawyer and as an accountant! His contention is that you should surround yourself with advisers suitable for the business you aspire to be, not the business you currently are.

Assignment 14.1

1. From the perspective of your business, do you believe that an acquisition will help you get where you want to go more quickly?
2. If the answer is 'yes', list the strategic reasons why acquisition makes sense.
3. Can you profile and even identify your acquisition targets?
4. If you are attracted by the idea of merging your business with another, have you considered fully the risk that one party might emerge dominant?
5. Would a joint venture make an attractive alternative to acquisition, as a means of expansion?
6. Are there assets or activities within the current business that could usefully be divested?
7. Are your advisers sufficiently skilled and experienced to support you in transactions of this kind?

fifteen
What are Your Options for Realizing the Value?

At some point on your entrepreneurial journey, you may well conclude that you want to exit the business and realize the value that you have built up over the years.

By the end of this chapter, you should have a clear understanding of the following key topics.

- Why do entrepreneurial business owners sell up and realize value?
- What are the options for value realization? We briefly look at a range of options including trade sales, selling to other managers, floating on a stock market, winding up and passing the business on through the family.
- Preparing the business for sale so as to maximize its attractiveness to potential purchasers.
- How privately owned businesses are typically valued.
- Using professional advisors.
- Life after the sale.

Why Realize the Value?

Every year, tens of thousands of entrepreneurs seek to realize all or part of the value in their business. The reasons for doing so are legion. Some want to retire, others are bored with the business and want to move on to something else, and others feel that their business has reached a point where association with a larger business is desirable or even essential. In quite a lot of instances the owners have taken the business as far as they are capable and it is for others take it forward. And, if you have taken venture capital funding, you may find that your investors become restless after a few years and look for a return on their investment.

A study at Cranfield on why entrepreneurs exit identified that the most common reason was retirement (51 per cent), followed by reasons to do with the strategy and development of the business (34 per cent), the entrepreneur wanting to explore other interests (8 per cent) and ill-health (7 per cent).

What are Your Options?

The routes to selling are also numerous and the one chosen will probably be governed by a number of factors, some personal and some economic. We have described below some of the most common options for selling the business open to the entrepreneur.

Winding Down

One option is simply to allow the business to wind down of its own accord, then close the business and sell off the assets. However, even if your business is not in the greatest of shape, or even financially troubled, selling an operating business, even one that is in trouble, almost always brings more money than closing it down and selling off the assets. Before you give up and conclude that no one would ever buy your business, consider that people buy businesses, even businesses with financial problems, for all sorts of reasons. Someone with more cash and another compatible business will be able to strip out cost, sell off unwanted assets and effectively add your customers to theirs. The combined business will be even stronger.

Private Sale

A very large number of businesses, particularly smaller ones, are sold privately to other individual entrepreneurs.

So-called 'sweetheart deals', where you sell out to someone you know or already do business with, are a popular strategy for retiring entrepreneurs. On the surface, this seems appealing since it can be done in a friendly way and should be straightforward once the price has been agreed. However, the reality is that they are almost always bad deals for the seller. In setting the original price, without an auction or controlled auction, you could be short-changed by as much as 50 per cent. Even having got your price, how can you be sure you will get your money? Warranties, missed earn-outs and bad tax advice could take much of that headline price out of your pocket.

An alternative, which at least creates an auction-like scenario, is to advertise the business through the press or a specialist business broker.

Trade Sale

A trade sale is where you sell some or all of your business to another business – usually a larger one and quite often one that is publicly traded. This is a very popular route, particularly for those entrepreneurs who are selling for strategic reasons since the larger acquiring business can often provide key resources to enable further growth (such as finance, access to markets, research and development, and so on), which the acquired business would not otherwise be able to afford.

As far as the acquiring business is concerned, the attractions of the acquisition are usually to do with some form of 'strategic fit' with their existing portfolio of products/services, or possibly taking out a competitor. There may be other reasons, such as access to particular people or skills, access to a more entrepreneurial culture, which are attractive to the acquirer also.

In the particular case of a publicly quoted company, there is an extra incentive to acquire privately owned businesses. Because the shares of an unquoted company are 'illiquid', that is they cannot be bought and sold easily, they are viewed as being less valuable than shares of a similar type of quoted company. So, whereas a quoted company's shares might trade on a P/E (price–earnings) ratio of 12 or more, a similar unquoted company would be more likely to be valued on a P/E of 4. Thus, if your profits were £250,000 and your company was unquoted, it might be valued at £1 million (4×£250,000), whereas a public company undertaking identical activities could be valued at £3 million (12×£250,000). Were a public company to buy your company for £1 million and absorb its profits into its own, the value of the acquiring company could rise by £3 million, without any change in the level of business undertaken. That is £2 million more than they paid in the first place!

Clearly, the more desirable your business is to the acquirer, the better the price that you will achieve. Therefore, it is worthwhile thinking carefully about what types of business might be a good fit with yours and actively approaching them, usually through an adviser, with a proposition.

For these reasons, a trade sale usually results in a better price than a private sale. On the other hand, the acquirer very often demands that the existing owner-manager stays with the business for a minimum period (a 'lock-in'), sometimes up to two years, so that a successful transition can be made. Part of the price that the acquirer is paying is usually linked to performance during this period in what is known as an 'earn-out'. However, be warned – do not let too much of the purchase price be subject to an earn-out. There is a lot of evidence that in the majority of situations earn-outs are never paid – the acquirer finds a way to avoid paying it!

Selling to Your Existing Management Team

Just as larger companies often sell off parts of their operations to the existing management team of that particular unit, so can you sell your business to your management team. This is known as a management buy-out or MBO.

MBOs are very popular with venture capital providers. The reasons are not hard to see. The business is usually well established and profitable, and the people in the best position to run the business are probably there already. The existing team can then be incentivized with shares and options to take the business to even greater heights. The result is much happiness and wealth all round! This is one of the reasons why developing a truly effective management team around you is so crucial to growth and building value.

On the other hand, smaller businesses can often find it difficult to attract much venture capital interest in funding a buy-out. The reason is usually that the venture capitalist believes the owner-manager makes all the key decisions, leaving the management to 'obey orders'. As the venture capitalist has no intention or desire to manage the business, it will be necessary to convince them that the existing management team can really run the business without you.

Selling to an Incoming Management Team

A close relative of the MBO is the MBI, or management buy-in, where you sell the business to an incoming manager and management team. This may be an appropriate route if you believe that your current management team lack expertise and/or experience. By injecting new management resources, the business is better placed to continue to grow and the new managers can share in the future profits and value.

As with MBOs, MBIs are popular with venture capital firms. Usually, the venture capital firm will have had a successful relationship with the buy-in team in a previous venture. Alternatively, a business angel with experience in your industry or market may fund the buy-in and take an active role in the future management of the business themselves.

There are also combinations of MBIs and MBOs where some of the business's existing management team join with a new incoming manager to buy the business. This arrangement goes under the strange sounding title of a BIMBO!

Passing the Business on Through the Family

If your inspiration is to build up an enduring family business, then you may plan to pass the business on to the next generation. However, beware the old adage 'clogs to clogs in three generations'. Only one-third of family businesses reach the second generation, less than two-thirds of these survive through the second generation while only 13 per cent survive through the third generation!

Although blood might be thicker than water, at the end of the day, the family managing the business have to be both capable and seen to be capable by the employees of the family business. It is not uncommon for resentment to build up in family businesses where key non-family managers are passed over in favour of unproven family. On the other hand, the average life cycle of a family business is 24 years, which is about the same as any other type of business.

Although these statistics illustrate the fragility of the continuing family business you should not despair: more than 50 per cent of US corporations, including some of the largest multinationals (Heinz and Campbell's Soup, for example), are family owned.

If you have children, or other family members, involved in the business, they may well be the right people to take it over. Even if there is no obvious family succession candidate, it might be worth casting your net beyond the immediate family. One business founder wrote to all his family and relations, asking if anyone would like to join him. A stepdaughter accepted the challenge and quickly became a key member of the management team.

But you will need to plan very carefully how you will extract any value you want or need from such an arrangement. It may be that you can allow the succeeding family members to pay for the company over a number of years. Alternatively, you might be content to retain a shareholding and take your reward by way of a dividend. On balance, a clean break is usually best, but in any event clear arrangements for payments agreed in writing is a prudent arrangement to ensure family peace.

Selling to the Employees

Selling the business to the employees is not exactly the most popular notion in entrepreneurial circles. And yet, recent research by the Centre for Tomorrow's Company has found that employee-owned companies outperform companies with other forms of ownership. The example below certainly makes interesting reading.

Tullis Russell has 1,200 employees making every sort of specialist paper, from that required to insulate high-voltage cable to that used to print postage stamps. David Erdal, the sixth generation of the Erdal family to run the company, spent a year on the factory floor before going to Harvard Business School, where he was the resident 'left-wing weirdo' in an annual intake of 800. He was the only one of 14 of his generation of the family working in the business and was appointed chairman of the company at the age of 37.

One of his jobs was to reconcile the interests of the family (25 interested parties), who had not been able to sell their shares since 1874, and who wanted to get their money out, with the future interests of the employees. There was nothing the matter with capitalism, he had decided, the problem was it created very few capitalists. 'A lot of rubbish is talked about capital taking the risk, therefore it must get the rewards. All managers know that a large part of their role is to shift the risk away from capital to the employees. If the share price is in danger of going down, you cut their wages or sack them.'

Erdal decided that the best way to satisfy both sets of interests was for the family to sell their shares to the employees with the deal being financed from the company profits.

Two far-sighted provisions in UK company law made the deal work for both sides. The family could sell their shares to a qualifying employee share trust (Quest), financed by the company, and reinvest the £19.3 million they received without paying capital gains tax. Had they sold for cash to an outside bidder this tax would have come to about £7 million. By forming a Quest, the employees could finance the buy-out from pre-tax profits, all money (capital as well as interest) being allowable against tax. If there had been a management buy-out, the company would have had to repay the debt from after-tax money, which would have cost another £6 million. As it was, the employees put up no money themselves. The family also agreed to give the buy-out a fair wind by allowing the payments to be spread over nine years.

As a result, the employees and the employee benefit trust now control Tullis Russell, owning 60 per cent of the shares. The rest are owned by a charitable trust set up by the family after the Second World War. This charitable trust, Erdal claims, gives stability to the company because it is a genuine long-term holder of shares. It has the power of veto over the future sale of the company, and it can veto the choice of directors put forward by the board. Nevertheless, the company is still very clearly management led, which is the single most important factor in any business.

At Tullis Russell, things are going from triumph to triumph. 'It patently works without me', Erdal is on record as saying. Profits have quadrupled over the last few years to more than £7 million, after £2 million of profit sharing. The management hopes to increase production to 200,000 tons a year in five years without buying any new paper machines, up from 117,000 tons this year, and 64,500 four years ago. This is among the fastest growth rates in the industry.

Going Public

Perhaps the 'ultimate accolade' for any business is to float on a public stock exchange. In so doing, the shares of the company are publicly listed and can be traded by anyone. This provides a reward for both the owners and investors and also allows access to further fund-raising possibilities by issue of new equity shares.

There are two possible types of stock markets on which to gain a public listing. In normal economic circumstances, a full listing on the London Stock Exchange, the New York Stock Exchange or any other major country's exchange calls for a track record of making substantial profits with decent seven-figure sums being made in the year you plan to float. A full listing also calls for a large proportion of the company's shares being put up for sale at the outset. In a frothy market, such as at the height of the Internet bubble, these rules can be set aside.

In more recent times, many major countries have formed so-called junior markets such as New York's Nasdaq, London's AIM or the Nouveau Marché in Paris. These markets were formed specifically to provide risk capital for newer ventures and have an altogether more relaxed atmosphere. They are, therefore, usually a much more attractive proposition for entrepreneurs seeking equity capital.

Public flotation tend to generate more value for the current shareowners. A perfectly respectable private business that might have been sold privately on a multiple of six times annual profits could float for anything between two and three times that sum. Why? Well, the logic is fairly simple. Placing shares on a stock market makes the company's shares liquid. In other words, shareholders can buy and sell at will, or nearly so. For the same reason, if you have raised any of your finance through either a venture capital firm or a business angel, then sooner or later the subject of a stock market float will come up.

On the other hand, since the shares are to be traded publicly, the markets have many safeguards. These safeguards place great demands on the company that is attempting to float. For example, to float on one of the major exchanges, you will need to appoint a sponsor (usually a merchant bank), a stockbroker, a reporting accountant and a solicitor. All of these will need to be well-respected firms, active in flotation work and familiar with your company's type of business. Such advice does not come cheap! As a result, floating is a very expensive and lengthy process which also places huge demands on the senior management team.

In fact, both the sales values achieved and the costs of floating vary significantly even between different stock markets, as the table below shows (Table 15.1).

A final word of caution: if you have to pull the flotation for any reason, it can be like slipping down a long snake back to the bottom of the snakes and ladders board. Only about 10 per cent of companies who withdraw a flotation ever manage to go public at a later date.

From the start of his new business, Nigel Apperley was keen to develop an Internet brand for photographic equipment. Early in 2000, *The Sunday Times*, the UK's leading Sunday newspaper, reported that the best place to buy a Fuji MX1700 was InternetCamerasDirect.co.uk. The brand was taking off. As a result of press coverage

TABLE 15.1 Where to Float ... and Why it Matters

Market	Number of stocks	Flotation cost	Entry requirements	Minimum market capitalization	Comparable PEs
AIM	350	£0.5 m	Low	None	1
London Stock Exchange	2,500	£1 m+	High	£1 m+	1
techMARK	200	£0.75 m+	High	£50 m+	×3
New York Stock Exchange	2,600	£7 m	Very high	£12 m+	×2
NASDAQ	5,500	£6 m	Very high	£10 m+	×5

Source: Exchange Details.
AIM, alternative investment market; PEs, price–earnings ratio.

such as this, allied with keen pricing and effective sourcing, sales had been doubling every month.

With all the hype surrounding the Internet at the time, all of a sudden the prospect of a flotation appeared realistic, and Nigel saw the opportunity to raise a large sum of money on AIM. He wanted to raise £10 million in return for 49 per cent of the business and to use this capital injection to build the business internationally. It was important to present a credible team to the market, and with this in mind he went about recruiting a board.

He called an old friend, Paul, who was previously company secretary at Hickson Group plc. Paul was three-quarters of the way through his MBA at Bradford, not so far from InternetCamerasDirect's head office. Paul agreed to come on board as a director and company secretary. Next, Nigel decided he needed a chairman. Through his connections at Cranfield School of Management, Nigel approached John Constable, professor of strategy and non-executive director of Sage plc, to join the board in return for 2.5 per cent of the equity in the company. Nigel then approached the finance director of a publicly listed chain of wine bars. He also agreed to join, in principle, at flotation. With the top team agreed, Nigel set about writing the business plan.

In January 2000, at which point the Internet stock market bubble was still at its peak, Nigel started approaching brokers to explore the appetite for a flotation. Unsurprisingly, given the market conditions at the time, their initial reactions were of keen interest. Based on these responses, the management team were extremely bullish. 'We think it'll be worth more than Lastminute.com', said Apperley, referring to another Internet business due to float the next month.

But it was not to be. In the spring of 2000, Lastminute.com became one of the last pure Internet businesses to float in the UK, and the way it was priced and shares were allocated caused some resentment among private investors. Suddenly, market sentiment towards Internet business-to-consumer (B2C) propositions changed. By the turn of the year, floating InternetCamerasDirect was a non-starter and even Lastminute.com was finding life on the public markets uncomfortable.

As it turned out, both InternetCamerasDirect and Lastminute.com have flourished in the years since the Internet bubble burst. By 2003, Lastminute.com was profitable and was held up as a prime example of an Internet business that 'survived'. Meanwhile, InternetCamerasDirect obtained finance for growth from other sources and continued to increase it sales to a point where it had reached a turnover of £20 million.

Preparing the Business for Sale (Dressing to Kill)

Whichever route you choose, if you are thinking about selling, it certainly pays to plan ahead and prepare your business to look its best. The process is not dissimilar to selling a car. Which car sells quickest and for the best price – the tatty wreck with no service history and missing paperwork, or the professionally valeted one with full service history and all the paperwork in order? No prizes for guessing! So do the same with your business – make it look good! Your buyer will look at your last three years' performance, at the least, and it is important that your figures for these periods are as good and clean as possible.

Taking the last point first, private businesses do tend to run expenses through the business that might be frowned upon under different ownership. One business, for example, had its sale delayed for three years while the chairman's yacht was worked out of 'work in progress'! There can also be problems when personal assets are tucked away in the business, or when staff have been paid rather informally, free of tax. The liability rests with the business, and if the practice has continued for many years the financial picture can look quite messy.

The years before you sell up can be used to good effect by improving the performance of your business relative to others in your industry. Going down the profit and loss account and balance sheet will point out areas for improvement.

Once the business is firmly planted on an upward trend, your future projections will look that much more plausible to a potential buyer. You should certainly have a business plan and strategic projections for at least five years. This will underpin the strength of your negotiations by demonstrating your management skills in putting together the plan, and show that you believe the company has a healthy future.

Some entrepreneurs may wonder if such an effort is worthwhile. Perhaps the following example will show how financial planning can lead to capital appreciation for the founder.

A 34-year-old owner-manager built up a regional service business in the United States that had a 40 per cent compounded annual growth rate for the five most recent years. He employed an experienced chartered accountant as his chief financial officer. This person developed budgets for one- and three-year periods and a detailed business plan charting the company's growth over the next five years. The owner's objective was to be ready to sell his business when the right offer came along.

A UK company interested in acquiring a leading service company in the region, and finding a manager with the potential for national leadership, carefully analysed the company and came away impressed with management's dedication to running its business in a highly professional manner. Because the previous year's after-tax profits had been $500,000 on sales of $10 million, the UK company offered $4.5 million on purchase and $4.5 million on attainment of certain profit objectives (which were well within the growth trend). The transaction closed on these terms.

The $9 million offering price, representing 18 times net earnings, was 50 per cent higher than the industry norm and clearly justified the owner's careful job of packaging his business for sale.

Valuing the Business

Whatever route you decide to take to selling the business, will involve placing a value on it.

One way to measure value is to work out what the various assets of the business would be worth on the open market. So, vehicles, premises, equipment and any other assets could be professionally valued. From that sum, you would take any outstanding liabilities to creditors, bank borrowings, tax authorities and redundancy payments due. This might make sense if the business is actually going to stop trading, but it is unlikely to produce the best value.

The real value that most businesses have is a capacity to make profit. Acquirers, while they may be interested in the assets of a business, will pay many times more for the ongoing profit stream that the same business can generate. At any rate, that is where the debate about value will start.

The ratio most commonly used here is the price to earnings (or P/E) ratio. This means the number of times annual profits a business is valued at. If you look up a company's performance in the financial press, you will see a P/E ratio calculated in the following way:

Price to earnings = share price/earnings (or profit) per share

The P/E ratio expresses the market value placed on the expectations of future earnings, i.e. the number of years required to earn the price paid for the shares out of profits at the current rate. So, if the share price of the business in question was £10, and the earning per share was 80p, then the P/E ratio is 12.5. Which is another way of saying the company is worth 12.5 times this year's profits. If you look up another company in a different industry sector, you might find a quite different multiple in force. At the height of the Internet boom, the record P/E ratio was 135! More usually, P/E ratios are less than 20.

Differences in P/E ratios between industries indicate the different perceived growth prospects of the industries concerned. Differences in P/E ratios between businesses in the same industry indicate that the markets believe that one business has better growth prospects than the other.

The public stock markets are where the frameworks for values are set. So, if your business is in the food sector, and P/E ratios there are about 12, then that is where outsiders will start when they think about valuing your business.

After this, a few things can get added – and a few things can get taken away! The first seriously negative event is the discount that will be applied because your business is not on the stock market. Privately owned businesses are generally viewed as being worth at least a third less than a publicly quoted firm listed on a stock exchange. That is because shares in a publicly quoted company are much more liquid, i.e. there are more shares and more buyers and sellers.

If the privately owned company is a 'one-man band', or is seen as overly dependent on one person (e.g. the current owner-manager), then the ratio might be halved again. The reasoning here is that the customers are probably loyal to the current owner-manager and may not come over to any new owner. There is no certainty that the business will have a profitable life without the current owner. Other factors, such as a small customer base or reliance on just one or two customers, will drive the valuation.

As a result, a potential buyer will adjust the industry-standard P/E ratio and then multiply this adjusted figure by the operating profit to give an indication of the value of the business.

On the positive side, any expense seen as being unnecessary to running the business can be added back into operating profit before the sum is done. So, if you have three family members on the payroll who are performing no useful purpose, or if you are taking out more than a new owner would have to pay to have the business managed for them, then that sum would go back to swell the operating profit and, hence, the value of the business.

One last factor that affects private business valuations is the economic cycle. At the bottom of the cycle (a downturn), smaller privately owned businesses sell on average multiples of between 6 and 8. At the top of the cycle (a boom), the same business may sell on multiples between 10 and 12.

All these figures are illustrative only. Every business sale, and every circumstance, has unique elements to it that can greatly affect the final outcome. As you can see, perceptions are at least as important as figures when it comes to valuations!

Professional Advice

Nothing written in this chapter should be construed as a substitute for taking professional advice. Most people sell a business only once in their lives. The best professional advisers in the field sell a dozen or so each year. There is a valid argument that using a third party to sell your business can make the negotiations less traumatic and leave you with more time to continue running the business. If you are not a natural negotiator then let someone else do it for you.

However, you will probably know as well as any professional advisor who may be keen to buy your business – it is probable that you have been fighting them for years! Getting the best value for your business may involve getting expensive corporate finance advice to maximize the price, in the minimum amount of time. In addition, a good tax and pension strategy can double the end value you receive and legal advice on warranties can make sure you get to keep the money.

Second Thoughts

Quite often the whole process of selling up can be too much for a lot of owners. There may be strong feelings of guilt. What will happen to the employees after you have gone? Will there be redundancies? Will the business be relocated, etc.? Although it is right to be concerned about these, you should remind yourself that during the difficult years it was you that remortgaged your house, guaranteed the bank loans, did not take a proper wage, etc., to keep the business going and keep them in work. It was you that worried about the business difficulties over the years and could not tell your staff for fear of unsettling them. Being an owner-manager can be a lonely experience and you did it, so when it comes to realizing the value you have every right to do it with a clear conscience.

Do make sure that you have thought through your future before setting a price on the business and go through the process of selling. The amount of money you will need to secure your future will depend on your age and the age (and size) of your family. Three million pounds is a lot of money for a 65-year-old with no mortgage and no dependent children. On the other hand, £3 million is not enough for a 35-year-old with three young children to educate, a large mortgage to pay off and another 40+ years of life to fund.

Also be sure you really want to sell up – there is no turning back after it is done! It might be that you want a better deal for yourself within the business. Perhaps you want to cut down from five days a week to three days and give yourself more leisure time. If this is the case, do not sell up! Change the deal for yourself – bring in a personal assistant or delegate more to others, stick with the business you love and make it work better for you.

Of course, there will be nagging thoughts about whether you have achieved the best value. If, for example, you sold your business for £10 million could you have got more? Let us leave you with a few words of wisdom that we heard when this same question was asked during a group discussion on this very topic. 'You know that you have got the best price for your business when you would not buy it back for the same amount that you are selling it for, armed with the knowledge that you have about your business, its prospects and the state of the economy ahead.'

Afterwards

What happens after you exit rather depends on your goals in selling up. If you are retiring, then your plans should be well laid beforehand. If you are staying on as a member of a larger group, then you need to be prepared for corporate rather than entrepreneurial life. This can be hard, and few people make the transition successfully.

Many entrepreneurs who have sold up seek to find another venture to start and/ or grow. Sometimes, it can take years to find the right opportunity to get back into business. What many have found helpful is to set themselves up as a sort of one-man venture capital and management consultancy business. By putting the word out that they are interested in buying or backing ventures in the field they understand best, they receive a steady stream of proposals and presentations, from which they hope to fund their next venture.

Irrespective of your future plans, and even if you are walking away with a large cheque, your experiences may bear a close resemblance to a bereavement. You have probably invested a great deal of your time, and a huge amount of emotional energy, into your business. And now, it is not yours any more! Do not underestimate the significance of this change!

But the most important thing to say, if you have got this far, having started, grown and then sold your business, is CONGRATULATIONS!

Assignment 15.1: Realizing the Value

1. Prepare two lists, in balance sheet style, setting out the pros and cons of selling up now and in say five years' time.
2. If you had to get out of your business for any reason, which exit route would you favour?
3. What value would you put on your business now and in say five years' time?
4. What will you do after you exit?

sixteen
Writing Up Your Plans

Up to this point all your efforts have been focused on gathering and analysing the information needed to create and confirm your strategy for growth, assess the capability of your team to implement this growth and identify and quantify the human, physical and financial resources you will need to deliver it. The logical conclusion to this process is to incorporate it in to a written document – a plan for your business.

By the end of this chapter, you should have a clear understanding of the following key topics:

- Why write a plan for your business?
- How to write up and present your plan for your business.
- Living life after the plan has been written.

What Sort of Plan do I Need and Why do I Need It?

The biggest selling business books are usually books on business planning. Look through most serious bookshops and you will see numerous books on the subject – most of them pontificating on how to write the perfect business plan. You may have noticed, however, that up to this paragraph we have made no mention at all of business plans but have carefully chosen to use the words 'plan for your business'. We believe that each business is different and has it's own unique plan for the future. It would therefore be wrong to try to shoehorn every business into a 'one size fits all' business plan. If the current (and foreseeable) challenge is to find a way to improve your market share then in all truth you need a marketing plan, which will detail what to do and what resources you will need to achieve this. If your challenge is staff retention then you probably need a properly thought-through human resource plan. If you have a fast-growing market for your products and you have run out of capacity then you need a physical resource and human resource plan. In some circumstances, the immediate need is not for a full-blown business plan but a specific plan for the immediate need.

However, at some stage most businesses will have arrived at the situation where a complete rethink is needed and in these instances a business plan is appropriate. The real benefits of preparing a business plan are:

- Planning gives you a chance to make your mistakes on paper before you make them for real – if you prepare the plan for your business and get several others to review it you will either get wholesale support (great) or wholesale or partial concern (which you also need to hear).
- Writing a plan is a great way to flesh out your ideas – when you start to commit your thoughts to paper you start to see the flaws and weaknesses much more easily.
- Writing a plan is a great way to share ideas with your management team – get them to prepare parts of it and they will feel more involved and committed to the strategy.

And you will definitely need a business plan if you are going to need any form of external funding. Without a business plan, no bank or potential equity partner will look seriously at your proposition. However, for the most part business plans are written almost entirely for internal use. Produced by the board they are used to show the analysis of the business that they have carried out, and outline the strategy for growth, the financial milestones, the key actions to be taken and the resources needed to achieve success.

What Does the Plan Look Like?

In many ways the intended audience will determine the final look of the plan. In its simplest form your plan could be a few words and numbers on the back of a cigarette packet. In a small craft-type business with a handful of employees, this may be all that is needed to create and share the plan. However, in a larger, more sophisticated and resource-hungry business, we would expect to see a lot more. In that case, you may need most of what is shown below in the 'standard' contents page for a conventional business plan.

'Standard' Contents for a Conventional Business Plan

The following list sets out the 'standard' contents for a conventional business plan, i.e. the type of document you might need if you were intending to raise external funding. It covers all the areas that a conventional business plan is likely to need. However, please treat it with caution!

Just to repeat, the most important aspect of the document you produce is that is it *your* document. In other words, it needs to do the job that you want it to do for your intended audience. You may then want to view the 'standard' contents list as a menu from which you choose the relevant content for your plan.

'Standard' Contents List

1. Executive summary (one or two pages)
   - the purpose of the document and the intended audience;
   - what the business does, who it does it for and what are its distinctive benefits;
   - a summary of the current headline numbers (sales, profit, staff);
   - the ownership of the business;
   - current key staff;
   - the overall aim and timescale of the plan;
   - the vision for the business;
   - short- and long-term objectives;
   - main strategies to be employed to achieve those objectives;
   - key change initiatives which will be required;
   - summary of financial forecasts (probably in a table);
   - how the plan will be funded and where the funding will come from.
2. History and current position
   - when the business started;
   - key events in the history of the business;
   - what the business does (products/services), the market segments it serves and the key distinctive benefits it brings to customers in those segments (current business purpose);
   - evolution of ownership and the current ownership stakes;
   - the current key management team and their roles.
3. Vision, aims and objectives
   - the vision for the business;
   - the period of the plan;
   - objectives by the end of the planning period;
   - interim objectives;
   - if appropriate for the intended audience and purpose, the personal goals and drivers of the owner-manager(s).
4. Product or services
   - description of the products or services which the business provides and the applications thereof;

- comparison with competition and how the business wins;
- distinctive benefits (e.g. proprietary position, value added services);
- whether the business 'makes or buys' the products/services and sources of supply;
  - future product/service development;
  - opportunity;
- timescale and cost estimates before ready for market.

5. Market, customers and competitors
   - clear description of the market segment served, the size of the segment and the growth forecasts of that segment;
   - likely future trends in the market segment (political, economic, social, technological, legal, environmental, etc.) and the opportunities and threats that these will bring;
   - descriptions of customer needs and the distinctive benefits delivered by the business's products/services;
   - customer decision-making criteria;
   - review of the supply chain within the market and the business's position/role within it;
   - the business's customers:
     - How many and who are they?
     - Why do they buy?
     - ABC analysis.
   - competitors:
     - direct and indirect;
     - strengths and weaknesses compared with the competitors;
     - likely response to plan.
   - future target market segments:
     - rationale;
     - size and growth forecasts;
     - attractiveness of products/services;
     - knowledge of new segment.

6. Marketing and selling
   - how the business is positioned in the market segment;
   - how existing customer relationships are maintained;
   - how new customer enquiries are generated;
   - how enquiries are converted to sales;
   - the current sales team;
   - pricing policy;
   - promotional activities;

- distribution channels;
- choice of location (if relevant);
- future plans for improving marketing effectiveness;
- future plans for improving sales performance;
- sales forecast for the period of the plan.

7. People and organization
   - organization structure – current and future;
   - current management roles and who fulfils them;
   - leadership capability within the business;
   - review of the current management team and how it needs to be enlarged or developed;
   - skills, attitudes and capabilities:
     - review of current requirements;
     - identification of future requirements.
   - review of approaches for recruiting, retaining, rewarding and motivating staff and any planned changes;
   - identification of key new recruitments required, how the recruitment will be undertaken and where the new recruits are likely to come from;
   - training and development plan.

8. Operations
   - review of internal operations and processes required in order to deliver the key elements of the 'customer promise' and the order winners and order qualifiers to the appropriate level;
   - resources required (e.g. people, money, equipment, premises, raw materials) and sources of supply;
   - output limitations and scaling implications;
   - performance and trade-offs in terms of speed, cost, dependability, flexibility and quality;
   - runners, repeaters and strangers.

9. The plan for change
   - identify the key change projects required within the next year;
   - for each change project, identify the key drivers and constraints, the people/ groups who are likely to be affected and how the change process will be managed;
   - for each change project, identify the resources required and estimate the time and costs.

10. Acquisition, mergers, joint ventures and divestments (if appropriate)
    - rationale and logic;
    - target profile;
    - plans for search.

11. Financial review and forecasts
    - review of current financial performance including key ratios and breakeven;
    - assumptions underpinning financial forecasts;
    - forecasted profit and loss, balance sheet and cashflow for the period of the plan;
    - discounted cashflow and/or payback period for any major investment;
    - sensitivity analysis.
12. Financing requirements
    - funds required and timing;
    - how the funds will be used;
    - if external funding is being sought:
        - the deal on offer;
        - payback period and return on investment;
        - anticipated gearing and interest cover;
        - exit routes;
13. Business controls
    - financial;
    - sales and marketing;
    - operations;
    - other.
14. Appendices (could include any or all of the following):
    - management team biographies;
    - names and details of professional advisers;
    - technical data and drawings;
    - details of patents, copyright, designs;
    - audited accounts;
    - consultants' reports or other published data on products/services, markets, etc.;
    - orders on hand and enquiry status;
    - detailed market research methods and findings;
    - organization charts;
    - action plans.

At first glance this all looks pretty scary stuff. Just to repeat: this is the full list of everything that could conceivably be included in a full-scale business plan – the sort that you may want to present to a venture capitalist. You should look carefully through the list above and select what you need for your plan – not necessarily all of it!

Perhaps some further guidance may help set you more at ease. Your plan should typically:

- cover an appropriate planning horizon – three to five years is fairly typical;
- be no more than 15–20 pages plus appendices; if the main body of the plan is looking too big, consign as much as possible to the appendices, which should be bound up as a separate document, for example your detailed financial projections could go in the appendices;
- include a contents page with each page numbered and referenced;
- use large margins, double spacing and a font no smaller than 10 point Times New Roman (no fancy fonts);
- use short sentences and paragraphs with headings, subheadings and bullet points where appropriate;
- do use a spell checker and get some one else to read it before you send it out – they will find the mistakes you do not find.

Before you Start to Write your Plan

It would be sensible just to recap and make sure that you have encapsulated your key objectives. You will have first looked at this during chapter 6 when you started to look at 'Where are you going?' If you are certain that these are agreed and not in conflict then you can proceed with preparing your plan.

Look back at the earlier chapters and the output from the assignments. These contain much of the content you will need for your plan. Start to slot this material into the headings that are in the 'Standard' contents list above. If there are gaps, decide whether you need to complete these sections – in which case further work is required – if not, move on.

However, before you write or cut and paste too much of the content, do bear in mind that if your plan is intended for an external audience, then it should be:

- *Fully researched and documented*: Compare yourself with a solicitor in court. How much weight does his or her assertion have compared with a solid witness statement – very little? Make sure that your plan has been fully researched and that all the supporting information/evidence is included. If you make a statement like 'Our customers will buy our new product in similar volumes to the old one' you are leaving yourself open to dispute.

  If, however, you make that same statement and back it up with documented market research, either independent or in house (e.g. customer survey, competitive product analysis, etc.), it is far more likely to be accepted. Do not include detailed market research, competitor analysis, product specifications, and detailed financial forecasts/accounts within the main body of the plan. Signpost them in the plan but include them in the appendices. This leaves readers the option to refer to them if they want to – either at the time of reading or later.

- *Appropriate*: The key thought that you must remember at all times as you prepare your plan is 'Does the reader need to know this?' Do not let your enthusiasm carry you over the top. For example, if you are preparing your plan to raise money it would be appropriate to include projected balance sheets and funding requirement. On the other hand, if your plan is required by your landlord before granting you a lease (enlisting external support), this information is likely to be inappropriate as would be market research, customer surveys, etc. Tell the landlord only what is neccesary.

- *Understandable*: Do not let your plan appear to be written in a foreign language to your readers. For example, if your product is quite complex and technical do not assume that the reader has the same level of knowledge as you. Where appropriate, explain/define specialist terms that are unlikely to be known to the reader – either in the text itself or in a glossary in the appendices. Do not fall into using jargon specific to your business. However, by using clear English you should be able to explain even complex information to the average person. It is your responsibility to ensure that your plan and all its complexities are understood by an intelligent reader who may not have any specific experience of your industry/product/service.

- *Passed the reality test:* Do not let your plan be another example of a spreadsheet exercise gone mad – this is where the profit and cash flow projections show amazing figures from day 1. You may rightly be confident about your business proposition but your readers have something known as common sense – they can tell truth from fiction. In all probability, they have seen similar businesses to yours before and they will know what is realistic and what is not. Do not forget that at some stage you have to deliver what your plan outlines – do not make it impossible for yourself. All your statements and financial forecasts should be based on either past experience or supportable assumptions. At the same time, do not make light of any business difficulties – they should be highlighted and a solution offered.

- *Smart and professional appearance*: It may sound obvious but do not let your high-quality business proposition be let down by its appearance. If your plan looks smart it will create a better impression on readers – it will make them feel that you are smart, business like, well-organized, etc. Fortunately, with the widespread availability of word-processing software, spreadsheets, and business planning software, laser printers and colour printing there is no excuse for poorly presented material.

Presenting your Plan

You may need to present your plan to a bank manager, other external funder or even your staff. Here are a few things to focus on in these circumstances.

How You Want to Run the Meeting

It is your plan and your meeting so take control. If you are seeing the bank manager you have probably got one hour at the most – a little bit longer if you are seeing a venture capitalist. Find out in advance how long the meeting will last. Plan both the time and the content. Our experience is that the best use of a one-hour slot is as follows:

- 0–20 minutes: introductions and outlining your plan;
- 21–50 minutes: discussion and answering questions on the plan;
- 51–60 minutes: concluding discussions based around decision.

Use this as a guideline. Do not talk for too long – watch out for the body language of your audience. Yawns and closed eyes should tell you it is time to move along quicker and get them more involved. If you have taken your management team along with you, work out in advance how they will be introduced and what they will do. They do not all have to present – they may be there to answer technical questions. As the owner-manager, you should introduce your team explaining how you wish the presentation to proceed. Make sure that you conclude your team's presentation.

If you get nervous at the prospect of making presentations, get help. There are plenty of good books on presentation skills. Speak clearly and try and be as relaxed and as natural as possible. Do not appear cocky, overconfident or grovelling – these do not work. Also do try a dummy run of your presentation (and answering likely questions) before you do it for real – and possibly make mistakes.

Questions and Answers

Expect questions and be prepared for them: it is normal. Do not assume that questions are a criticism of your plan: they are not. You will certainly be questioned about the contents of the plan: these may be used to check facts, make clear areas of uncertainty or deal with omissions. Other questions may be used to clarify additional points you have mentioned in your presentation. If you are fully familiar with your business and the plan, then you should be able to deal with most questions easily.

However, there may be some questions that you cannot answer, for example some commercial factor which you did not know about or may have overlooked. Do not try and bluff it out – this is a high-risk strategy. If there is a problem within your plan and it is highlighted, acknowledge it and outline how you will deal with it. An acceptable response might be to say, 'I do not know the answer to that, but I will find out and let you know'. If you are not certain how you might deal with the problem, ask the questioner how they might suggest you dealt with it.

Keep your answers short and to the point.

If it seems that there are no further questions, or you are running tight on time, do move the meeting along with 'If there are no further questions' or 'We are running a bit short on time and there are some other important areas that we need to cover so can we . . . ?'

Appearance and Timing

Wear something that makes you feel comfortable and is appropriate to the meeting. For example, if you are a plumber and you are meeting the bank manager to arrange a small overdraft, you would not need to wear a suit – if you did it might make both you and the bank manager feel uncomfortable. On the other hand, if you are a furniture designer and you are making a presentation to a venture capitalist to raise, say £5 million, then you would be expected to wear a suit. The impression that you must give is that you care – do not turn up in your worst work clothes.

Make sure you leave yourself enough time for important meetings like this. Allow plenty of travel and getting lost time – especially if you are going somewhere you do not know. Also, do try to arrive at least five to ten minutes early so you can relax and be in the right frame of mind for the meeting. If there is more than one of you making the presentation, arrange to meet the others at a convenient place close to the meeting half an hour before your appointment. This way you can be sure you all arrive on time together or at least be aware of any unforeseen problems before you enter the meeting.

A couple of final points on the plan presentation. Although it is your plan and your meeting, do not forget to observe the usual social niceties. At the start of the meeting, wait to be shown to your seat(s) and do wait to be invited to start your presentation. Your audience should have received your plan in good time and have read it – but do not assume this. Ask them at the start of the meeting if they have read the plan. If they have not you will have to contain you disappointment or anger and spend a bit more time on this area in your presentation.

If, at the end of the meeting, they have not given you a decision, do not be afraid to ask them 'What happens next?' so that you are aware of the follow-up procedure. You should also ask them to indicate when you will receive a decision and how it will be communicated to you. It is always worthwhile sending a polite letter to the recipient of your plan thanking them for their time and that you look forward to receiving their decision soon. Do not be afraid to phone them up if you have not heard their decision within, say, two weeks.

Communicating and Living the New Plan

Your plan has achieved its first objective: secured the money, got board approval, clinched the lease, etc. So now what do you do? You have got to deliver against your plan because there are a lot of people out there with high expectations: new investors, the bank, new landlord, staff, etc.

If you did not involve your managers in the preparation of your plan, then your plans may come as a bit of a surprise to them. Almost certainly they will not know the detail of the plan. Further down the line, there will be staff who are blissfully ignorant of your plans and what may be expected of them. You have to get them all on board so that they are all rowing together – and in the right direction. Depending on the size of your business, then the communication process could be as follows.

Tim Holmes employs about 25 people in his marketing communications business. His senior management team comprises five people. Each year when Tim produces his annual plan he follows a tried and tested process. He involves all his senior managers in producing the plan. Tim sets the overall objectives and communicates these to the team. They then work on a plan that can deliver against these. A sales forecast is prepared – not by Tim but by his new business manager and operations manager. The accountant prepares a cost budget and a series of profit and loss forecasts (with sensitivity analysis). Eventually, a full plan is prepared with the involvement of the senior managers. So what about the other 20 employees – how do they find out about the plan? They have a conference off-site, where Tim and his senior management team present the new business plan to them. They spend a day together – play silly games, have fun – but by the end of the day everyone knows what is expected of them. Any changes of strategy are explained. If there are to be any new work practices then separate workshops are organized during work time to explain these. Action plans are drawn up, responsibilities assigned and follow-up monitoring meetings held.

This process of involving and communicating the plan works for Tim – but what do you do? There are basically two ways of communicating your plan:

1. *Company meeting*: You gather the whole business unit, which could be the whole company or just a division, factory, department, and present the plan to everyone. Bearing in mind the mixed nature of the meeting (tea person through to managers) do not present in detail but in broad brush. After the main meeting, use your subordinate managers to hold team meetings to explain the next level of detail.

2. *Cascading meetings*: You gather your senior managers and introduce the plan to them. Because of the nature of the meeting the discussion will be in some detail. The senior managers will then be responsible for holding separate meetings with supervisors and staff to explain the plan to them. Depending on how large your business is, there may be several levels of meeting.

You should use whichever approach is appropriate to your size of business and your personal style. The end result should be the same – everyone in the business knows in appropriate detail what the plan is.

Monitoring Progress

If your plan is intended to help you raise finance, then nobody is going to give you money without being convinced that you will use it properly. You may have prepared a winning plan but the proof of the pudding is in the eating (or in your case the delivery). Your plan must show what systems you have in place to monitor and control your progress. These will include a whole range of business controls.

Financial Controls

Budgets

Regardless of whether you are a limited company, partnership or sole trader, you need to know where you are and how this compares with where you want to be. From your detailed financial projection should come a budget for the next 12 months. This is a key tool for monitoring your actual financial performance. Our suggestion would be that you take your profit and loss forecast and use this as a monitoring tool by showing each month's actual results and variance against budget. The example in Table 16.1 shows the current month position (month 3) and the year to date position (which in this case is the sum of all the three months so far this year).

In this example we can see that:

1. Sales are below budget for both month 3 and for the year to date.
2. Cost of sales is above budget for both month 3 and for the year to date.
3. Stationery is above budget for both month 3 and the year to date.

The actual versus budget comparison has revealed these three variances which now need to be investigated to find out:

- why they happened;
- what can and will be done to stop them from happening again.

Fortunately, there has been a favourable variance – heat and light is below budget. Also, since there is nine months left to run before the year-end there is time to stop the rot.

The key figures you will need to know (and how frequently you will need to use them) are:

- cash and bank position (daily – if in overdraft, weekly otherwise);
- aged debtor analysis – who owes you money and how old that debt is (weekly unless in overdraft then daily);
- aged creditor analysis – as above but shows who you owe money to;
- stock (where appropriate) – this is what you make sales from so make sure you have sufficient to make anticipated sales each month (weekly);
- profit and loss (monthly);
- VAT/PAYE/NI liabilities (quarterly/monthly);

TABLE 16.1 Beechwood Enterprises Profit and Loss Forecast: Year ended 31 May, Year 1

	Month 3			Year to date		
	Budget	Actual	Variance	Budget	Actual	Variance
Sales income	20,000	15,000	−5,000	80,000	70,000	−10,000
Less cost of sales	10,000	11,000	1,000	40,000	50,000	10,000
Gross profit	10,000	4,000	−6,000	40,000	20,000	−20,000
Expenses						
Rent	1,000	1,000		3,000	3,000	
Salaries	10,000	9,000	−1,000	30,000	27,000	−3,000
Heat and light	1,000	900	−100	3,000	2,700	−300
Stationery	500	600	100	1,500	1,700	200
Total expenses	12,500	11,500	−1,000	37,500	34,400	−3,100
Net profit before tax	−2,500	−7,500	−5,000	2,500	−14,400	−16,900
Tax						
Net profit after tax	−2,500	−7,500	−5,000	2,500	−14,400	−16,900

- balance sheet (at least quarterly but ideally monthly);
- key operating figures: break-even, key costs, sales, etc. (monthly).

Key Ratios

Do not forget that as part your earlier financial analysis you worked out a series of key ratios. You can now use these to control and monitor the day-to-day performance of the business. For example, if your key ratios stated that debtor days were going to be, say, 45 days and actual days are running at 55 days, what does that tell you about the business? Things are getting worse and you are taking longer to collect your money. So what is the answer? Start to look at the whole process from invoicing through to the money ending up in your bank account. There are a whole host of reasons why this may happen – isolate the problem and act.

Your Next Plan

This may seem like a strange thing to be saying – just after you have prepared your current plan. However, plans are not forever – they do have a 'sell by date'. Certainly, within a year you will need to be preparing your next plan update, if only because you have completed the first year. In a way, this will be a check to see if your plan is still valid and roll it on another year. This will involve making your old year 2 the next year's budget. This may mean some additional detailed work to prepare budgets and action plans. You may at the same time want to redo the final year of your plan – to give the full three- or five-year view.

Of course, it is possible that for one reason or the other your business is way off course. Sales and profits may be well below forecast. In that case, your original plan may not be valid and a fresh plan is required that takes account of the current factors.

Even if sales and profits are above those forecasted in the plan, you should still review the plan. It may be possible that a more ambitious plan can be prepared and achieved.

Assignment 16.1: Writing up Your Plan

1. Write up your plan for your business.
2. Decide how you will communicate, implement and monitor your new plan.

Index

literature 40; and growth 3–4; sales promotions 169–70; word-of-mouth 167–9
Maslow, Abraham 101
Material World 255
meddlers 118
meetings management 274–6
mentoring 203
mergers 285–91
mezzanine finance 253–4
misconduct 213
MMR 95, 111–12
Mobile Media 287–8
moments of truth 163
morale of staff 101
Morgan, Lara 159
motivation: of entrepreneurs 107–12; of management team 187–90; and retention of staff 100–2

net profit/net profit percentage 55

objectives: and business growth 4; financial 138, 138; market 138, 139; people and management 139; SMART 137
O'Donovan, Miles 255
Olsen, Karen 287–8
on-the-job training 201
operating profit/operating profit percentage 54
organization of the business 74; and the business environment 74–6, 75; growth model 76–80, 77
organization pictures 142–3
organizational structure 87, **88**, 89, 94–6, *97*, 98–9
outsourcing 247
owner-managers: as barriers to growth 123–4; future role of 267–9; leadership transitions 114–16; need for change 221; template of role 121–3; types of relationships with staff **116**, 116–18; use of time 120, *121*
ownership, sense of 102

Pacific Direct 17, 159, 282
Pareto analysis 34, 38
Patel, Mayank 293
Paterson Printing 198–9
people *see* staff
performance indicators 44, 46
performance management: appraisals 195; goals and targets 194–5; and organizational goals 192–4, **193**; prior to dismissal 213, 214–15; reviews 195, 197
person specifications 183–4
personal business outcomes *131*, 132
personal life outcomes *131*, 132
personnel *see* staff
PESTEL analysis 23–7
planning: for challenges of growth 5; for growth 3; *see also* business plans

Point Source 84, 86, 95, 109–10
Pointer, David 84, 86, 109–10, 132–4
Pollard, Moira 111–12
Porter, Jason 270–1
postcard from your future 134–6
power sharing 86–7
prices: increasing 150, 246; and margin optimization 166–7
Prime Response 270
Pro-Activ Textiles 19
product mix, improving 150
product portfolio analysis **155**, 155–9, **156**, **158**
productivity, improving: cutting costs 148–9; impact of change 221, 223; improving product mix 150; increasing margins 149; increasing prices 150
profit per employee 56–7
profitability: 80/20 rule 242–4, *243*; Ashcroft Deli 57; cost reductions *242*, 242–4; gross profit/ gross profit percentage 54; incentivize around profit 244–5; increasing margins 245; net profit/ net profit percentage 55; operating profit/ operating profit percentage 54; outsourcing 247; pricing 246; profit per employee 56–7; reducing time wastage 243–4; return on capital employed (ROCE) 55–6; return on shareholders' capital 56; smart working 246–7; training to prevent mistakes 244; value added per employee 57–8; zero-based budgeting 244
psychometric testing 185
purpose of the business: Cobra Beer 12; defining 13–14, **14**; Hotel Chocolat 13, *13*; statement of 14

quality 162–4
quick ratio (acid test) 59

ratios: Ashcroft Deli 57; average collection period (debtor days) 60–1; average payment period (creditor days) 61–2; circulation of working capital 63–4; current ratio 58–9; financial 50; as financial controls 321; gearing 64; gross profit/ gross profit percentage 54; interest cover 64–5; net profit/net profit percentage 55; operating profit/operating profit percentage 54; profit per employee 56–7; quick ratio (acid test) 59; return on capital employed (ROCE) 55–6; return on shareholders' capital 56; sales growth 52; stock (inventory) control 62–3; value added per employee 57–8; worksheet 51
recognition system 190–2
recruitment and selection processes *99*, 99–100, 182–7
redundancy 213
Reed, Richard 268
Renardson, Chris 111

websites 170–3; competitors 40
Williams, Richard 221–3
Wiseman, Brian 262
word-of-mouth marketing 167–9
work/home balance 112
working capital: average collection period (debtor days) 60–1; average payment period (creditor days) 61–2; calculating requirement for 234–7, *236, 237*; circulation of working capital 63–4; stock (inventory) control 62–3
World Challenge Expeditions 111

zero-based budgeting 244

eBooks – at www.eBookstore.tandf.co.uk

A library at your fingertips!

eBooks are electronic versions of printed books. You can store them on your PC/laptop or browse them online.

They have advantages for anyone needing rapid access to a wide variety of published, copyright information.

eBooks can help your research by enabling you to bookmark chapters, annotate text and use instant searches to find specific words or phrases. Several eBook files would fit on even a small laptop or PDA.

NEW: Save money by eSubscribing: cheap, online access to any eBook for as long as you need it.

Annual subscription packages

We now offer special low-cost bulk subscriptions to packages of eBooks in certain subject areas. These are available to libraries or to individuals.

For more information please contact webmaster.ebooks@tandf.co.uk

We're continually developing the eBook concept, so keep up to date by visiting the website.

www.eBookstore.tandf.co.uk